100 Animated Feature Films

BFI Screen Guides

Andrew Osmond

A BFI book published by Palgrave Macmillan

First published in 2010 by
PALGRAVE MACMILLAN

on behalf of the

BRITISH FILM INSTITUTE
21 Stephen Street, London W1T 1LN
www.bfi.org.uk

There's more to discover about film and television through the BFI. Our world-renowned archive, cinemas, festivals, films, publications and learning resources are here to inspire you.

Palgrave Macmillan in the UK is an imprint of Macmillan Publishers Limited, registered in England, company number 785998, of Houndmills, Basingstoke, Hampshire RG21 6XS. Palgrave Macmillan in the US is a division of St Martin's Press LLC, 175 Fifth Avenue, New York, NY 10010. Palgrave Macmillan is the global academic imprint of the above companies and has companies and representatives throughout the world. Palgrave® and Macmillan® are registered trademarks in the United States, the United Kingdom, Europe and other countries.

Cover image: *The Adventures of Prince Achmed* (Lotte Reiniger, 1926, Comenius-Film/BFI)
Designed by couch
Set by Cambrian Typesetters, Camberley, Surrey
Printed in China

This book is printed on paper suitable for recycling and made from fully managed and sustained forest sources. Logging, pulping and manufacturing processes are expected to conform to the environmental regulations of the country of origin.

British Library Cataloguing-in-Publication Data
A catalogue record for this book is available from the British Library
A catalog record for this book is available from the Library of Congress

10 9 8 7 6 5 4 3 2 1
19 18 17 16 15 14 13 12 11 10

ISBN 978–1–84457–340–0 (hbk)

Contents

Acknowledgments

My thanks go to Rebecca Barden and Sophia Contento for commissioning and supporting this book, and to the wonderful staff at London's BFI library where much of the research was done. Other thanks go to Michael Barrier, Crystal Bogle, Jonathan Clements, Benjamin Ettinger, Helen McCarthy, Justin Johnson, Bill Plympton (for kindly answering my questions about *Idiots and Angels*, 2008, during a flying visit to the Animated Exeter festival in 2010), and Blue Neon and Niffiwan for help on East European animation.

Introduction

The animated feature film is one of the most unruly changelings in cinema. It encompasses a myriad of styles, techniques and subject matter, some purposefully stretching animation's definition to its limits. There are many competing visions of animation, and fans and artists will probably never agree on what it *should* be. Some directors included in this book, such as the Czech surrealist Jan Svankmajer and *Avatar* (2009) director James Cameron – and yes, it does feel strange to mention both in the same sentence – deny they make animated films at all. Through their history, animated films have been often buried under successive stereotypes, from the Disney bluebirds of past decades to the knowing in-jokery of CGI films.

Yet the animated feature has rarely been as celebrated, or enjoyed such a high profile, as it does today. There's a high awareness among cinemagoers that it's not a genre but a diverse medium; that it doesn't always come from Disney, Pixar or America; and that it's not necessarily aimed at children or family audiences. The new pluralism is reflected in features such as the British/French *The Illusionist* (produced in Edinburgh by a French director, 2010), France's *Persepolis* (co-directed by an Iranian woman and a French man, 2007), Japan's Oscar-winning *Spirited Away* (2001), Israel's *Waltz with Bashir* (2008), and the Irish/French/Belgian film *The Secret of Kells* (2009). Together with American box-office hits from *WALL·E* (2008) to *Kung Fu Panda* (2008), they excite discussion and speculation about where the medium – *not* genre – will go next.

There have always been more animated feature films than most people think. Disney's *Snow White and the Seven Dwarfs* (1937) is routinely referred to as the first, but there were several precedents in cut-out and stop-motion animation. The earliest known surviving animated feature – which, thankfully, is now easy to see on DVD in restored form – is Germany's cut-out *The Adventures of Prince Achmed* in 1926, directed by Lotte Reiniger. By a happy alphabetical accident, it is the first entry in this book. There were also several lost films from Argentina which were *probably* feature length, discussed in the entry on *El Apostol* (1917). The first animated *star* in a feature film, though, was surely King Kong in 1933, whose stop-motion body and mattes-and-models Skull Island towered over any of the picture's live-action elements.

From 1937 until the 1990s, animated features around the world were dominated by Disney. Of course, other films and many other *kinds* of film, were made in this time. Some were critically acclaimed, or were local hits, or gained loyal fan followings. Some were truly alternative visions, from Jiří Trnka's balletic stop-motion *A Midsummer Night's Dream* (1959), to Ralph Bakshi's coarsely drawn *Fritz the Cat* (1972), to Katsuhiro Otomo's future epic *Akira* (1988). But these landmarks were separated by language, generations and cultural expectations. When it came to feature animation, Disney was the world's denominator.

The Mouse

This is the point where any writer on animated features must declare where he or she stands on what one biographer snidely called 'The Disney Version' of popular culture. For the record, I respect and admire much, though not all, of the studio's work, and especially the quintet of films Disney released in fewer than five years: *Snow White*, followed by *Pinocchio* and *Fantasia* (both 1940), *Dumbo* (1941) and *Bambi* (1942). Yes, the films can be cute and mawkish, most notoriously in the characters' drawn faces and cartoon-saucer eyes. (Eyes, perhaps more than anything else, tend to repel viewers from particular forms of animation, as a skim of reviews of *The Polar Express*, 2004, or of Japanese cartoons will attest).

At their best, though, Disney films use their cuteness as a starting point in works of cinema bravado, thematic power and spiritual depth. A film such as *Bambi* demands to be taken *seriously*, which is why the critic Manny Farber tried strenuously to garotte it as a traitor to cartoondom. In a celebrated *New Republic* review, 'Saccharine Symphony', Farber called *Bambi* a bid to 'ape the trumped up realism of flesh and blood movies', betraying the unpretentious purity of Mickey Mouse and Donald Duck (soon to be toppled in the short-film pantheon by Bugs and Daffy). Some cartoon aficionados extend this argument to denounce *all* feature-length animation, save the occasional brand from the burning: Disney's *Dumbo*, perhaps, or Ralph Bakshi's *Heavy Traffic* (1973).

Such critical assaults – to be revisited later – are far more engaging than those lazily based on revisionist biographies of Walt Disney. These generally portray him as racist, fascist and/or otherwise warped, and have a politically correct standing for pundits who view Disney as the corporate-sexist-imperialist dragon. Then it stands to *reason* that its founder must have been, for example, monstrously anti-Semitic, his films encoding his bigotries. My favourite example of extreme Disney academia is Matt Roth's paper, '*The Lion King*: A Short History of Disney Fascism', published in the film journal *Jump Cut* in 1996.

Roth argues seriously, for instance, that when in *Pinocchio*, the puppet rescues his creator Gepetto from the whale Monstro, the 'Nazi-inflected' scenario uses the father figure Gepetto to stand in for the Fatherland, while Monstro represents the international Jewish banking system. Such lunacy seems impervious to the tedious facts, such as that some of Walt's top employees were Jewish, including those who went on record after his death to deny he showed any prejudice. All I can do is refer the reader to the Bibliography in this book, which includes sounder starting points that treat Disney as more than one man's megalomania.

Disney's history after *Bambi* went through several phases. Following *Bambi*, Disney had several years of commercial decline, caused by the war and Walt's over-ambition. I have included one entry from this period, on the bizarre 1944 film *The Three Caballeros*, made for the South American market. Disney returned to prominence with 1950's *Cinderella*, but Walt himself was less involved as he moved into live-action films, TV, theme parks and even town planning. He died in 1966, while his studio was in production of what would be one of its most enduringly popular animated films, *The Jungle Book* (1967).

According to *The Disney Studio Story* by Richard Holliss and Brian Sibley, Walt's brother, Roy O. Disney, wanted the unit wound down after Walt died. Bill Anderson, the Vice President in charge of production, claimed he asked Roy to send him an official memo, which never came. However, the Disney animated films over the next twenty years are usually only mentioned now in bad-old-days contexts. Many young animators were hired by the studio in this time, and many bailed or were dismissed. The dropouts included some of the biggest future names in animation: John Lasseter, Brad Bird, Henry Selick, Tim Burton and Don Bluth.

I have included one Disney film from this 'dark' time, 1977's *The Rescuers*, which was the first Disney I saw in the cinema, aged five. I grew up with several Disneys now widely considered the worst (though I missed *The Black Cauldron* in 1985, which notoriously earned less than *The Care Bears Movie* the same year). Contrary to some accounts, these films were still enjoyed by children. *The Fox and the Hound*, for example, earned around $50 million in 1981. The next year, though, Disney was subject to a boardroom *coup*, instigated by Walt's nephew, Roy E. Disney, who was unhappy with the studio's direction. (Roy O. Disney, his father, had died in 1971.)

Following the *coup*, the next Disney regime was led by Michael Eisner, Jeffrey Katzenberg (from the Paramount studio) and Frank Wells (from Warner Bros.). According to James B. Stewart's book *DisneyWar*, Eisner and Wells wanted to shut down Disney's animation, while Katzenberg, on his account, was indifferent. That left Roy E. Disney as its main defender (ironic, given that his father had wanted to close it). Katzenberg, though, was soon fascinated by the medium and began exerting a creative influence of his own, as reflected in the entries on *Aladdin* (1992) and *Toy Story* (1995).

The Eisner regime saw an upswing in Disney's prestige through the successes of *The Little Mermaid* (1989), *Beauty and the Beast* (1991), *Aladdin* (1992) and *The Lion King* (1994). Was this 'gold standard' on a level with *Snow White* or *Bambi*? Not to an adult sensibility, but then Disney also released *The Nightmare before Christmas* (1993), a Gothic stop-motion film different enough to appeal to people who disliked the new Disney style. Two years later, the studio released another 'unDisney' film by an outside party. This was *Toy Story*, the first computer-animated feature film.

Post-Disney

Made by the young Pixar studio, *Toy Story* was visually kinetic, with a buddy-film dynamic, and very funny. It was also a better Disney heir than that studio's in-house *Pocahontas* (1995), or *The Prince of Egypt* (1998), a Bible epic from the rival DreamWorks studio. DreamWorks was co-founded by David Geffen, Steven Spielberg and Katzenberg, whose Disney career ended after Frank Wells died tragically in 1994. Eisner blocked Katzenberg's succession to the number two spot, and the ties were severed bitterly. The establishment of DreamWorks confirmed there were now several animated games in town. Feature animation was no longer just a fight for Walt's legacy.

In fact, it was as much a fight for the legacy of *The Simpsons*. The animated TV sitcom débuted in 1989, and quickly changed expectations of what animation could offer in terms of jokes for adults. (This was reflected in the show itself, with its switch of emphasis from the brattish Bart to the middle-aged Homer.) Coincidentally or not, *The Simpsons'* knowing, audience-flattering tone was mirrored in features as early as Disney's *Aladdin*, then fed into the first batch of computer-animated films: *Toy Story*, DreamWorks' *Antz* (1998) and, most successfully, *Shrek* (2001).

At the same time, non-Hollywood animation was rising. Disney itself helped change the violent, cultish image that Japanese animation had in the West, distributing the family films *Kiki's Delivery Service* (1989) and *Spirited Away*, made by Tokyo's Studio Ghibli and directed by Hayao Miyazaki. For its part, DreamWorks signed up with Britain's Aardman Animations to fund the plasticine features of Nick Park, director of the Oscar-winning *Creature Comforts* (1989) and *The Wrong Trousers* (1993).

By the 2000s, Disney's animation was declining, unable to compete with Pixar, DreamWorks and other computer-animated studios. From 2002, Eisner began shutting down Disney's traditional animation units, even before the flop of the costly film *Treasure Planet* (2002). But as traditionally animated features faded at Hollywood, they were imported from overseas. France's very unDisney *Belleville Rendez-Vous* (2003, aka *The Triplets of Belleville*) won critical attention; so did the Disney-distributed *Spirited Away*.

Both films were marginal at the Western box office, but they had high cultural cachet in an increasingly glutted market. In 2006, there were around a dozen CGI family films released in Britain and America alone, ranging from Pixar's blockbuster *Cars*, to France's refined fairytale *Azur & Asmar: The Princes' Quest*, to cannon fodder dross such as *The Wild* and *The Ant Bully*. The same year saw such adult films as Richard Linklater's *A Scanner Darkly*, which premièred at Cannes, and Satoshi Kon's *Paprika* at Venice.

Another snapshot

At the 2010 Oscar ceremony, there were five nominees for the category of Best Animated Feature. This had only come into being in 2001, and not without controversy – many fans saw it as a Hollywood ploy to ghettoise animation away from 'real' films. The nominees in 2010 were an especially interesting mix: *The Princess and the Frog*, *Up*, *Coraline*, *Fantastic Mr Fox* and *The Secret of Kells*.

The Princess and the Frog was a traditionally drawn Disney musical – indeed, the first traditionally animated Disney of any prominence for five years. In 2005, Michael Eisner had left Disney, having mothballed hand-drawn features and alienated the Pixar studio, which was preparing to break up with Disney. However, Eisner's replacement Robert Iger secured a *rapprochement*, then bought Pixar out in a $7.4-billion deal. John Lasseter, the director of *Toy Story*, became the Chief Creative Officer of both Disney and Pixar and promptly brought Disney's hand-drawing back.

How strange that only fifteen or twenty years earlier, many people in America and Britain would have said that a traditionally drawn Disney film was the *only* kind of animated feature, or the only kind that mattered. Now the critical darling was not *The Princess and the Frog* but *Up*, the tenth feature film from Pixar, computer-generated like its previous titles. Since 2001, Pixar had won four Best Animated Feature Oscars, for *Finding Nemo* (2003), *The Incredibles* (2004), *Ratatouille* (2007) and *WALL·E* (2008). Disney's own in-house films had won none.

The puppet films in competition, *Coraline* and *Fantastic Mr Fox*, were directed by Henry Selick and Wes Anderson respectively. In 1977, Bruno Edera had written the book *Full-Length Animated Feature Films*, a survey of the field as it seemed then. In Edera's view, the stop-motion puppet film had probably had its day. 'None of the new (animated) film-makers will make much use of puppets,' he wrote, 'and it remains to be seen what will happen to this particular branch of the medium.'

But stop-motion had lasted. A puppet film, *Wallace & Gromit in The Curse of the Were-Rabbit*, had won the Oscar in 2005, beating yet *another* stop-motion film, *The Corpse Bride*. Apart from *Coraline*, all of them were animated in Britain, now challenging Eastern Europe as the hub of puppet production. If anything demonstrated animation's plurality, it was the survival of this 'dying' art.

And then there was the dark horse. *The Secret of Kells* was a largely hand-drawn film directed by Tomm Moore of the Irish studio Cartoon Saloon. The production was spread internationally, with contributions from Brazil, Belgium, Hungary and France. The French investor, Les Armateurs had supported

Kells as a successor to its previous hit, *Belleville Rendez-Vous*. Like *Belleville*, *Kells* was an unDisney animated film in an unDisney style; even its end was no conventional happy ever after.

All the nominees were brought together in a spoof interview reel in which Fantastic Mr Fox, voiced by George Clooney, grouched about animation's lowly critical status. ('These are all cartoons … I thought we got nominated like a real movie!') In the event, *Up*, which surprised no one by winning the Best Animated Feature prize, was also nominated for Best Picture. So was James Cameron's *Avatar*, a film *not* entered in the Animated category. (Both films lost to the live-action *The Hurt Locker*.)

Animation or not?

'I think the thing that people need to keep very strongly in mind is that (*Avatar*) is not an animated film,' Cameron said.

> These actors did not just stand at a lectern and do a voice-part, and then animators went off for the next two years and created the entire physicality of their performance … . Every nuance, every tiny bit of the performance that you see on the screen, was created by the actors. They had to run, they had to leap, they had to fight, they had to do all the things that you see them doing in the film, and that's where the power of the performance comes from.

Animation fans, though, knew that Cameron was describing an old, old principle that had developed a decade only or so after animation itself. Today it's called motion capture or performance capture, and done with electronic motion sensors attached to the actors. In previous decades, it was called rotoscoping or motion-reference, and involved animators tracing live-action film frames and turning them (more or less freely, depending on practical constraints and the artist's gifts) into animation.

You can find increasingly pervasive rotoscoping in Disney's films from *Snow White* onwards, in Ralph Bakshi's *The Lord of the Rings* (1978) and *American Pop* (1981), and in digital form in *The Polar Express* and *A Scanner Darkly*. In all these films, as in *Avatar*, the aim was to reproduce the performance of a live-action actor in animation – or, as sour animation fans would phrase it, to create pseudo-animation based on live action.

The problem with rotoscope, as the historian Michael Barrier explained in his book *Hollywood Cartoons*, is that it does not 'distinguish the important from the unimportant. Lines in an animator's drawing could evoke a figure's shifting centre of gravity, giving that figure weight and mass; in a tracing, they could do no more than locate body parts.'

The caricaturist Al Hirschfeld made similar points when he critiqued Disney's *Snow White* on its first release, but he had a more fundamental complaint. 'When cartoons approach that close to actuality,' he wrote, 'real people and real backgrounds had better be used.'

Brad Bird, the acclaimed director of the traditionally animated *The Iron Giant* (1999) and the Pixar computer films *The Incredibles* and *Ratatouille*, talked about both rotoscoping and motion capture in 2007. 'I think the dirty little secret of most mo-cap (motion capture) is that the really, really good stuff has been massaged a lot by animators,' Bird said. 'And that's what people don't talk about, and I think that does a tremendous disservice to animators.'

'There's nothing wrong with animation,' Bird continued.

Animators are not technicians. They're artists, they think about performance ... . The best mo-cap that I've seen has all been messed with by animation, in much the same way as the best rotoscope done in Disney's time was mucked with.

Bird was speaking before *Avatar* but his comments seem borne out by a piece on the film in *3D World* magazine. It noted that 40 per cent of the Na'Vi aliens' facial movements were actually hand animated.

But the rotoscope issue brings up deeper arguments about what animated films should and shouldn't be. For some critics, the value of the animated feature lies in how well it can exploit the unique qualities of animation, those unreplicable in any other form. The consensus is that this means creating characters who act *without* the rotoscope, who in Barrier's words 'seem to act of their own volition and occupy the screen with the presence of real creatures'.

A recent book, Thomas Lamarre's *The Anime Machine*, swims against the tide, arguing that cartoon acting is less fundamental to the medium than the 'multiplanar' images of animation and the interaction between characters and backgrounds. Indeed, the creation and exploration of fantasy worlds is a vital part of many animated features, to the extent that in the Japanese films by Hayao Miyazaki, characters feel defined by the surroundings, rather than the reverse. However, Lamarre's wider arguments and conclusions are less compelling.

A coruscating critique of animation past and present, in the tradition of Farber and Hirschfeld, is 'John K Stuff', the blog of John Kricfalusi, who created the mould-breaking TV cartoon *Ren and Stimpy* in 1991. Kricfalusi pushes a powerful manifesto for real cartoons. He mocks the visual and narrative formulae of animated features, and denounces 'decadent' house styles, scripted (rather than storyboarded) cartoons, simulated spectacle and Disneyesque 'believability'. Like Farber, he ultimately seems to be calling less for *better* animated features than for *no* animated features at all, sweeping the bastard form away in favour of compact caricature. However, Kricfalusi also says he would like to make his own animated feature, but doubts any studio would let him break out of the Disneyfied strait-jacket.

Today's audience, meanwhile, accepts films as different as *Shrek*, *A Scanner Darkly*, *The Secret of Kells*, *Princess Mononoke* (1997) and *The Illusionist*. The animated feature was a hybrid even when Walt Disney had a virtual monopoly on the form, somewhere between the short cartoon and the live-action feature, and it always leaned more towards the latter. It may have been stunted by the world's most powerful studios – Disney, Pixar, Ghibli, DreamWorks – yet it has surely not survived and thrived just by unhappy accident. A changeling by nature, it will continue to mutate with the rest of cinema, but its future must hold more than *Avatar*.

Other visions

Given the high level of production today, it's not surprising that there are many more interesting animated films around than there used to be, or a greater range. It's debatable if this equates to a 'golden age' of animation, but the volume of production has never been higher. Around 1960, there might have been four or five animated features made around the world in a good year. Now there are typically dozens, facilitated by international co-production, off-the-shelf software and world-animation festivals.

As of writing, the biggest such event is the Annecy International Animation Festival in France, which was founded in 1960. In 2008, its Animated Feature Film competition had two joint winners: *Sita Sings the Blues* by Nina Paley and *Idiots and Angels* by Bill Plympton. Both were American independent films, animated *single-handedly* by their creators, Plympton with drawings and Paley with Flash animation software. The runners-up and out-of-contest features, meanwhile, included France's *Go West, A Lucky Luke Adventure*; Germany's *The Three Brigands*; India's *Return of Hauman*; China's *Zhang Ga!*; and Denmark's *A Tale of Two Mozzies*.

While *Idiots and Angels* and *Sita Sings the Blues* are both in this book, I missed seeing the other films, which have not had an Anglophone release as of writing. On the other hand, I *did* see Belgium's lame CGI film *Fly Me to the Moon*, which won an Anglophone release and was promptly panned by reviewers. As with live-action cinema, it is hard to gauge how many 'good' films we are missing from elsewhere in the world. Some foreign-language animated features are more incompetent than the most despised Anglophone titles, due to their lack of resources or staff experience. I saw numerous lesser-known non-English films for this book that disappointed, though it would be unfair to name names.

From a Western viewpoint, the big discovery since the 1990s has been Japanese animation, and particularly the films of Hayao Miyazaki, who was directing wonderful animated features two decades before he came to world attention with his epics *Princess Mononoke* and *Spirited Away*. In Japan, Miyazaki's Studio Ghibli has distributed several films that were inspirations to its founders, Miyazaki and his colleague Isao Takahata (*Grave of the Fireflies*, 1988). The films include France's *Le Roi et l'oiseau* (1980), Russia's *The Snow Queen* (1957), America's *Hoppity Goes to Town* (1941) and Britain's *Animal Farm* (1954).

Doubtless there will be many more animated films released in the years to come. Hopefully many more hitherto-overlooked films will be snapped up by Anglophone distributors. In this book, I have mostly confined myself to films that the Anglophone viewer can see fairly easily with a multiregion DVD player. For example, both China's *Nezha Conquers the Dragon King* (1979) and Hong Kong's *My Life as McDull* (2001) are available on Asian DVDs with English subtitles. About two-thirds of this book's entries cover what might be called mainstream films in Britain and America; that is, popular cinema hits or widely reviewed and disseminated films.

Almost half of the entries are American, with East Asia accounting for another quarter (mostly Japanese films, plus *McDull* and *Nezha* from Hong Kong and China). Britain, France and Czechoslovakia are represented with around half a dozen films each, with the balance made up of individual titles from Russia, Norway, Italy, Ireland, Israel, Canada, Australia and Hungary, plus *Achmed* and *El Apostol*, the pioneering films from Germany and Argentina. The selection is shaped by my own tastes, as the entries make clear, but I hope it is not wholly capricious.

For readers looking for a comprehensive overview of world animation, and an indication of how much more is out there, the indispensable books are *Cartoons: One Hundred Years of Cinema Animation* by Giannalberto Bendazzi and *Animation Art*, edited by Jerry Beck. Both deal with feature-length animation and animated shorts (a form of animation which Bendazzi considers far more artistically valuable), with Beck's book bringing in television as well. In comparison, this book is a skewed and partial appreciation of the medium, but I hope of some worth of its own.

The Adventures of Prince Achmed
Germany, 1926 – 66 minutes
Lotte Reiniger
[Cut-out silhouettes]

DIRECTOR/ANIMATION Lotte Reiniger
SCORE Wolfgang Zeller

The making of the world's oldest surviving animated feature was seen at first hand by a boy called Louis Hagen. (As an adult, he would flee to England as a Jewish refugee, become a decorated glider pilot and write a bestselling war memoir, *Arnhem Lift*). Hagen could hardly *not* have seen the production of *The Adventures of Prince Achmed*. It was made at his German family villa, by his beautiful art teacher, Lotte Reiniger. Hagen's father, who shared his name, was a bohemian banker who chose to support Reiniger, an artist trained in theatre and film. Reiniger had studied under Max Reinhardt and Paul Wegener, but found herself drawn to silhouettes, shadow plays and animation.

The senior Hagen proposed that Reiniger should animate a feature, financed by himself (money had little worth during German hyperinflation) and made in an attic studio over the garage of his Potsdam villa. Here Reiniger animated her characters, which appear on screen as black cut-out silhouettes, while her husband Carl Koch operated the camera. (Koch later worked with Renoir on *La Grande Illusion*, 1937, and *La Règle du jeu*, 1939.) Different layers of animation were shot on vertically stacked glass sheets, an ancestor of the multiplane camera.

Berthold Bartosch, who would later make a celebrated French political animation, *L'Idée* (*The Idea*, 1932), handled the special effects involving wax, sand and soap. His partner on *Achmed* was Walter Ruttmann, the future director of *Berlin: Symphony of a Great City* (1927). Walter Turck arranged the brightly tinted, print-like backgrounds, in a film taking its hero from Arabian minarets to Chinese mountains.

The junior Hagen remembered that when his villa's lunch-bell rang,

> We heard all kinds of moans and groans, as if they had been in a torture chamber … . The studio wasn't very high and all the animation work had to be done at floor level, so they worked on their knees. You can imagine, if you spend hours crawling, it's bound to be painful when you get up.

In *Achmed*'s story, a composite of Arabian Nights tales, the Prince contends with sorcerers, spirits and monsters, and eventually teams up with Aladdin (who in this version loves Achmed's sister). Ruttmann complained about the fantastical material – 'What has this got to do with 1923?' he asked – but the film was timely. *Achmed*'s production overlapped with Hollywood's *The Thief of Bagdad* (1924), starring Douglas Fairbanks, and anticipated at least four cartoon-feature landmarks: *A Thousand and One Nights**, *The Thief and the Cobbler**, Disney's *Aladdin** and *Azur & Asmar: The Princes' Quest**.

Achmed, like all Reiniger's silhouette animation, is tactile *à la* stop-motion. There's a physicality to the opaque figures' filigreed outlines, their frilly dresses, unkempt beards and jointed limbs, which the viewer can *imagine* manipulating. There's also a palpable electricity between the characters. An evil wizard grasps the hand of a princess; the taboo in this touching feels greater played out by silhouettes. Later the heroic Achmed woos a cowering girl, their motions of longing and repulsion framed in a grove with seashell curves.

The eroticism is plain, as it is when Achmed finds a bawdy bevy of man-hunting maidens (snaffling a last kiss from them as he flees) or steals the wings from a faunlike fairy bathing nude (the same girl he woos later). *Achmed* never subverts the fairytale convention of princesses as prizes for heroes, but nor does the film hide its sexual tensions. The BFI DVD of *Achmed* also includes a striking extract from Reiniger's 1935 short, *Galathea*, in which a woman statue ferociously rejects her Pygmalion.

Within Reiniger's innately magic animation, a capering simian sorceress commands the elements like Mickey Mouse in *Fantasia**. The rival wizard creates a flying horse from primal liquid shapes. The horse bears Achmed helpless into the starry heavens in a thrilling but scary scene, while the heroine's bird nature foreshadows the oeuvre of Hayao Miyazaki. The villain folds origami-style into a bat; a tree unfolds into a man-eating monster; and a mountain vomits up enough creepy crawlies to populate Skull Island.

Another BFI DVD, *Lotte Reiniger – The Fairy Tale Films*, focuses on the children's shorts which Reiniger made in England. Two of them, *Aladdin and the Magic Lamp* and *The Magic Horse* (both 1954), combine *Achmed* footage with new animation. Far stranger is Reiniger's 1928 *The Death Feigning Chinaman*, which is also included on the fairytale DVD. Originally planned as an episode of *Achmed* itself, the short features a comedy corpse, gallows humour and a gay theme. Reiniger explained that she wanted two men to kiss, 'so children – some of whom would be homosexual and some who would not – could see it as a natural occurrence and not be ashamed'.

Akira
Japan, 1988 – 124 minutes
Katsuhiro Otomo
[Drawings (with brief CGI)]

DIRECTOR Katsuhiro Otomo
PRODUCER Ryohei Suzuki, Shunzo Kato
STORY Katsuhiro Otomo, Izo Hashimoto
SCORE Shoji Yamashiro
DESIGN Kazuo Ebisawa, Yuji Ikehata, Koji Ohno
ANIMATION Takashi Nakamura, Yoshio Takeuchi, Hiroaki Sato

In July 1988 – both the real date when *Akira* opened in Japan and the fictional dateline at the start of the film – Tokyo was burned away by a great sphere of light. But in Katsuhiro Otomo's epic animation, creation and destruction are part of one organic process. Our first sight of *Akira*'s city, Neo-Tokyo, is of a bleeding red shape, suggesting a heart, lungs or guts. Teen gangs, the city's *true* life-blood, rule the streets on huge phallic motorbikes, blurring into neon speedlines down tarmac veins between skyscrapers. Armed police battle rioters, terrorist gangs adding to the mayhem. And in a giant-sized nursery, housing a top-secret state project, three withered children await the return of their divine brother, Akira … .

Otomo's film was a cult hit in the West because of its stunning spectacle and shocking images. For all its political subtexts, *Akira* is a visceral trip which became a punkish piece of British pop culture and a midnight movie in America. Harry Knowles, the founder of the *Ain't It Cool News* website, remembered, 'College theatres got hold of that film and just played it over and over and over.' Its cartoon violence looked transgressive to everyone who hadn't seen Ralph Bakshi's early films (see p. 75) or the more recent *Heavy Metal* (1981). *Akira*'s most nakedly exploitative moment, reminiscent of *Robocop* the previous year, comes during the manic opening scenes where an already horribly maimed man is shredded by bullets. From there on, though, bloodletting is secondary to Otomo's grander vistas of destruction.

Considered as a Japanese animation, *Akira* is a fluke. Director Otomo was primarily a creator of comic strips (his *Akira* manga, unfinished when he made the film, would run to 2,000 pages). When *Akira* entered production, Japan was in its booming bubble years. The film had an unprecedented budget of around $10 million (huge for anime), a seventy-strong staff, technology allowing for character lip-synch, and the resources to make 'full' animation on twelve or twenty-four frames a second. Even Studio Ghibli films use semi-limited character animation, which is why they're less smooth than their Hollywood counterparts. *Akira*'s characters also move far more individually than Ghibli's, though their explosive fury rarely modulates into anything like pathos.

Otomo's vision was inspired by 1970s Tokyo. 'There were so many interesting people … . Student demonstrations, bikers, political movements, gangsters, homeless youth … . In *Akira*, I projected these elements into the future, as science-fiction.' Halfway through the action, a colonel character brings about a military *coup*, echoing an actual (failed) insurrection in 1936. A universe is born in an Olympic stadium, as the 1964 Olympics had heralded the rise of post-war Japan. The images of tanks on 'Tokyo's' streets – as in films such as *The Flying Ghost Ship* (1969) and the later *Patlabor 2* (1993) – reflect the fears of another militarisation in the 'pacifist' country. 'We're in East Ginza', a soldier reports, placing the action in Tokyo's best-known shopping district.

The film compresses Otomo's manga into two dazzling but confused hours. Subplots and support characters are truncated or forgotten: plot points are vague or contradictory. The abridged story is in line with

earlier SF anime films, such as *Space Battleship Yamato* (1977) or the *Mobile Suit Gundam* trilogy (1981–2), though these were edited down from TV cartoon serials rather than comic strips. And yet *Akira's* messy plot and information overload are its fascination. More than any SF film since *Blade Runner* (1982), Otomo's film hurls viewers into a world bleeding from the screen in multiple hinted backstories.

The round-faced boy leads, the cocksure Kaneda and the monster-victim Tetsuo, are believable teenagers, oscillating between sentimental comradeship and murderous hate. The other characters are under-explained and under-developed, but they're solid on-screen presences, especially the commanding, bull-like colonel who knows Akira's secret. The spectacle is driven by the explosive breathing and clacking percussion of the musicians Geinoh Yamashirogumi, as Tetsuo mutates into a killer teen demi-god, fighting through tanks and helicopters, then battling a supergirl on a huge metal globe while giant pipes and energy beams take out the infrastructure. 'It would be great if a film were just one big scene, with no divisions,' Otomo said.

But Otomo also stresses Tetsuo's enraged vulnerability. We're shown the boy's nightmare, a ghastly, beautiful scene where he crumbles into rubble in a playground while Kaneda smiles obliviously. Even when Tetsuo wakes, he's attacked by the psychic kids disguised as childish toys. In another scene, he can't save his girlfriend from a sexual assault, which is brutal and believable without a trace of exploitation. Afterwards, the boy is shown flailing and staggering screaming on the street, clutching his head, a terrible portrait of teen impotence. The blipvert images that punctuate his fit – flashforwards to the end of the film – include a subliminal glimpse of the girl's death, which he's doomed to cause.

Finally, Tetsuo's puberty sends him back to babyhood as he swells into a liquefying giant, mewling, puking and excreting its way into oblivion. The coda is a New Age trip through a vortex of smashed skyscrapers, book-ending the film with twin Armageddons. Even the destruction is beautiful: the buildings buffeted by roiling winds, the sea pouring through concrete wreckage, the sky reflected in a thousand dead-eyed windows.

Aladdin

US, 1992 – 87 minutes

John Musker, Ron Clements

[Drawings with CGI]

Disney's hit *Aladdin*, made on the upswing of the studio's fortunes in the 1990s, skewed Hollywood cartoon features in new if not necessarily artistic directions. Its star turn, though, was a one-off. *Aladdin*'s Genie, an S-curved blue stream of cacophonous consciousness, was realised by animator Eric Goldberg and perpetually psyched comedian Robin Williams. 'The frame speed of animation guarantees that where Williams goes, an instantly compatible image follows,' wrote *Sight and Sound*'s Farrah Anwar. 'If he chooses to shoot from a glitzy chat-show host to a heavyweight political figure via a mischievously shaded Jack Nicholson, the film stays with him and has the temerity to ask for more.'

The character's introduction would have made Walt proud. 'The ever-impressive …' (Genie is Schwarzenegger from *Pumping Iron*, 1977) '… the long-contained …' (Genie strains against the cube that's trapped him) … 'often imitated …' (Genie ventriloquises a dummy) '… but never duplicated-duplicated-duplicated' (Genie throws up a swirl of doubles) … 'Genie of the LA-AMP!' (The duplicate Genies applaud, while the original turns into TV host Ed Sullivan.) It might not have moved fans of the wildest Hollywood animators – Tex Avery, for example, or Bob Clampett – but its self-promotion was flawless. In a flash, Disney cartoons had gone from fairytale to Friday night, swimming in a soup of catchphrases and celebrity lookalikes.

As with *Shrek**, one of *Aladdin*'s progeny, the film was only doing what cartoons had done decades before. Bugs Bunny, for example, had faced off a caricatured Edward G. Robinson and Peter Lorre back in 1946 (a Friz Freleng short called *Racketeer Rabbit*). Classic Disney features had one-liners for grown-ups; in *Pinocchio**, Jiminy Cricket demands, 'What does an actor want with a conscience anyway?' *Aladdin*, though, made these gags a talking and selling point of a family blockbuster, much as *The Simpsons* (1989–) had done for a family sitcom.

The directors claim the humour was guileless, without commercial agendas. However, it's hard to believe Jeffrey Katzenberg, Disney's CEO, didn't know what he was doing when he aggressively overhauled *Aladdin* in development. Originally, Aladdin would have been young, not much older than *The Jungle Book**'s Mowgli, and his main concern would have been to please his mother, with a tent-pole song called 'Proud of Your Boy'. This young Aladdin is visible in the film; freeze the moment in the 'Friend Like Me' song when the hero is pressed down by Genie's finger.

Legend has it that Katzenberg's reaction to the young Aladdin was a curt, 'Eighty-six the mother. Mom's a zero.' The mother was utterly erased from the film. From then on *Aladdin*'s themes shifted from parent–child to buddy-bonding, even keeping in a homoerotic Williams quip: 'Oh Al, I'm getting kind of fond of you, kid; not that I want to pick out curtains or anything.' We're told that Aladdin has layers and esteem issues, which is something that cartoons convey best when the characters are middle-aged and ugly (the

DIRECTOR/PRODUCER John Musker, Ron Clements
STORY John Musker, Ron Clements, Ted Elliott, Terry Rossio
SCORE Alan Menken
DESIGN R. S. Vander Wende
ANIMATION Glen Keane, Eric Goldberg, Mark Henn, Andreas Deja

Beast, Buzz Lightyear, Mr Incredible, Homer Simpson), though not always even then (Shrek). But Peter Schneider, Disney's head of feature animation, conceded that *Aladdin* was courting teens, with a buffed-up hero they might want to sleep with. Note the way that Aladdin suddenly gains a mature cheekbone when he first kisses his love interest, the voluptuous Princess Jasmine.

Many reviewers thought Aladdin and Jasmine fared about as well against the Genie as Snow White did against the dwarfs. In some scenes, the pair seems almost drawn for mockery – look at their shiny-sappy expressions in the 'Whole New World' song, though in fairness that's followed by some of their *best* animation, when Jasmine challenges Aladdin while they rest on China's Forbidden City. Sensibly, their romance is told as a story of escape, discovery and adventure, the film pitching between exuberant and crass. There are theme park rides (a zooming magic-carpet dash was inspired by Disneyland's 'Star Tours'

flight simulator), shouty scenes (a parrot sidekick is deafeningly voiced by comedian Gilbert Gottfried), and TV toon pacing (the frantically busy last act).

When I saw *Aladdin* at a London retrospective screening in 2010, the print had the controversial version of the opening song, 'Arabian Nights', including the notorious lyric, 'They cut off your ear if they don't like your face.' (The first draft had been, 'They'll hack off your lips if they don't like your smile.') In 1992, *Aladdin*'s panto-burlesque Arabia, chock-full of harem dancers, pointy Viziers and ape-like palace guards, was denounced by Arab groups, and the 'ear' line removed from British prints. Given the stink, it's poignant to watch Genie animator Eric Goldberg on the *Aladdin* DVD. He explains that he took Williams's Yiddish exclamations (the Genie's first word is 'Oy!') to mean that what the film is *really* all about is the friendship between an Arab and a Jew.

Alice
Czechoslovakia/UK/Switzerland/West Germany, 1988 – 84 minutes
Jan Svankmajer
[Live-action and stop-motion. Shown on British television in six segments.]

The avant-garde Czech artist Jan Svankmajer has been in many animation books before this one, a fact he may view with annoyance or amusement. For Svankmajer insists he's not an animator at all. 'Animators tend to construct a closed world for themselves,' he says, 'like pigeon fanciers or rabbit breeders. I'm not interested in animation techniques or in creating a complete illusion, but in bringing life to everyday objects. Surrealism exists in reality, not beside it.'

Svankmajer was influenced by Georges Méliès, and like Méliès he spent decades channelling his ideas through short films, dating back to 1964. In Svankmajer's usually stop-motion masterpieces, clay heads eat each other; shoes and socks gain eyes and teeth; and stones and dolls perform intricate ritual dances. Released under the suspicious gaze of the Communist authorities (which penalised Svankmajer more than once for his works' suspect content), his films do less to bring the inanimate alive than to breach the barriers between living and unliving. Svankmajer respects dreams, pre-rational childhood and the magical properties of objects and structures, down to the living textures of raw stone, which people imbue with consciousness over years and centuries.

By the 1980s, Svankmajer had a world festival following, and *Alice*, his first feature, found backers outside the Iron Curtain. Britain's Channel 4 contributed nearly half the budget. As Clare Kitson recounts in her book, *British Animation: The Channel 4 Factor*, *Alice* was an underhand production, passed off not as a film but as an 'audiovisual display'. At the first full screening, the foreign backers were met by angry Czech officials insisting, too late, that a feature film was *forbidden*.

Alice (called *Something of Alice* in Czech) interprets *Alice's Adventures in Wonderland* as a violent, solipsistic nursery game. Much of its action takes place in stone passages (it was shot at a former Prague bakery) or in doll's houses that shrink outside and in. Apart from a glimpse of Alice's sister, her face unseen, the sole human is Alice herself, played by a blond, blank-faced little girl. Even she becomes a stop-motion doll for long sequences, while her Wonderland adventures continue without a break. (Svankmajer directed them first, while he was looking for his human actress.) The doll's face is immobile, yet seems more expressive than the real girl's. Mercifully it's the doll-Alice, not the real one, who's attacked by skull-headed chimeras in a stomach-churning scene whose imagery recalls Starewitch's *The Mascot* (see p. 175).

Svankmajer's creations (designed by him and animated by Bedrich Glaser) blur the line between affectless characters and uncanny effects. You may feel more fleeting empathy with a bit of ambulatory meat (a Svankmajer motif) or with a heap of leaves rushing into a desk drawer, than you do with the madly chittering White Rabbit, puckish and malign. (Alice chases him into the story after he escapes a taxidermist's vitrine.) Carroll's Caterpillar becomes a sock-puppet, building itself with dentures and eyeballs. The Mad Hatter is a Czech marionette, tea dribbling from its wooden torso, as sawdust does from the White Rabbit's

DIRECTOR/STORY/DESIGN Jan Svankmajer
PRODUCER Peter Christian-Fueter
ANIMATION Bedrich Glaser

stitching. (Tragically, Svankmajer doesn't do the Cheshire Cat.) All these creatures are Alice herself – she says their lines, the camera focusing on her lips, or rather another girl's lips, as 'Alice' herself lost a tooth during the shoot. But the child's transformations mean she herself is another bit of Wonderland, just one more figment of dream.

The *New Yorker*'s Terrence Rafferty deemed *Alice*

> a film for children of a certain kind, for the quiet solitary ones who spend hours in conversation with their dolls … whose play will, over the years, perhaps turn into a lonely, obsessive craftsmanship, of the sort animators have.

Amusingly, Svankmajer claimed that Swiss parents dragged their children out of the cinemas, threatening to sue the distributors for such a disturbed and disturbing film. In Britain, Channel 4 serialised *Alice* at lunchtimes over a holiday week. As Kitson says, it was arguably a better way to see *Alice* than watching its one-note strangeness straight through.

Svankmajer replaces the charm of Carroll's prose with savage Punch and Judy violence (a slapstick siege of a doll's house goes on forever). The music-free soundtrack consists of harsh creaks and bumps, while dialogue is atomised into Alice's flat, piecemeal line-readings ('"Your hair needs cutting", said the Mad Hatter'), around compulsively repetitive action. At times, it's reminiscent of early computer text adventures, with their atonal pseudo-narratives. The end departs from Carroll, with a mischievously political moment where Alice won't read a scripted confession, but she's last seen becoming a tyrannical Queen of Hearts. Svankmajer firmly believes that kids are cruel. In one of his later features, *Little Otik* (2000), a carved tree-trunk comes to life and devours a hapless social worker, the monster's baby coos and chuckles punctuated by the splat of human organs against a door.

Alice in Wonderland
France/Britain/USA, 1948 – 83 minutes
Dallas Bower
[Live-action with stop-motion]

The previous entry described how Czech animator Jan Svankmajer's version of *Alice* was made covertly, in defiance of the Communist authorities. It wasn't the first time that an *Alice* film was threatened with suppression (a word Lewis Carroll defined as being put into a canvas bag and sat on). Nearly forty years before, a French *Alice* was taken to court, not by an authoritarian state, but by the world's most powerful cartoon studio. The charge: impersonating a Disney film!

Actually, the *Alice* in question (its live-action directed by Dallas Bower, but essentially the creation of its producer and progenitor, Russian-born animator Lou Bunin) reversed Disney's approach. If Disney strove to conceal the seams and joins in its cartoon worlds, to make its cartoons a *cohesive* illusion, then Bunin's film flaunts the dichotomy between real and animated. The creatures of Wonderland are unearthly puppets, only semi-linked to our reality. Their uncertain scale, their gaping and grinning expressions that turn the merely crude into the assertively rude, suit *Alice*'s anarchy. The girl is real, a puckishly charming *ingénue* played by British actress Carol Marsh, the innocent foil to Richard Attenborough's baby-faced killer in *Brighton Rock* (1947).

In 1945, Bunin struck a blow for Hollywood stop-motion, animating the opening scenes of MGM's musical, *Ziegfeld Follies*. However, his footage was pruned back, suggesting that Hollywood recognition of stop-motion was still limited after *King Kong**. Bunin's dream, though, was *Alice*. He produced the film in France, with some financial backing from Britain's Rank Organisation. The cast was nearly all English, a Nice set stood in for Oxford in the live-action prologue, and the picture was double-shot in English and French.

The prologue tackles the problem faced by every *Alice* adapter; imposing a dramatic structure on the material without losing its magic. Bunin's solution is impishly French, making *Alice* an overtly republican spoof on Britain's monarchy and aristocracy. Thus we start, not with Alice at the rabbit hole, but with a royal visit to Oxford by a battle-axe Queen Victoria, played stridently by Pamela Brown. Today, she looks uncannily like Margaret Thatcher; when Alice's father thanks her for taking an interest in his children, she replies smoothly, 'I expect you to take an interest in mine.' Of course, she's puppeted as Wonderland's Queen of Hearts (with Albert as her King), a royal trout with a permanently upturned nose.

Lewis Carroll also appears in the prologue, played by a stammering Stephen Murray. A fellow free spirit for Alice, he muses, 'Animals and nonsense … . What could be pleasanter.' Rocked asleep on a boat, Alice drifts off as Carroll begins his tale; her fall down the rabbit hole is soporifically gentle. We switch to cut-out-style sets and geometric designs. From now on, the script is loyal to Carroll, keeping much of his dialogue and nonsense verse which Alice trills with the Wonderlanders (her singing is dubbed by Adele Leigh). Of the puppets, the standouts are Carroll's secondary figures: a jointly grotesque Duchess and baby, a monstrously unreal giant puppy, and a Mock Turtle tragedian, all clasped hands, hitching sobs and bulb-faced histrionics.

DIRECTOR (Live-action) Dallas Bower
PRODUCER Lou Bunin
STORY Henry Myers, Albert E. Lewin, Edward Eliscu
SCORE Sol Kaplan
DESIGN (PUPPETS) Bernyce Polifka
ANIMATION William King, Ben Radin, Oscar Fessler

The anti-establishment stings slide in; the Queen's court is packed with social climbers, with Carroll the shifty Knave in the deck. At the end, Alice accuses the Knave of stealing the royal tarts, as Carroll did for her in the real world. Yes, says the miscreant, but *she* is the Knave, and he himself is Alice – as of course Carroll is, being the teller of her story. It anticipates the by-play between grown-up authors and their child avatars in *Comet Quest** and the live-action *Dreamchild* (1985). The latter film is an Alice-Carroll metafiction, scripted by Dennis Potter, which uses Jim Henson's sophisticated animatronic puppets for the Wonderland creatures. By *Dreamchild*, the original *Alice* is just a springboard for new reality-shifting dramas, such as *Coraline** and *Spirited Away**.

The Disney studio, though, objected to Carroll becoming common currency. Bunin's film was made at the same time as Disney's prettified cartoon version, and the Mouse said the public would be gulled into seeing the wrong film. The matter was fought out in Manhattan's District Court, where Disney lost. The *Alice*s raced each other round the States in 1951; neither was a hit, but Bunin's film dropped out of sight, even its prints fading thanks to an untried colour process. Yet it's Bunin's film, not Disney's, which keeps Carroll's puckish spirit.

Allegro non troppo
Italy, 1977 – 85 minutes
Bruno Bozzetto
[Live-action and drawings (with brief stop-motion)]

In music, 'allegro non troppo' means 'fast, but not too much'. It's a modest title for a reckless-seeming homage, a response to the most hubristic cartoon ever made. Like Disney's *Fantasia**, this Italian film sets classical music to animation, so why not call it *Fortissimo*, or *Vivacissimo*? Perhaps director Bruno Bozzetto was banking on the audience's love of underdogs. *Fantasia* began with the black-jacketed Philadelphia Orchestra sitting down to play, so *Allegro non troppo* starts with a cleaning lady wiping down the stage. Such is the place of the non-Disney animator; but it also reminds us of Disney's Snow White and Cinderella, before their fairytale rags became riches.

Bozzetto's film is less a spoof than a humorous commentary, extending the adult content in *Fantasia* that Disney cloaked in fantasy, and injecting a European pessimism which Walt wouldn't have tolerated. What *Allegro non troppo* is *not* is anti-Disney, in the manner of Tex Avery or *Shrek**. Bozzetto saw *Fantasia* eleven times: 'Walt Disney left an indelible mark on my childhood.' Before *Allegro*, Bozzetto had made a slew of cartoons and features, many starring the hapless Mr Rossi, who was created as a cipher for the Italian Everyman. Rossi cameos in *Allegro*, where he's drawn as a doodle on paper, then blithely burned to a crisp.

Much of *Allegro* is live-action (the animation lasts about fifty minutes). The live-action framework is a slapstick, occasionally Pythonesque farce as the film-makers struggle to make their picture with a geriatric woman orchestra and an enslaved animator. (The latter is played by Bozzetto's collaborator Maurizio Nichetti, who would later direct *The Icicle Thief*, 1989, and co-direct the part-animated *Volere Volare*, 1991.) Many reviewers found the live-action obnoxious, and it was reportedly trimmed on some prints. The purpose of these 'shabby and wacky' scenes, Bozzetto said, was to counterpoint *Fantasia*'s over-dignified interludes with Leopold Stokowski and Deems Taylor. *Allegro*'s live-action is in black and white, so that the colour animation stands in the same relation to it as Oz does to Kansas in *The Wizard of Oz* (1939).

There are seven cartoon segments in the film, three of them outstanding. The first uses Debussy's 'Prélude à l'après-midi d'un faune', a languorous stroking of lust in an unserious Arcadian mythoscape that inevitably recalls the coyly sexualised world in *Fantasia*'s 'Pastoral Symphony'. Bozzetto's twist is to make the faun an ageing roué whose spirit can't lift his flesh. When he sees a nude nymph, he's so excited that he stands upside-down, and his tummy puddles round his head. In a landscape flowering with *double entendres*, there's no smutty happy ending; the faun shrivels into his dotage. There's more lust in a lesser segment which uses Stravinsky's 'The Firebird' (later animated in Disney's *Fantasia 2000*). Here, hell is endless pink-hued pornography, as giant breasts pour from TV screens.

The remarkable 'Bolero' sequence took a year to create. Astronauts discard a Coke bottle on a barren planet and life evolves, at first undulating over the landscape as bubbles with eyeballs before chimeric creatures emerge, flowers billowing into dinosaurs. Gradually a villain is glimpsed in the fauna, a

DIRECTOR Bruno Bozzetto
STORY Bruno Bozzetto, Guido Manuli, Maurizio Nichetti
ANIMATION Bruno Bozzetto, Giuseppe Lagana, Giancarlo Cereda, Guido Manuli, Paolo Albicocco

sneaky serial-killer ape. It's a misanthropic joke, more savage than any of Hayao Miyazaki's eco-fables, though perhaps to balance it, we see an angelically innocent Adam and Eve in the 'The Firebird' episode. The sequence parodies Fantasia's 'The Rite of Spring' and the start of *2001: A Space Odyssey* (1968), but the beautiful morphing images, intelligently built through Ravel's repeated theme, are a paradigm of animation as a rhythmically sustained, narratively muscular conceit.

The film's most iconic piece, though, is set to Sibelius's 'Valse Triste'. A mangy, saucer-eyed cat, its stripes straining against its haunches, skulks around the remnants of its home. Despite, and partly because of, its Margaret Keane-esque eyes, the cat's face and body are enormously expressive, while the timeshifting scenario anticipates the operatic 'Magnetic Rose' in the Japanese *Memories**. As with the best Disneys, the art is good enough that the manipulation (lazily equated with kitsch) feels like a by-product – surely Bozzetto's tribute to the Disney of his youth. At the segment's end, we cut to the live-action orchestra of hag ladies dabbing their eyes and wailing 'Bravo!' It feels less like smugness than the self-conscious harrumph of a director shyly trying on Walt's mantle.

American Pop
US, 1981 – 96 minutes
Ralph Bakshi
[Rotoscoped animation with live-action]

Released in 1981, *American Pop* was the sixth animated feature by maverick director Ralph Bakshi, nine years after his X-rated début, *Fritz the Cat**. It should have been his seventh, but his 1975 *Hey Good Lookin'* was shelved by Warners, though a revised version opened in 1982.

Before *American Pop*, Bakshi had made the first cinema version of J. R. R. Tolkien's *The Lord of the Rings* (1978). Notoriously, it cut the book in half (the planned Part 2 was never made), while its hobbits, wizards and goblins were plainly live actors, gesticulating manically behind an ink and paint veneer that was sometimes barely there. Bakshi made *American Pop* on the rebound from *Rings*. 'It was time for me to get back to something personal again.'

A stylised history of its subject, *American Pop* is told through generations of fathers and sons. Its scope and structure may have been influenced by the second *Godfather* movie (1974). Bakshi's film begins as the story of a Jewish boy and his mother, fleeing Russia's Cossacks to America in the 1890s. The mother dies in a New York sweatshop fire, referencing the Triangle Factory disaster of 1911. The boy grows up amid ragtime and vaudeville, marries a singer, falls in with the Mob and loses his wife to a letter-bomb.

The focus shifts to their son, a pianist who fights in World War II as we cut between the carnage in Europe and Americans gyrating to 'Sing Sing Sing'. *His* son grows up with the Beat poets, odysseys to San Francisco, writes great songs, and succumbs to drugs. The last scion takes the story to the (then) present day, as he sells cocaine against a background of safety-pins and Johnny Rotten. The ending is ambivalent, but Bakshi at least suggests that heritage survives the melting-pot. The last 'hero' passes a Rabbi who, unknown to him, resembles his great-great-grandfather. The strutting, coke-dealing punk has the ear to catch the Hebrew chants, lower his sunglasses and snap to the rhythm of his forefathers.

Like *The Lord of the Rings*, *American Pop* is rotoscoped, the gaudily traced performances defined by overstatement that make many scenes look like filmed theatre, though the backgrounds evolve evocatively through the decades, from sepia to psychedelia. Much of the film has the depth of a comic-strip panel, telegraphing reversals of fortune like a brassy biopic, while the fictional family cornily creates real songs from 'As Time Goes By' to 'Night Moves'. But as fans noted, the film itself plays like a rock ballad, making it easier to enjoy its shamelessly dealt cues on second viewing. *American Pop*'s pseudo-history makes a far better fit for Bakshi's techniques than Tolkien's literal myth-making.

The film has adult content (it was 'AA' in Britain) but the violence is restrained and the sex implicit, unlike Bakshi's more raucous work. The broadest joke may be the title, which looks like a sour pun. Through the film, gifted sons pay the price for their egoist fathers. Even in the sepia 1890s prelude, a Rabbi patriarch abandons his family and dies for his piety, murdered finishing a prayer. (Interestingly for a film whose

DIRECTOR Ralph Bakshi
PRODUCER Ralph Bakshi, Martin Ransohoff
STORY Ronni Kern
SCORE Lee Holdridge
DESIGN Louise Zingarelli, Johnnie Vita, Marcia Adams, Barry Jackson
ANIMATION Lillian Evans, Carl Bell, Craig Armstrong, Debbie Hayes

females mostly die or disappear, the screenplay was by a woman, Ronni Kern.)

Bakshi had moved beyond the anti-Disney jibes of *Fritz the Cat*, but his stylised story could be a satire on all of Walt's plucky orphans, finding their place in the world. However, two later cartoon films kept some of *American Pop*'s real-world sweep while losing its commentary. Don Bluth's cutesy mouse film, *An American Tail* (1985), starts with Jewish rodent refugees fleeing Russia for the Dream; and *Millennium Actress* (2001), a Japanese magic-realist romance by Satoshi Kon (p. 212), tells Japan's story through the history of cinema rather than music.

Animal Farm
UK/US, 1954 – 72 minutes
John Halas, Joy Batchelor
[Drawings]

In the British cartoon of George Orwell's *Animal Farm*, the word of Communist revolution is spread by a jowly Old Major pig, who looks and sounds like Winston Churchill. Orwell might have liked that irony, if not necessarily the cartoon (he died before its release). The actor Maurice Denham, who provided the film's barnyard vocals, claimed the voice fitted the 'lovely old pig'. But it seems to reflect how even a cartoon that was funded by the CIA wouldn't conform to straightforward rhetorical agendas. After the Churchillian Major is killed by his own oratory, and collapses and dies on screen, the film's sparse dialogue is dwarfed by a cacophony of brays, squawks and squeals, a mass of individuals who'll never surrender.

Premièring in New York in 1954, *Animal Farm* came from Britain's Halas and Batchelor studio, named for its married founders John Halas and Joy Batchelor. The Hungarian Halas had worked with a pre-Hollywood George Pal. Batchelor was an illustrator-animator from Watford. Before *Animal Farm*, their studio was known for its government-sponsored shorts, such as 1949's *The Shoemaker and the Hatter*, a political fairytale about the virtues of free trade. Amusingly, *Animal Farm* is equally energetic in showing the exploitative trade between humans and pigs.

Animal Farm is often called the first British cartoon feature, though there are two other contenders. In 1927, the director Anson Dyer completed a forty-minute film, *The Story of the Flag*, about the history behind the Union Jack and other British flags, but his producer sliced it into six shorts. It was Dyer's later studio in Stroud, Gloucestershire, described as a 'drab, colourless, three-storey Victorian house', would become the base for *Animal Farm*'s production. (The film employed seventy people, when there were fewer than 200 working in British animation.) Before *Animal Farm*, Halas and Batchelor's studio made 'instructional' feature animations for official use, starting with *Handling Ships* (1945) for the Admiralty.

In Orwell's *Animal Farm*, the animals revolt against their tyrant farmer and establish a Communist-style state. However, they're betrayed by their leader, the sly pig Napoleon, and they end up worse off than ever. An allegory for the Russian Revolution and the rise of Stalin, the tale was subtitled 'A Fairy Story'. Many critics saw a similar irony in *Animal Farm*'s adaptation as a cartoon. *The Animated Bestiary* by Paul Wells quotes a contemporary journal, *Cine Technician*, on the film: 'The incongruity of recognisable horrors of some political realities of our times are emphasised and made more troubling by the apparent innocence of the surrounding frame.'

The cartoon draws on Disney's lyrical and dramatic tropes, stretching them into new territory. If Disney's first bold run of films hadn't stalled in the 1940s, perhaps it might have made *Animal Farm* after *Bambi**, which was at least figuratively red in tooth and claw. But for contemporary viewers, *Animal Farm* was showing things Disney would never have dared to, such as the shocking animal executions or the cruel fate of the Herculean horse Boxer, last seen still struggling for freedom as he's carted off to the knacker's

DIRECTOR John Halas, Joy Batchelor
PRODUCER Louis de Rochemont, John Halas, Joy Batchelor
STORY Lothar Wolff, Borden Mace, Philip Stapp, John Halas, Joy Batchelor
SCORE Matyas Seiber
ANIMATION John F. Reed, E. Radage, A. Humberstone, R. Ayres, H. Whittaker, F. Moysey

yard. Such scenes would have had a terrible extra meaning for the half-Jewish Halas, who lost a brother and other relatives in the Holocaust.

The film's painterly backdrops make surfaces into colours, often speckled, splotched or daubed. The animals' faces are less expressive than their bodies, which vividly highlight what it is to have four legs. When the pig Snowball (Orwell's analogue for Trotsky) runs frantically for his life, his plump back becomes a jiggling curve. The horse Boxer's pathos is inseparable from his burdened bulk, but the most expressive face-acting comes from his donkey ally, Benjamin. A moment when Benjamin regards his stricken friend in a storm stands comparison with Disney. The lighter, more cosily Disneyesque sequences, led by a cute duckling, are only interludes. (The credited animation director was John F. Reed, who'd worked at Disney, but who later broke with Halas and Batchelor on bad terms.) The film starts and ends in the heat of anger, more visceral than Orwell's prose.

Animal Farm's secret funding by the CIA as Cold War propaganda is detailed in Daniel Leab's book, *Orwell Subverted: The CIA and the Making of* Animal Farm. Yet, while there are changes to Orwell's text – for example, the film reduces the evil Napoleon to a greedy thug – the streamlined story inadvertently deepens the lament that the revolution didn't work (and might it have, had Snowball guarded himself better?). The changed ending, where the animals enact a counter-revolution, muddies the moral ground, but it's hard to imagine any film catching the despair of Orwell's last lines. Even so, the very last frames in the film show Benjamin stepping slightly forward from his allies. A hint, perhaps, that the 'hero' donkey is doomed to become the next animal tyrant?

Antz
US, 1998 – 80 minutes
Eric Darnell, Tim Johnson
[CGI]

Woody Allen plays an ant, or rather he plays Woody Allen as an ant in *Antz*, the animated début for the Hollywood studio, DreamWorks. Allen is introduced in character on a therapist's couch (well, leaf). 'My mother never had time for me,' runs his monologue. 'When you're the middle child in a family of five million, you don't get any attention …'.

Antz did get attention, partly by having an absurdly starry voice-cast: Allen, Sharon Stone, Sylvester Stallone, Gene Hackman, Jennifer Lopez, Christopher Walken, Danny Glover and Anne Bancroft, *plus* cameos by Dan Aykroyd and Jane Curtin. The film press was also exercised by claims that DreamWorks had stolen a march on a rival. After *Toy Story** three years earlier, the Disney-backed Pixar studio had embarked on its own insect CGI film, *A Bug's Life* (also 1998). When *Antz* was announced, Pixar's John Lasseter publicly accused DreamWorks of poaching the idea. The issue was ramped up when DreamWorks bumped *Antz's* release forward, beating Pixar's insects into cinemas in what many commentators saw as a brazen spoiler.

DreamWorks denied copying Pixar. In fairness insects, like toys, were an obvious choice of subject for early CGI, thanks to their lack of fur or flesh. (A French TV CGI cartoon, *Insektors*, 1994, predated both films.) Whatever the truth, the high-profile clash established something hitherto unknown for Hollywood cartoon features: a brand war. Other studios and directors had challenged Disney (see *Alice in Wonderland**), but now the studio was threatened by a rival with comparable marketing clout, and the star names to go with it.

Gratifyingly, *Antz* and *A Bug's Life* make a fascinating compare-and-contrast. In *A Bug's Life*, the ants are enslaved by gangster-style grasshoppers. The ants *know* they're slaves, but need an assortment of misfits (ant and non-ant) to teach them to fight back. In *Antz*, the oppressor is society itself, with Z (Allen) starting out as the lone dissident in his *Metropolis*-style anthill. The dystopia is more Aldous Huxley than George Orwell; we glimpse cute baby larvae being given either workers' pick-axes or soldiers' helmets. The soldier ants fight termites, but the war has been set up by a mad general (Hackman) who plots to cull the weaklings. The film's satirical and sexual innuendoes were pitched to the knowing, post-*Simpsons* crowd.

For much of the way, *Antz* focuses on Z's kvetching individualism ('What about my needs, what about *me*?'). Despite the adultified dialogue, it's not so different from contemporary Disney cartoons, typified by needy protagonists with 'I want' songs (Allen has a snatch of 'Almost like Being in Love'). More interesting is *Antz's Life of Brian* twist. Z selfishly flees the anthill, and is built up into a saviour by the masses back home, who spontaneously generate phrases like, 'Workers control the means of production.' The rebellion is resolved, not with Allen-style bathos, but with a fine-tuned inoffensive plot fudge, like Pixar's *WALL·E* a decade later.

The climaxes to both *Antz* and *A Bug's Life* show the ants saved by their collective natures, though *Antz* has the better flimflam symbolism, as the ants build their bodies into a giant tower. On the DVD

DIRECTOR Eric Darnell, Tim Johnson
PRODUCER Brad Lewis, Aron Warner, Patty Wooton
STORY Todd Alcott, Chris Weitz, Paul Weitz
SCORE Harry Gregson-Williams, John Powell
DESIGN John Bell, Raman Hui
ANIMATION Rex Grignon, Dennis Couchon, Sean Curran, Donnachada Daly

commentary, however, *Antz*'s directors inadvertently point up a contrast between the films. Both films' finales involve water: a flooding anthill in *Antz*, a rainstorm in *A Bug's Life*. In *Antz*, the water physics become human-scaled, with the flood presented like the Red Sea in *The Prince of Egypt**. The storm in *A Bug's Life* is far more elaborate, as raindrops explode like blobby bombs on the ants fleeing in convincing disorder.

It's the characters, though, that show up the different cartoon sensibilities, despite both casts having restrictive bug suits. The *Bug's Life* ants are zippy and elastic (especially their mouths), with only two legs. The *Antz* insects have heavier, less cute faces and *four* legs. Pixar's bugs have more energy, but the leads' anodyne voices underscore their resemblance to muppets. *Antz*'s characters are equally comparable to puppets, but with moments of presence from the often half-lit insect faces, and especially from Stallone's big-lipped stand-in. Even Stone's brittle, haughty heroine has a certain arch-browed, curved-mouth charm. Z, though, is a bust, little more than a creepily charmless marionette blessed with Allen's unmistakable tones.

A Bug's Life earned more than double *Antz*'s takings, but the critical split was fairly even, many reviewers preferring *Antz*. However, it was soon eclipsed by DreamWorks' vastly more popular *Shrek**. Most of *Antz*'s true surprises – such as a bleakly funny battlefield reveal showing a 'wounded' soldier ant to be a severed head – now feel as out of (studio) character as the similarly grotesque moments in Pixar's début *Toy Story*.

El Apostol (The Apostle)
Argentina, 1917 – unknown
Quirino Cristiani
[Cut-outs]

DIRECTOR/ANIMATION Quirino Cristiani
PRODUCER Federico Valle
DESIGN Diogenes Taborda

In English, 'cartoon' means political caricature as much as funny animals, but graphic satire rarely figures in feature films. There are some exceptions in British animation; the Old Major pig in *Animal Farm** bears a suspect resemblance to Winston Churchill, while Tony Richardson's live-action *The Charge of the Light Brigade* (1968) has exquisite *Punch*-style sequences of Victorian empire-building, animated by Richard Williams's London studio (p. 205). On the other hand, Ralph Bakshi's raucous *Coonskin* (1975) presents America as 'a huge-titted nympho tease who shoots venereal bullets', in the words of critic Kim Newman.

However, there's evidence that the first few animated features may have all been political cartoons, beginning with *El Apostol* (1917). They were made in Argentina, the first by the illustrator-animator Quirino Cristiani, who made *El Apostol* when he was barely twenty. Cristiani is also credited with the first *sound* animated feature, *Peludopolis* (1931). All these films are lost, and it took cartoon historians such as Bruno Edera and Giannalberto Bendazzi to bring them to world attention. In 2007, the animator Gabriele Zucchelli directed an excellent documentary feature, *Quirino Cristiani: The Mystery of the First Animated Movies*, including interview footage of Cristiani himself.

In 1900, when Cristiani was four, he, his mother and siblings migrated from Italy to Buenos Aires to join Cristiani's father, who had gone there for work. (Viewers of vintage anime may find the situation familiar; Isao Takahata (p. 82) made a 1976 TV saga, *From the Apennines to the Andes*, about a poor Italian boy's quest taking him from Genoa to Argentina.) A free spirit, Cristiani studied zoo animals to improve his pictures and drew satirical cartoons for newspapers. His move into animation was prompted by Federico Valle, a pioneering Italian cameraman who'd filmed from Wilbur Wright's plane.

Valle funded *El Apostol*, whose cut-out figures anticipated *The Adventures of Prince Achmed** nine years later, though *Achmed* used silhouettes rather than Cristiani's political caricatures. The designs were by the cartoonist Diogenes Taborda. Cristiani handled the cut-outs by two different methods; he moved jointed figures laced with thread, and he replaced individual figures in sequence. Zucchelli's documentary includes a contemporary 'making-of' film about *Peludopolis*, in which Cristiani uses the replacement method to show two characters dancing.

El Apostol took ten months to make, opening on 9 November 1917. The film was described by Cristiani as an 'amiable' caricature of President Yrigoyen, the leader of Argentina's Radical Party, who pledged to fight corruption. In the story, Yrigoyen dresses as an apostle of Argentina's redemption and climbs Mount Olympus. After talking politics with the gods, Yrigoyen acquires Zeus's lightning bolt and smites Buenos Aires – a twenty-one-foot high model city created by the French architect Andres Ducaud, complete with cabs and coaches on wires. Finally, Yrigoyen awakes; we have been watching his dream.

El Apostol was a hit, playing in Buenos Aires for six months. Cristiani's follow-up, *Leave No Trace* played for a single day. It concerned the sinking of an Argentinian ship by a German U-boat (Argentina was neutral in World War I) and it opened in 1918, the same year as Winsor McCay's angry US short, *The Sinking of the Lusitania*. The more comical *Leave No Trace* was jinxed by its name. The government, fearing diplomatic frictions with Germany, confiscated it.

Also in 1918, Ducaud made *The Republic of Plenty*, while Valle produced *Gala Night at the Colon*. The latter used puppets, but Zucchelli points out that the surviving stills show no strings, suggesting that the puppets may have been moved by stop-motion. In the 1920s, the bohemian Cristiani founded a nudist colony, before returning to animation with *Peludopolis*. Again the subject was Yrigoyen, who'd returned to office in 1928. (The title came from the politician's nickname, 'El Peludo', or the hairy armadillo.) Two years later, Yrigoyen was deposed by General Uribu, whom Cristiani had to write into *Peludopolis* as its hero.

The running time of these early films is undocumented, leaving it uncertain if they're true features. Zucchelli argues that they probably would have been as long as a typical feature of the time, perhaps sixty or seventy minutes. (*El Apostol* would have been projected at sixteen or eighteen frames per second.) Zucchelli adds, though: 'To me, counting the minutes is less interesting than the fact that animation was no longer a curiosity among newsreels. It was a movie for which people bought tickets just to see the film.'

For the record, the historian Bruno Edera claimed the first animated feature was Italian, *The War and the Dream of Momi*. Edera also claims the film was released in 1916, a year before *El Apostol*. *Momi* (which other sources date to 1917) combines live-action with animated puppet battles, the latter handled by Spain's Segundo de Chomon. However, the film may have been less than thirty minutes long, judging by an unofficial internet copy, with Chomon's bellicose puppets on screen for perhaps half that time.

Avatar
US, 2009 – 163 minutes (extended to 170 minutes in a 2010 revise)
James Cameron
[Live-action and CGI]

According to legend, had things been slightly different, Hollywood's first feature-length cartoon wouldn't have starred Snow White but a princess of Mars. In the 1930s, a young cartoon director called Bob Clampett approached Tarzan creator Edgar Rice Burroughs about animating the author's sci-fi hero, John Carter. In Burroughs's stories, Carter is a former Confederate soldier, re-embodied on Mars with superhuman powers. 'A hero who can leap twenty feet into the air with ease, who fights four-armed green men astride eight-legged mounts!' boasted Clampett's showreel. 'John Carter does all this for an incomparably exotic Martian princess, whose skin is tinged the colour of reddish-copper.'

Actually, Clampett's *John Carter* wouldn't have been a feature. It was pitched as a set of animated shorts, comparable to the Fleischer studio's *Superman* films (see p. 41). Despite Burroughs's support, MGM turned *Carter* down, leaving Clampett to become a giant at Warner Bros. instead. (His classics include Daffy Duck's best short, *The Great Piggy Bank Robbery*, 1946, and the now-unshowable *Coal Black and de Sebben Dwarfs*, 1943.) A new *John Carter of Mars* is scheduled for 2012; it will be an effects-laden Disney spectacular, directed by *WALL·E*'s* Andrew Stanton.

However, *John Carter* has already inspired another sci-fi blockbuster, James Cameron's *Avatar*. 'The Edgar Rice Burroughs books, H. Rider Haggard – the manly, jungle adventure writers … I wanted to capture that feeling, but updated,' Cameron told *Entertainment Weekly*. John Carter is now Jake Sully (Sam Worthington), a twenty-second-century ex-marine who ships out to the planet Pandora. A lush forest world, Pandora has trees like skyscrapers, mountains that float in the air, and great birds and beasts. It also has a race of towering blue-skinned aboriginals, the Na'vi, who have tails, fight with bows and arrows, and are psychically linked to Pandora's Gaea-goddess.

The wheelchair-bound Sully projects his mind into an artificially grown Na'vi body. In this form, he meets a native woman warrior (Zoe Saldana, blazing throughout) and promptly falls for her. In *Avatar*'s most vivid moments, the characters seem uplifted from stereotype to archetype: the blunt, ignorant hero explorer, the exotic tiger-woman leaping into a firelit glade and loosing an arrow in mid-air. Invigorated by Pandora's wonders, Sully is reborn as a true Na'vi to fight the humans despoiling the planet.

It's a respray of the hero-going-native myth, but the very literalism of Cameron's vision gives force to the metaphor, as we see bodies rebuilt and synthesised. The army grunts steer giant anthropomorphic fighting robots; the Na'vi bio-bound with Pandora's flora and fauna. In a ballsy central set piece, the villainous humans bring down the Na'vi's titanic tree-home in a cascade of smoke and debris. This is a 9/11 perpetrated by American fire-power, and its obviousness doesn't belie its dramatic and thematic power. *Avatar* is post-colonialist fantasy, with the Na'vi as Native Americans; it's also Saint Paul in space, as Pandora's goddess chooses Jake as her instrument.

DIRECTOR/STORY James Cameron
PRODUCER James Cameron, John Landau, Eileen Moran
SCORE James Horner
DESIGN Rick Carter, Robert Stromberg, John Rosengrant, Neville Page
ANIMATION Richard Baneham, Andrew R. Jones, Paul Kavanagh, Daniel Barrett, Alex Burt, Mike Cozens, Jan Philip Cramer, Ben Forster, Robyn Luckham

The Na'vi are created with motion-capture, human actors turned into CGI figures. When *The Polar Express** used the same approach five years earlier, its characters were panned for looking inhuman. Conversely, *Avatar*'s flat-nosed, fluorescent-skinned aliens could almost be actors with unusually good *Star Trek* prosthetics. One reminder this *is* motion-capture is the presence of a maternal scientist played by Sigourney Weaver, who was in Cameron's *Aliens* a quarter-century before. When she appears in Na'vi form, she seems magically rejuvenated back to that time, albeit with blue skin and a tail.

Previous motion-captured stars had caricature and exaggeration – Gollum in *The Lord of the Rings* trilogy (2001 on), the 2005 King Kong. Both characters were realised by New Zealand's WETA studio, which handled most of *Avatar*'s effects. WETA mixed motion-capture with manual computer animation (key-framing). The latter accounted for 20 per cent of the Na'vi's body movements and 40 per cent of their faces (see the Introduction). Yet these 'cartoon' characters are no longer fabulous monsters or anthropomorphisms, despite their introduction in a luminous night scene more Barrie than Burroughs. It's only when the Na'vi share the frame with humans that we see them briefly as Harryhausen-type giants.

Pandora's other fauna are mostly standard beasts, super-panthers and rhinos, though there are some pleasingly demonic hyenas (sadly cutesified later) and an arresting sequence where Jake tames a sneering dragon on the brink of an impossible chasm. The flying, though, is less dynamic than in cartoons such as *Laputa** or *How to Train Your Dragon**. The epic fantasy compositions are presented in unprecedented depth and detail, filling the largest IMAX screens. The actors performed on bare stages, but Cameron viewed them through monitors in real-time virtuality, already framing the aliens against their supersized wilderness, when they're not proudly sustaining their close-ups.

The magnificent spectacle is sometimes lowered to the level of a theme park, and like most epics, there are disasters of dialogue and imagery. The slack middle act where Jake bonds with Neytiri resembles a bad Disney song montage, and the Na'vi's swaying religious rites rank among sci-fi's most ludicrous moments. Yet *Avatar* marks a tipping point in virtual-effects cinema. Both its characters and *mise en scène* are mostly drawn, designed and animated, and yet *Avatar* was *not* sold or received as an animated film. Rather, it puts us on Pandora for 'real', literally grounded in the details; Jake joyfully kicking up the dirt on his first Pandora run, or the grasses blowing wildly under a military 'copter.

Azur & Asmar: The Princes' Quest
France, 2006 – 99 minutes
Michel Ocelot
[CGI]

It takes more than goodwill to break Disney's spell. The storytelling of French director Michel Ocelot is so unlike Hollywood animation that one critic said of Ocelot's first feature, *Kirikou and the Sorceress* (1998), that, 'I felt the same restiveness as when I was a child and chanced upon an award-winning Czechoslovakian cartoon on TV.' For children's cartoon films with such slow rhythms, you must go to *Bambi** or *My Neighbour Totoro**, and even they have funny critters absent from *Azur & Asmar*. But Ocelot does marvellous monsters: a crimson-maned lion, a Roc-sized peacock, dressed up in his film's scorching colours.

Azur & Asmar is an 'Arabian Nights' fable of races, cultures and languages in harmonious overlap. Azur and Asmar are two boys, raised as brothers in medieval Europe. Azur is pale and blue-eyed, the son of a widowed lord, while Asmar is the dark-skinned son of an Arab maid. Natural rivals, Azur and Asmar fight and quarrel, but they have a strong brotherly bond. Angered by their rough-and-tumble, Azur's father banishes Asmar and his mother, but Azur journeys to Asmar's country to win the magic Djinn princess. Naturally, he must compete with the wronged and angry Asmar. Equally naturally, the boys end up fighting side by side.

Ocelot is identified with such uplifting fables (so much so that it's shocking to see his bawdy 1987 short *The Four Wishes*, about a quarrelling couple who sprout a profusion of genitalia). He spent his childhood in Africa, and remembers looking out of a window onto a Guinea landscape, seeing people walking by and being captivated by their beautiful dark skins, their costumes and head-dresses. *Kirikou* and *Azur & Asmar* use flat but radiant blocks of colour to make extraordinarily pleasing picture-book compositions, far from the quasi-realism of Pixar and DreamWorks.

Azur & Asmar is Ocelot's first CGI film (*Kirikou* was drawn), using restricted perspectives, characters in formal poses, and background décors of arabesque patterns. The characters are rooted in the antique silhouettes of *The Adventures of Prince Achmed**, most evidently when Azur and a child-princess actually *become* silhouettes in the branches of a tree. The human bodies are flat, only faces and hands in 3D. The radiant garments are flatly rendered, key-framed without cloth simulation.

The film's pleasure is in its leisurely telling. There's no voice-over, yet the narrative voice supersedes its heroes' personalities. The scenes where Azur and Asmar squabble and fight, then bond instinctively in shared adversity, are charming and true, though the characters never evolve past types. Unlike *Kirikou*, though, *Azur & Asmar* has a strong support cast. A comically bigoted rogue called Crapoux reveals unexpected pathos; the child-genius princess is delightfully unsappy.

Ocelot evokes a land of spice-scented markets and vast flower gardens, navigated in different ways. Azur, feigning blindness, crashes and stumbles drunkenly, while the princess slides and sprints through the picture. Some viewers may mistake Ocelot's unshowy stylisations for inertia, and his straight-backed heroes make one miss the irreverent Sabu of *The Thief of Bagdad* (1940). But inside the film's bookishness, there's no lack of charm, warmth and splendour.

DIRECTOR Michel Ocelot
PRODUCER Christophe Rossignon
STORY Michel Ocelot, George Roubiceck
SCORE Gabriel Yared
ANIMATION Laurent de la Chapelle, Christophe Barnouin, Magali Bouchet, Jean-Claude Charles

Bambi

US, 1942 – 70 minutes
David Hand
[Drawings]

By 1942, Disney was at war. On the day of Pearl Harbor, the studio's sound-stage had been commandeered by the US army for vehicle and anti-aircraft gun maintenance, with three million rounds of ammo stored in the parking lot. Mickey and Donald were starring in public-information films about chemical warfare, while propaganda shorts included a resprayed *Three Little Pigs* (1933) with a Nazi wolf.

Of *Bambi*'s cast, Friend Owl, who swoops through the softly radiant forest at the film's start, appeared on an army-commissioned insignia … wielding a machine gun. Flower the skunk popped up on another, in a gas mask. At *Bambi*'s world première in London in August 1942, the climactic forest fire must have struck a chord with the Blitzed audience. A film with no on-screen humans was now attached to humanity's greatest conflict, whether Walt and his audience liked it or not.

Bambi: A Life in the Woods was written in 1923 by the Jewish-Austrian novelist and playwright Siegmund Salzmann, writing as Felix Salten. Disney was introduced to the book in 1935 by MGM director–producer Sidney A. Franklin, who'd purchased the rights but was flummoxed by how to turn the deer drama into live-action. Walt announced the project days after *Snow White*'s triumphant première, by which time Salzmann's book had been banned by the Nazis.

It was the headiest time in Disney's history, of unbelievable creative ambition and fecundity. Not content with one feature follow-up to *Snow White**, Walt ploughed ahead with three: *Bambi**, *Pinocchio** and *Fantasia**, while he was also developing *Alice in Wonderland* and *Peter Pan* (1953). But the golden period ended when war broke out in Europe. The foreign markets vanished and *Pinocchio* and *Fantasia*, released in 1940, both flopped. In 1941, a bitter strike soured the studio and coloured Walt's reputation ever after. *Bambi*'s core animators were unaffected, but the strike delayed the later stages of an already sluggish production, even before Pearl Harbor.

Bambi made extensive use of the costly multiplane camera, giving depth to scenes such as the glorious opening forest reverie. Meanwhile, artists struggled to give the cartoon animals realistic anatomies (*Snow White*'s deer were flour sacks in comparison). The deer's faces, they learned, did not squash and stretch; those principles were better applied to their haunches, 'shoulders' and toe-tips to convey a 'massive swelling and thrusting up in the body', as Frank Thomas and Ollie Johnston put it in their book, *The Illusion of Life: Disney Animation*.

While the picture men studied fawns in a purpose-built studio zoo – and a deer carcass in a noisome art class – costs rose and nerves frayed. Walt made swingeing cuts to the film, reducing the animators to tears, but the last-ditch economies weren't enough. *Bambi* was yet another flop, and Disney entered its 'mashed potato and gravy' years of cheap package films (see p. 209).

To say that *Bambi* is about frolicking woodland animals is like saying *The Lord of the Rings* is about little men with hairy feet. Everyone knows the cute scenes; baby Bambi stuck on a fallen tree-trunk (one of

DIRECTOR David Hand
STORY Perce Pearce, Larry Morey, George Stallings, Melvin Shaw
SCORE Frank Churchill, Edward Plumb
ANIMATION Frank Thomas, Milt Kahl, Eric Larson, Ollie Johnston

the test animations that convinced Walt to make the film) or the rabbit Thumper's seduction by a girl bunny, his libido displaced to a helplessly pedalling paw. The children, led by Thumper, are all stumbles, laughter and chatter. The adults move cautiously and speak sparsely, sometimes with devastating weight: 'Man … was in the forest'; 'Your mother can't be with you any more.'

The focus is squarely on the beautifully drawn animals, their surroundings pushed back into pearly mist and negative space. The backgrounds were inspired by Tyrus Wong, whose sketches encouraged his fellow artists to soften and blur the branches and grasses of *Bambi*'s world. Impressionism blends with expressionism in bursts of colour. The forest fire is a shivering yellow painting, towering over the trees; the screen brightens to red-orange as the deer herd flees man; Bambi's fight with a rival stag is all struggling silhouettes, rimmed by livid golds and icy blues.

Scene flows to scene with absolute simplicity; the brief dance of Fall leaves as seasons pass links the film briefly to *Fantasia*. The terrible human villain is never seen, and the death of Bambi's mother – one of cinema's all-time traumas – is restricted to a gunshot, the bleakest of snowscapes and a heartbreaking tear. That Walt cuts from this to the silliest of spring-themed symphonies (with twittering bluebirds modelled on a 1933 short, *Birds in the Spring*) shows his trust and mastery of a medium that turns on a dime in a way unthinkable in live-action. The majestic final hero shot, of a stag standing proud and his father retreating, is Disney masculinity at its most iconic.

We laugh and we grieve, but mostly we marvel, at a faun's blinking introduction to a little April shower, to the miracles of snow and ice, to the magnificent herd representing the mystery of adulthood, bounding over Bambi's head with the clash of cymbals. Disney's point, admirably unspoken but transparent to a child, is that the fun and fear, the silliness and heartbreak, are all of a piece. This is a *real* grown-up cartoon.

Batman Beyond: Return of the Joker
US, 2000 – 76 minutes (original edit), 80 minutes (uncut 2002 edition)
Curt Geda
[Drawings]

In Pixar's superhero film *The Incredibles**, Helen Hunt's elastic matriarch warns her kids that super isn't invincible; they can be hurt, or killed. According to director Brad Bird,

> You make this connection between animation and superheroes. You think Saturday morning, where these very strange (cartoons) are designed around conflict and yet no-one dies or gets really injured … I think it's better if kids realise there's a cost, and if the hero gets injured and still has to fight, it's closer to life.

The Fleischer studio (see p. 87) made spectacular short *Superman*s for the cinema. In the runaway train film *Billion Dollar Limited* (1942), two characters plunge to their doom from a bridge; Lois Lane exchanges tommy-gun fire with gangsters; and Superman (weaker here than in his later incarnations) is bombarded with tear-gas and dragged downhill by the train. A few decades later, such feats were routinely vetoed by TV censors. For example, a Superboy TV cartoon was meant to show the junior hero stopping another train bare-handed, but it was changed in case kids tried doing the same.

A half-century of TV cartoon superheroes began with the likes of 1967's *Spider-Man*, with its 'Does whatever a spider can' song and psychedelic input from future auteur Ralph Bakshi (p. 75). Batman was voiced by Adam West in a Filmation cartoon, while Hanna–Barbera paired the character with Scooby-Doo. Superhero toons stayed kids' stuff, even while the comics turned violent; the 80s Batman strips *The Dark Knight Returns* and *The Killing Joke* were mainstream hits. The first cartoon to catch the dark trend was Japan's *Akira**, whose mutating, mass-murdering antihero suggested an unchained Hulk.

Tim Burton's live-action *Batman*, dominated by Jack Nicholson's scene-chewing Joker, led to the Emmy-winning *Batman: The Animated Series* in 1992. By TV standards this was a lavish cartoon, its noir, art-deco style (Warners called it dark deco) immortalised in the opening titles where Batman chases hoods through an impressionist urban netherworld, dispatching them in silhouette. With far stronger storytelling than Burton's films, it led to a cluster of linked shows, including the inevitable *Superman: The Animated Series*.

Batman Beyond grew out of an executive suggestion for a younger Dark Knight. The *Batman* cartoon team – Paul Dini, Bruce Timm, Alan Burnett and Glen Murakami – plumped for a warrior-trains-student story, as in the recent live-action *The Mask of Zorro* (1998). *Batman Beyond* is set in a Gotham City decades from now. The designers play down neon billboards in favour of ziggurats and sky-high flyovers. An aged Bruce Wayne, the first Batman, passes his mantle to seventeen-year-old Terry McGinnis. The streamlined Batman loses his cape (anticipating *The Incredibles*), and looks even more vampiric, with crimson wings. His mentor Wayne, still built like an American football player, is rasped by Kevin Conroy, who voiced Wayne/Batman in *The Animated Series*.

DIRECTOR Curt Geda
PRODUCER Alan Burnett, Paul Dini, Bruce Timm, Glen Murakami
STORY Paul Dini, Bruce Timm, Glen Murakami
SCORE Kristopher Carter
DESIGN Shane Glines, Glen Murakami, Bruce Timm
ANIMATION Shojiro Nishimi, Yoshinobu Michihata, Hiroyuki Aoyama, Nobuo Tomizawa, Atsuko Tanaka

A live-action *Batman Beyond* film was developed in 2000, with author Neal Stephenson approached as a consultant. Ultimately, though, the only *Beyond* film was the animated *Return of the Joker*, released to DVD that year. The decades-crossing plot involves the old and new Batmen, and the resurrection of Batman's clown-faced enemy the Joker, voiced by former Jedi, Mark Hamill. (Conroy said, 'It's almost as if he's possessed by the Joker; his whole face goes somewhere else, and you don't want to get too close.') Hamill's performance is manic and gleeful, but affectionate of the character; this Joker is both killer *and* clown.

Nonetheless, the doom-laden story echoed strips such as *The Killing Joke* and *A Death in the Family* where the Joker torments or kills Batman's nearest and dearest. Indeed, this is very much an invasion of the Batfamily; the pivotal image is of Batman's shadow falling over his 'children' in a gesture not of menace but protection. The film has an infamous flashback torture scene involving Batman's young ally Robin, going far beyond what was permissible on TV. Yet the torture is pivotal to the psycho-thriller story, and the payoff is redemptive.

There are exuberantly enjoyable action scenes, involving props such as a giant lava lamp and a weapons satellite raining fire (homaging an overblown set piece in *Akira*; it was actually drawn by the same Japanese animator, Hiroyuki Aoyama). The film's main limitation is it assumes a working knowledge of the Batman universe; for example, knowing who Tim Drake or Barbara Gordon are.

Once more, the superhero was censored. Warners executives vetoed the violence, and the initial DVD release was edited, with a crucial death scene re-animated off screen. However, a wave of interest from Bat-fans led to an uncut release in 2002, rated PG-13. Since then, more explicit superhero cartoons have appeared on DVD, such as 2007's *Superman: Doomsday*, busting out of the Saturday-morning slot for good.

Beauty and the Beast
US, 1991 – 84 minutes (extended to 91 minutes in the 2002 Special Edition)
Kirk Wise, Gary Trousdale
[Drawings with CGI]

Disney's *Beauty and the Beast* is a tale of transformation, narrated in the overtly stylised fashion of Broadway. Accounts of the film's production tend to foreground not directors Kirk Wise and Gary Trousdale, but animator Glen Keane, who supervised the reforming Beast, and lyricist Howard Ashman, who directed the singers from his sick-bed as he lay dying from AIDS. The musician Alan Menken deserves equal credit, but his lush style, unlike Ashman's pawky lyrics, was sadly institutionalised in subsequent Disney films.

Following 1989's *The Little Mermaid* (everyone seems to forget about *The Rescuers Down Under* in 1990), *Beauty and the Beast* cemented Disney's 'return' as an animation studio. Until *Up** and *Avatar** in 2009, it was the only animated feature nominated for a Best Picture Oscar, losing to *The Silence of the Lambs* in 1991. For sceptics, though, the new Disney was already brand-Disney. *Beauty and the Beast* was supposed to have been directed by London animators Richard and Jill Purdum (whose studio employed, among others, a young Sylvain Chomet, p. 46). The Purdums wanted a non-musical, reportedly 'dark' film, 'something not in the Disney mould', according to producer Don Hahn. They were let go, and Ashman and Menken brought aboard to repeat their musical success from *The Little Mermaid*.

Yet for all this creative rigidity, *Beauty and the Beast*'s first screening was in a uniquely metamorphic state at the 1991 New York Film Festival. This 'Work in Progress' (included on the DVD) interleaves pieces of finished animation with moving pencil sketches, static concept art and rough blockings, with the liquid mystery of Cocteau's *La Belle et la bête* (1946). In the giant ballroom, the titular dancers (hand-animated in the finished scene by James Baxter) are wire-frames moving in staccato, clockwork increments against the monochrome geometries of early CGI. The Beast – shown mostly in naked pencil tests – is a mass of snarling lines, dissolving into ensouled shades and scribbles, like *Forbidden Planet*'s (1956) Id monster.

The finished film lacks these dimensions, but it has a freshness and energy palpable in Belle's first swinging steps as she walks 'towards' camera with the presence of Julie Andrews, cueing her small provincial town to wake up and sing. Her song, 'Belle', is the radiant flipside to Menken and Ashman's tragicomic 'Skid Row' in the stage musical *The Little Shop of Horrors* nine years before. Even the villainous Gaston, a preening Adonis, is first seen uplifting the chorus with his chauvinist baritone.

Some of the animated crowd shots are trite and mechanical by classic Disney standards, especially in the finales to 'Belle' and 'Gaston', but they're easily outweighed by the flair of a jaunty, stand-shuffling French candlestick introducing the next number ('The dining room proudly presents … your dinner!'), or by the ballroom's swirling camerawork. This same flair makes Belle's overstated feistiness continually charming, now that its counter-stereotype has been thoroughly outmoded by the post-Disney heroines of *Belleville Rendez-Vous**, *Persepolis** and *Sita Sings the Blues**.

DIRECTOR Gary Trousdale, Kirk Wise
PRODUCER Don Hahn
STORY Linda Woolverton, Brenda Chapman, Burny Mattinson
SCORE Alan Menken
ANIMATION James Baxter, Mark Henn, Glen Keane, Andreas Deja

Back in the day, academics argued if *Beauty and the Beast* might be feminist (the man must reform to be fit for the woman; the woman's gaze is balanced against the man's in the 'Something There' duet) or not (it's still a fairytale marriage plot, and Belle happily loses herself against the Beast's chest or paw). Perhaps inadvertently, there's some looking-glass recursion about Belle's place in the story. We and the Beast know Belle is the answer to his predicament ('Who could ever learn to love a Beast?'). But the story is told *through* Belle, a wide-eyed adventuress and dreamer who might have almost conjured up the Beast, castle and all. These entwined framings add piquancy to the moment of (ostensible) free will when the Beast spurns their predestined story and frees Belle, sacrificing himself for love of her.

The critic Marina Warner wrote of Keane's Beast as 'male desire incarnate; he swells, he towers, he inflates, he tumesces'. But it's a displaced, sublimated desire beside Cocteau's literally smouldering Beast, or the throbbing cartoon Wolf of Tex Avery's *Red Hot Riding Hood* (1943). Disney's Beast hates and fears his monstrous body, like the incontinently ballooning boy in *Akira**. When he doesn't get his way, his roars give way to confused petulance in a snappy scene when he argues through Belle's door. (Keane based the Beast's comedic moments on Jackie Gleason in *The Honeymooners*, 1955.) Then he's coaxed into bathing, table manners and dance steps. In one sight gag, he's made up like the Cowardly Lion, though that's the limit. His manly honour is restored in a stormy rooftop battle, causing his saintly death and transfiguration in a crescendo of arched limbs and billowing linework. His human form is striking in the first reveal, until he speaks.

Keane drew another muscled Disney hero in 1999's *Tarzan*, but that character's physique outstripped his personality. CGI films have relegated monsters to comic or cuddly duties, while *Shrek** tried revising *Beauty and the Beast* by turning a beautiful princess into a homely ogress. Hayao Miyazaki's *Howl's Moving Castle* (2004) contrasted its hero's monstrous transformations with a girl's empowering human changes, from young to old and all points between.

Belleville Rendez-Vous (The Triplets of Belleville)
France/Canada/Belgium, 2003 – 80 minutes
Sylvain Chomet
[Drawings with CGI and brief live-action]

[The film was released in British cinemas as *Belleville Rendez-vous*, the name of its opening song. It was issued on UK DVD under the same name but also as *The Triplets of Belleville*, a translation of the French title, *Les Triplettes de Belleville*. It had the *Triplets* name in America.]

In 2009, I interviewed Pete Docter and Jonas Rivera, director and producer of Pixar's *Up**. The film deals with a curmudgeonly old man, left behind by his wife's death, and the extraordinary things he does after. I asked if the film-makers ever thought about widowing the wife and making her the main character instead. 'We did think about that,' said Docter. 'But we had developed this grouchy old man … . Maybe I'm sexist, but it just didn't seem appealing as an old woman, someone who would slam the door in people's faces.' Rivera concurred. 'It's almost movie logic; an old man gets more licence than an old woman.'

Six years earlier, though, the French director Sylvain Chomet made an Oscar-nominated feature about a dourly heroic granny. In the film, she odysseys to the towering city of 'Belleville' (a Frenchified New York) to save her kidnapped grandson, and encounters a benign three-crone coven of witchy musicians. Given the way *Up** goes, it's funny to see *Belleville*'s granny bop a boy scout painfully on the head.

Madame Souza, as our heroine is called, has a firm, querulous presence that's charismatic in itself. She only speaks three times, and we don't *see* her speak, which would be as wrong as Nick Park's dog Gromit suddenly growing a mouth. Souza's whiskery mouth is an obstinate line, contrasting with her busy black eyes. The comedy has minimal dialogue, taking its lead from Jacques Tati (there's a live-action clip from *Jour de Fête*, 1949) and the only significant speech is at the beginning and the end.

We start in France, where Souza adopts her orphaned-waif grandson, Bruno. The grief is lower key than in *Up*, but no less believable. A moment where Souza tries teaching Bruno to play the piano is moving; Bruno shakes his head helplessly and flees, while Souza plays a sad bottom note. She brightens him up by getting him a dog and bicycle (a reminder of his cyclist parents), and training him for the Tour de France. For a while, she communicates by blowing an insistent trainer's whistle. That and her huge orthopaedic shoe suggest the props of a clown whom no one would *dare* call funny.

The film is funny, of course, but Chomet doesn't indulge us; he spaces his gags out for the biggest laughs, and sprinkles them with vinegar. Disrespecting human dignity is one theme. Souza loves her grandson, but she has a unique way of showing it, toning his legs with a vacuum and egg-whisk and making him into, as critic Nick Bradshaw put it, 'the racing cyclist equivalent of a prize ox, all piston thighs and baleful eyes'. One villain is a human mouse, with a squeak and Mickey ears. The exhausted cyclists are compared to slaughtered pigs and horses. In the nastiest scene, a clapped-out cyclist (not Bruno) is casually murdered. We see the victim trembling, his eyes huge and rolling … and then, before the shot, Chomet throws in a whinny.

DIRECTOR/STORY Sylvain Chomet
PRODUCER Didier Brunner
SCORE Benoît Charest
DESIGN Sylvain Chomet, Evgeni Tomov
ANIMATION Nicolas Quéré, Emmanuel Guille, Antoine Dartige, Jean-Christophe Lie

The misanthropy is lightened by Souza's mini-heroics. When Bruno is kidnapped by the killers (wine-swilling Mafiosos), Souza chases them on a pedalo. We see the indomitable granny surmounting huge ocean waves in the film's defining image, accompanied by Mozart's *C-Minor Mass*. Even the bovine cyclists' purposeless pedalling is more authentic than the traffic jams and ceaselessly rattling trains of *Belleville*'s world. The climactic chase is built round the joke of the villains driving stretch-limo 2CVs which can barely turn corners and flip backwards on slopes like dominos.

The aged 'triplettes' whom Souza meets make STOMP-style music from fridges, vacuums and newspapers (Souza adds a bike wheel). The unplugged ethos is mirrored in the low-tech animation. *Belleville* opens with a bouncy, fantastical homage to Fleischer's 1930s 'Talkartoons', which included surreal classics such as *Minnie the Moocher* (1932) (see p. 141). In Chomet's tribute, Fred Astaire is devoured by dance shoes, banana dancer Josephine Baker is mugged by monkey-men, and the average viewer wishes it could go on longer. (*Who Framed Roger Rabbit** had the same problem: both films open *too* well.)

The prologue is in scratched monochrome, while the film proper consists of scratchily elegant drawings in brownish palettes, suggesting earth and sepia. The kooky players include coffin-shaped gangsters (who slot together like lego) and a literally spineless *maître'd*. The cute characters soon drop out, barring a grossly fat and lovable dog who takes some of the sting out of Chomet's insistence that Americans are all supersized barrage balloons. ('Because they are!' he snapped at one interviewer who asked.)

The last scenes sum up the film; a comic climax, a belly-laugh, a bittersweet coda consigning the tale to nostalgia, and a deadpan gag for viewers who wait through the credits.

Cinderella
US, 1950 – 74 minutes
Clyde Geronimi, Hamilton Luske, Wilfred Jackson
[Drawings]

The 1950s were book-ended by Disney princesses, *Cinderella* (1950) and *Sleeping Beauty* (1959). *Cinderella* saved the Disney animation tradition, or a semblance of it. It re-established Disney as the world's leading cartoon brand; small wonder later Mouse managements would use princesses to renew the line, with *The Little Mermaid* in 1989 and *The Princess and the Frog* two decades later. *Sleeping Beauty*'s failure, on the other hand, ended Walt's dreams of besting his younger self, the immortal, unreachable Walt who'd made *Snow White** a World War ago.

The Walt of *Snow White* was obsessed with making the perfect cartoon, to the point of pathology. One animator quoted by historian Michael Barrier described Walt at that time, 'like a madman, hair hanging down, perspiring … Christ, he was involved'. But Walt was burned by frustrations and flops, including his beloved *Fantasia**. By *Cinderella*, cartoons were making way for other toys. For much of *Cinderella*'s production, Walt wasn't even in America. Rather he was at Bristol harbour in England, overseeing Robert Newton and Bobby Driscoll on the first wholly live-action Disney feature, *Treasure Island*. During that time, *Cinderella*'s three directors mailed him memos, scripts and storyboards across the Atlantic.

Live-action was pervading Disney in other ways. The London release of *Cinderella* was double-billed with *Seal Island* (1948), the first of Disney's 'True-Life Adventures' nature films. *Cinderella* itself was largely pre-shot in live-action, not just as motion-reference for the animators, but as an economic way of defining cutting, staging and (in practice) viewpoints. The wholly cartoon scenes, as anyone could guess, were the cat-and-mice conflicts, mainly animated by Ward Kimball.

Cinderella's literal staging makes its live-action language overt, even as the cartoon effects can feel a trifle thin, if only by the standards of Disney's extraordinary heyday (for example, when Cinderella is multiply reflected in a cloud of bubbles). More striking are the frequent touches of noir. When Cinderella enters the stepmother's bedroom, she's framed by bars of shadow. There's more ostentatious chiaroscuro after her dress is destroyed by her spiteful sisters. Seen from above, Cinderella runs into the dwarfing dark of a hall, her figure illumined in one opening door, then another. The dress-tearing itself is a set of violent cuts, the rending implicit as Hitchcock might have liked.

For all these touches, many reviewers found the human scenes unbearably bland. Cinderella herself was variously called a blond non-entity, an American bobby-soxer and Snow White's doughy sister. Japanese director Hayao Miyazaki bemoaned the live-action approach: 'In trying to achieve a sense of symbolism by using an average young American woman as the model, (the Disney animators) lost even more of the inherent symbolism of the orginal story than they did with *Snow White*.' But the Cinderella character, drawn by Marc Davis and Eric Larson, actually stands up rather well for Disneyfied womanhood; she's mischievous, lightly ironic and a valued ally to the animals, not a passive idol like Snow White.

DIRECTOR Clyde Geronimi, Hamilton Luske, Wilfred Jackson
STORY Ken Anderson, Winston Hibler, Bill Peet
SCORE Oliver Wallace, Paul J. Smith
ANIMATION Eric Larson, Milt Kahl, Frank Thomas, John Lounsbery, Ward Kimball

Sadly, her Prince is a stiff, and the film fatally stalls during their ball encounter, though there's a surprising stress on Cinderella's female gaze in the staging and soundtrack (she leads the romantic number, 'So This Is Love'). The meeting is accompanied by ravishing night-blue art direction, spearheaded by Mary Blair. Its failure to save the scene should have been a warning to *Sleeping Beauty*, which often feels like nothing *but* design.

But *Cinderella* is really the adventure of the mice Gus and Jaq, both voiced by sound effects legend Jimmy Macdonald, who provided Mickey's falsetto after Walt. For me, nothing matches the greedy Gus's efforts to carry one *more* piece of cheese from the barnyard; at last he successfully braces the morsel against his teeth and totters away, straight into the leering cat Lucifer. The monster's golden moment is a game of Find the Lady, as Gus cowers under teacups. The cat picks up the *right* cup, puts it down, realises what he's done, and pulls a happy-sappy pose of tongue-wagging, paw-waving delight, flowing perfectly from the dancing rhythm. The snag; the floor-level antics suck the human world down the mousehole.

Cinderella, a lesser film than any of Disney's early masterpieces, is still one of the best four or five cartoon features that the studio would make in the next forty years. (*Sleeping Beauty* had treble *Cinderella*'s budget, and perhaps half its charisma, momentum and fun.) As an elegantly tamed *Snow White*, *Cinderella*'s cover version takes you back to the original. What if *Snow White*'s true successors, such as *Pinocchio** or *Fantasia**, had been as popular? Would Walt have stayed married to animation, not dallied with live-action and Mickey parks? Where could his dreams have led? It's like asking where would today's animation be had *The Simpsons* flopped, or *Toy Story**.

Comet Quest: The Adventures of Mark Twain
US, 1985 – 85 minutes
Will Vinton
[Clay stop-motion]

One of the most eloquent screen celebrations of a writer is the 1989 stop-motion short *Next*, by the British animator Barry Purves. In the film, a dapper Shakespeare takes to the stage and, without saying a word, gracefully performs a series of mimes or physical ciphers for each of his plays. In the best joke, a wooden bear trundles on from stage right; Shakespeare hastily exits, towing the bear behind him. Shakespeare is a puppet himself, but his smooth, precise movements define the film's meter as we pass through thirty-four plays in five minutes.

Will Vinton's feature-length portrait of the American humorist Samuel Clemens, or Mark Twain, doesn't have such elegant economy. The film is ingenious, though, and its best moments make touching use of fantasy to frame real life. Like Purves, Vinton works with stop-motion, but his characters, sets, skies and water are all made of clay. The characters' expressions can seem simple and rough-hewn, only to turn disarmingly nuanced. In his book *Clay Animation*, Michael Frierson notes how Twain was sculpted along the lines of *portrait-charge* or a loaded likeness, 'a large head with slightly exaggerated features on a small but detailed body'. But the medium makes even the overbearing Twain, his white whiskers bristling, feel contingent in form, like the fluidly reshaping scenery.

Written by Vinton's wife Susan Shadburne, *Comet Quest* starts with Twain's thoughts on Halley's comet. His birth coincided with the astral body; he declared, 'The Almighty has said, no doubt, "There go those two unaccountable freaks; they came in together, they must go out together."' He died when the comet returned. In the film, Twain, voiced by James Whitmore, builds a Verne-style airship for a rendezvous with the comet in the heavens. He takes along three earnest kids; Tom Sawyer, Huckleberry Finn and Becky Thatcher (Tom's sweetheart), characterised as Twain wrote them.

In the first scene, clay 'water' spills from a book on a library desk, melting it into the banks of the Mississippi. Like the previous year's *The Company of Wolves*, the surrealism smoothes the cavalier structure. Twain's aerial journey is less interesting than the extended interludes in which Tom, Huck and Becky witness visions from the author's writings. The longest of these is Twain's take on Adam and Eve, which Vinton animated as a featurette (*The Diary of Adam and Eve*, 1980) before the rest of the film. The story's cartoon whimsy (the Snake has sunglasses) is a good fit for a pettish comedy of the sexes.

Only when the reconciled Adam and Eve grow old do we see they're really Twain and his late wife. The pathos of these weathered oldsters foreshadows *Up**, though the mood is partly spoiled by a tweely synthesised score. Elsewhere in the film there's a version of Twain's comic story, 'The Celebrated Jumping Frog of Cavaleras County'; a visit to a heaven of supercilious aliens with telephone heads; and Twain playing a Gothic organ that's festooned with wailing faces.

DIRECTOR/PRODUCER Will Vinton
STORY Susan Shadburne
SCORE Billy Scream
DESIGN Joan C. Gratz, Don Merkt
ANIMATION Barry Bruce, Tom Gasek, Mark Gustafson, Bruce McKean, William L. Fiesterman

The script draws on another of Twain's interests, the divided soul, and applies it back to the writer. Vinton imagines that the genial, beloved creator of Tom and Huck has a dark doppelgänger, the despairing Twain of later life. Ravaged by tragedy, he lambasts humanity in works such as his posthumous 'The Mysterious Stranger'. Vinton's version is formidable. Satan, a headless figure holding a rippling mask, invites the children to make crude clay homunculi, resembling Aardman's character Morph. Satan brings the characters to life, then murders them all with passionless wrath. 'We can make more some time, if we need them.'

It's one of the clearest visions of animation as thanatos; the homely technique deepens the godly spite. (Vinton had previously used this effect for black comedy in his 1976 short, *Mountain Music*,

where a forest is annihilated by a rock concert.) Satan softly quotes Twain's text: 'Nothing exists save empty space and you, and you are but a thought.' Given that Twain's companions – Tom, Huck and Becky – are imaginings in his dream, his reply is a response to solipsism as well as to tragedy. 'The human race,' Twain declares, 'in all its poverty, has only one truly effective weapon: laughter.'

The film's US title is *The Adventures of Mark Twain*, not to be confused with a live-action biopic of that name. Vinton's best-known creations are the animated California Raisins, but *Comet Quest* is closer in spirit to his lyrical TV version of Antoine de Saint-Exupéry's *The Little Prince* (1979). In 2002, Vinton lost his Portland studio to new management, which renamed it Laika. Its first stop-motion feature, *Coraline*, is the subject of the next entry.

Coraline
US, 2009 – 100 minutes
Henry Selick
[Stop-motion with CGI; released in 3D]

Coraline's director Henry Selick, discussing stop-motion's application to scary subjects, said, 'Stop-motion brings a charm, a warmth – it takes a little bit of an edge off the darkest, most troubling parts of the story, and adds a little creepiness to parts that might be too sweet.' It's an interesting tweak on a venerable anti-Disney argument, that Disney neutralises dark and upsetting folk-tales and turns them into corporate cream puffs. Selick was fending off the opposite charge, that he had made a kids' film too frightening for children.

Stop-motion isn't *inherently* warm or charming, any more than the witchcraft it resembles. *Coraline* points this up in its opening sequence, in which inhuman metal fingers unstitch a cloth doll, gut it of stuffing, and rebuild it as a replica of the main character. The sequence recalls Svankmajer shorts such as *Jabberwocky* (1971), in which plastic dolls are daintily cooked and eaten *by other dolls*.

Not that eleven-year-old Coraline resembles a doll; she's an immensely expressive stop-motion heroine, well voiced by Dakota Fanning. She lacks the stonefaced poetry of Aardman's dog Gromit, but her liquid expressions, designed by Shane Prigmore, are always engaging. During production, computers handled her transitional expressions, her inbetweens, but even these had a material reality, being turned into 3D print-outs and attached physically to the puppet. On screen, Coraline has the dancing curiosity of a Disney princess, and the pouts and petulance of a normal kid.

In the film, Coraline's family move into a sprawling house, imprisoned by a rugged, rainswept Oregon landscape. Bored, Coraline fumes at her preoccupied parents, but by night, she's led through a door into *another* house. Not only is this one brighter and deeper (especially in the 3D version) but it also has better parents, who are welcoming, fun-loving and magic. The 'other' mother and father resemble her parents, but they have buttons for eyes (Coraline's own eyes are cartoonily round). It warns us that this isn't *Alice in Wonderland* but *Hansel and Gretel*, and Coraline is in the gingerbread house.

Based on a book by Neil Gaiman, *Coraline*'s siblings include Clive Barker's children's tale *The Thief of Always*, which was developed as an unmade CGI film; Paul Berry's stop-motion nightmare *The Sandman* (1991), about an eye-eating monster; and Miyazaki's *Spirited Away**, about the importance of getting names right. In *Coraline*, many of the girl's peers call her 'Caroline', spoonerising her identity and alienating her further from reality. Like *Spirited Away*, *Coraline*'s unusual structure can disengage some viewers. The film takes a long time setting and elaborating its magic trap before letting the girl see it.

Many fantasies work on 'little big' principles, where small spaces contain impossibly large ones (Narnia's wardrobe, Doctor Who's TARDIS). *Coraline*'s space shrinks through the film, its enticingly dimensional magic world leading nowhere and disintegrating at the climax. The film looks inward, with elegant match-cuts and mutating visual rhymes. A garden that blooms for Coraline in the first half becomes a carnivorous nightmare in the second. Reality is destabilised through transforming landscapes and the shifts

DIRECTOR Henry Selick
PRODUCER Henry Selick, Bill Mechanic, Claire Jennings, Mary Sandell
SCORE Bruno Coulais
DESIGN Jason Lajka, William Sturrock, Martin Meunier
ANIMATION Anthony Scott, Travis Knight, Trey Thomas, Eric Leighton, Phil Dale

from smooth to stuttery animation, as when dozens of jumping mice perform a dance for Coraline, using the Puppetoon replacement techniques of George Pal.

Selick added a boy to the story to let Coraline better express herself, but the film's real narrator is its score, written by Bruno Coulais, also responsible for 'L'Amour d'escargots' ('Snail Love') in the nature film *Microcosmos* (1996). In *Coraline*, Coulais takes a sequence where the bored girl explores her house and sets it to glossolalia choruses. These are more detached than composer Joe Hisaishi's pitter-patter play for a comparable scene in Hayao Miyazaki's *My Neighbour Totoro**. Both scores are fond of their subjects but Coulais's music is more childlike for children, more adult for adults, playing on the perceptions of each. (Coulais also composed for the cartoon, *The Secret of Kells**.)

Coraline improves on repeat viewing, though its fruity comic turns – especially two elderly 'Baby Jane' burlesque actresses, voiced by Dawn French and Jennifer Saunders – can distract from the delight. The film's heart is in Coraline's multifaceted relationship with her parents, especially her two mothers, both voiced by Teri Hatcher. The button-eyed mother summons up the predator terrors of *Snow White** or *Cinderella**, yet she's cancelled out by the abrasive yet touching relationship between Coraline and her *real* mother. The puppets charmingly convey the mutual similarities of parent and child in a film that's good-humoured and juicily creepy.

Dumbo
US, 1941 – 63 minutes
Ben Sharpsteen
[Drawings]

Both as cartoon fable and cartoon history, Disney's *Dumbo* was the story of 'The Runt Who Could'. Walt himself disparaged it as 'one of those little things we knocked out between epics'. It was a cut-price, swiftly made trifle, barely an hour long, made to claw back some of the funds drained by the production of *Pinocchio**, *Fantasia** and *Bambi**. Yet *Dumbo* trounced them all, critically and commercially, as its titular hero triumphs over the grown-up elephants who try to keep him from the limelight.

Why was *Dumbo* more popular? Its unpretentiousness has been cited, and its lack of horror (though its pink elephants are terrifying). Then there's its cartooniness; *Dumbo* turned away from ornate pseudo-realism to a cartoon reality where a stork sits on a cloud above a Florida with FLORIDA printed on the landscape. For myself, I think it's the proudly sentimental happy ending that's organic to the film. Other Disney endings were makeshift (Snow White being taken by her cardboard prince, Pinocchio becoming a real boy), or sombre (Bambi loses his mother forever, and only reproduces his childhood Eden through his offspring, from whom he's patriarchally distanced in the last shot). *Dumbo* ends with the big-eared elephant changing world history, but that's almost irrelevant; what matters is that he gets his mother back.

Dumbo returns to the spontaneous invention of Disney's shorts, the 'Silly Symphonies' especially. The fleet of storks delivering babies, the parade of circus clowns and animals, and the chuffing I-think-I-can train in a toy landscape are all natural short subjects. But *Dumbo*'s pacing is actually faster than many shorts, so that an enchanting playtime between mother and child runs directly into Dumbo's harassment by a buck-toothed boy (who plainly missed the coach to *Pinocchio*'s Pleasure Island), and then on into Mrs Jumbo's stampede, culminating in the traumatic parting of mother and child. So swift is the film that the last act, full of story and emotional twists (Dumbo's meeting the crows, his finding he can fly, the brilliant 'magic feather' placebo and the thrilling finale in the circus tent), takes barely ten minutes.

The film is also supremely eerie, taking Disney past the straight scares of *Snow White* and *Pinocchio*. While *Bambi* favoured post-Disney artistic devices – unseen villains, impressionistic forest fires – *Dumbo* goes for all-out cartoon craziness. Hulking roustabouts and leering clowns have energised routines. A cosmos of pink elephants emerges from bubbles, their grinning shapes evoking paper ribbons. They rush round the screen in racing cars and rollercoasters, a scary and hilarious vision of modern life gone mad. *Dumbo* is the best feature the Fleischers never made (the film opened just before that studio's flop, *Hoppity Goes to Town**). Ex-Fleischer animator Hicks Lokey worked on both the clowns and pink elephants.

But the scene long enshrined as Disney's zenith is 'Baby Mine', when Dumbo visits his imprisoned mother. The mother's feet are chained; their trunks must clutch and caress through iron bars. The elephants were drawn by Bill Tytla, inspired by his two-year-old son, and he turns Dumbo into a human baby before

DIRECTOR Ben Sharpsteen
STORY Joe Grant, Dick Huemer
SCORE Oliver Wallace, Frank Churchill
DESIGN John P. Miller, Martin Provenson, Maurice Noble
ANIMATION Bill Tytla, Fred Moore, Ward Kimball, John Lounsbery, Art Babbitt

our eyes. Those few seconds of moving drawings, with the circles and crescents of Dumbo's eyes and mouth in heartrending flow as the trunks curl and our tears fall, are widely seen as character animation's Holy Grail.

Then again, some of my own favourite scenes, such as the lumbering fall of the elephants' ungainly pyramid (largely drawn by John Lounsbery) and the happy antics of the drunken mouse Timothy (drawn by Fred Moore), are sternly singled out by historian Michael Barrier, who sees them as some of *Dumbo's* worst animation. Other parties condemn the film's cackling 'black' crows with their minstrel overtones – 'good old family racism', sneered the TV cartoon *Family Guy* (1999–) in a swipe at the film – yet they still come over as the smartest, wittiest and most tolerant characters on screen. Their crazy steps and shuffles were by Ward Kimball; it's hard to imagine them ever being written out of history.

A lack of documentation leaves it unclear how involved Walt was in *Dumbo*, though historian-animator John Canemaker cites studio notes on a story conference (about the pink elephants), suggesting that Walt was focused and detail-orientated. Barrier, though, argues that *Dumbo's* best animation, where an artist like Tytla could fully identify with the character he drew, made Walt redundant. It was a case for a new cartoon cinema; *La politique des animateurs*?

Halfway through *Dumbo*, the circus clowns sing of hitting their boss for a raise ('Oh, we're going to get more money, Because we know we're funny!'). The scene was drawn by Art Babbitt; soon after, he'd confront Walt through a megaphone on the picket line in the 1941 Disney strike. Bill Tytla, his friend from before Disney, would be with him. It would not end well, and by the time *Dumbo* opened to acclaim, Disney – the man and the studio – had changed forever.

The Emperor's Nightingale
Czechoslovakia, 1949 – 72 minutes
Jirí Trnka, Miloš Makovec
[Stop-motion with live-action framing scenes]

DIRECTOR Jiří Trnka, Miloš Makovec
PRODUCER Bohumír Buriánek
SCORE Václav Trojan
DESIGN Jiří Trnka, Milena Naubauerova, Karel Sobotka
ANIMATION Bohuslav Šrámek, Břetislav Pojar, Jan Karpaš, Zdeněk Hrabě, Stanislav Látal

In his online book, *How to Succeed in Animation*, the American animator Gene Deitch describes coming to Czechoslovakia for the first time. It was 1959, and he would work there for the next half-century.

> One of the first things I noticed about the way (the Czech animators) worked, is how they related to the figures they were animating. They referred to them in just that way, that they were animating *figures* … . The mouths did not move as they spoke dialogue, and the eyes did not really look … . There was no real development of character. All of those things were secondary to a symbolic approach to storytelling.

The foremost Czech animator was Jiří Trnka, who'd co-founded the great Prague animation studio Bratri v Triku (Trick Brothers). Born in the aftermath of World War II, the studio would produce more than 1,600 titles. (British viewers may remember the Mole cartoons.) However, Trnka himself favoured puppet animation, creating a sister studio where he could develop the medium his way. Czech puppetry goes back centuries, and Deitch and other commentators see this heritage as underpinning the country's cartoons.

Ladislas Starewitch (p. 174) and *King Kong**'s Willis O'Brien created puppet beasts with curling lips and flashing teeth. Trnka's toy people had neither.

> From the beginning, I had my own conception of how puppets could be handled – each of them to have an individual but static facial expression … . In practice, this has tended not to enhance the realism, but rather conduce to naturalism.

Trnka was clear how his figures should differ from drawn cartoons. 'The very nature of (drawn) cartoon figures calls for continual motion. It is not possible to stop them, and neither is it possible to bring them into a state of contemplation.' In *The Emperor's Nightingale*, based on Hans Christian Andersen's story, an impassively baby-faced emperor sheds a tear as he hears the nightingale's song. Without a moving mouth, it's left to the turn of the emperor's head, to close-ups, pull-outs, dissolves and shadows to connote unsayable feelings.

Made in the late 1940s, the film coincides with France's *Le Roi et l'oiseau**, another Andersen story treated in a very unDisney way. (Trnka illustrated books of fairytales, Andersen's included.) In *Nightingale*, a lonely live-action boy shut in a mansion dreams that he's the cosseted Chinese emperor, surrounded by glittering knick-knacks and robotically filing courtiers who occasionally scurry in panic. A real robot clangs cymbals, remorselessly measuring the clockwork days.

Even the nightingale is travestied by technology. A mechanical golden bird supplants it because it sings the same song to order, 'Without life, without meaning.' (What would Trnka have made of cartoon videos?)

Soul-sick, the emperor is being taken by Death at his bedside when the true nightingale saves him.

Nightingale is easy to look at, despite its drab DVD appearance (a consequence of the film's conversion from Agfacolor to Technicolor when it went to America). The English narration was written by the poet Phyllis McGinley and spoken by an eloquently avuncular Boris Karloff. The haunting music is by Trnka's regular collaborator Václav Trojan. British viewers of a certain age will think of children's music-box animations: *Camberwick Green* (1966), *Bagpuss* (1974). The emperor's palace is full of soft hanging threads, with fronds, cacti and twigs for the exteriors.

Yet Trnka's slow play of stolid toys is hard to *watch*. In the first half, the soporific pace is only relieved by gentle jokes and fleeting turns; a honking frog with an umbrella, a simian-looking astronomer.

When the nightingale appears, Trnka's minimalist evokings of feeling are sporadically arresting, rising to a crescendo of montaged small gestures as Death approaches. The shift into menace is understated, with the sense of the awful only puppets convey. The emperor trapped in his bed is frightened and frightening. Even when the darkness passes, Trnka gives us a lingering tour of Death's garden of tranquil shadows, as if bidding us not to forget.

Philistine viewers, though, may be relieved that the puppets in Trnka's later *A Midsummer Night's Dream** move more and contemplate less. The political subtexts of *Nightingale*'s omnipresent rules and railings are more pungent in Trnka's later shorts. The most famous of these is *The Hand* (1965), Trnka's sardonic Orwellian fantasy, which is perhaps the most iconic and universal political animation ever made. It was Trnka's last film; he died in 1969.

The Fabulous World of Jules Verne
Czechoslovakia, 1958 – 83 minutes
Karel Zeman

[Live-action, stop-motion, and other techniques. Some editions of the US release feature an extended introduction by the broadcaster Hugh Downs.]

The magic of Verne's novels lies in what we would call the world of the romantically fantastic adventure spirit; a world directly associated with the totally specific which the original illustrators knew how to evoke in the mind of the reader ... I came to the conclusion that my Verne film must come not only from the spirit of the literary work, but also from the characteristic style of the original illustrations and must maintain at least the impression of engravings.

DIRECTOR/STORY Karel Zeman
PRODUCER Karel Zeman, František Hrubín
SCORE Zdeněk Liška
DESIGN František Màdl, Vilém Janik
ANIMATION Arnost Kupcik, Jindrich Liska, František Krčmář

In his day, Prague film-maker Karel Zeman (1910–89) was seen as the heir to Georges Méliès, the silent-screen magician who fired a rocket into the eye of the moon. Today, Zeman seems just as much a precursor to today's digital unrealities, worlds that glory in stylised, artificial fantasy. That doesn't mean *Avatar**, *The Lord of the Rings* trilogy (2001 on) or even *The Matrix* (1999), whose fake world barely registers under the violent superheroics. Rather it means the candy-coloured collages of *Speed Racer* (2008, by *The Matrix*'s Wachowski brothers); the stormy Greece of *300* (2006); the hard-boiled monochrome of *Sin City* (2005); and the neon circuitry of *Tron* (1982).

Zeman, though, wasn't interested in violence, or spectacle in the modern blockbuster sense. Instead, he had an animator's love of handicrafts and the draughtsman's line. In *The Fabulous World of Jules Verne*, real actors and live-action sets are mashed up with drawings that indeed evoke engravings. Many of the images are overlaid with black parallel lines, mimicking an artist's hatching, and re-echoed in the pin-striped costumes, décor and models.

But it's Zeman's mix-and-match effects that are truly special. In one shot, we might be watching a photo of the hero sitting inside an animated steam car. In the next, we're looking at the real actor sitting in what's apparently a real vehicle, though we quickly lose track of which bits of a shot are 'real' and which are miniatures, *trompe l'oeil* scenery, mechanical props, cut-outs or stop-motion puppets. Like the work of Zeman's countryman Svankmajer (p. 16), this is true surrealism, not elevating dreams to reality but always the reverse.

Zeman first made his name with a range of stop-motion shorts, including the popular 'Mr Prokouk' series and *Inspiration* (1949) whose figures were made of glass manipulated by heating. In 1955, Zeman made a feature-length dino-fantasy, called *Journey to the Beginning of Time* in the US, where a group of (real) boys row down a river and see an array of stop-motion creatures. As in *Fantasia**, there's a set piece battle between a T-Rex and a stegosaurus.

Zeman was dissatisfied. 'The spectator can tell the difference between real and faked surroundings when he wants to,' he said. 'A realistic representation of fantasy is beginning to have a sensational and cheap

look.' By *Verne*, his live actors were almost incidental. 'My heroes were not allowed even to sneeze or scratch their heads; they had to adapt themselves completely to their unreal surroundings.' In the film, they act with a rigid reserve, in line with decorous Czech puppetry.

Jules Verne is set in what we would now call a steampunk world, full of never-were inventions. A miniature zeppelin is flown by a single pedalling pilot; more pedalos are driven underwater by divers, complete with hand-bells; a mini-sub swims with mechanical flippers; and there's a giant super-cannon WMD. In the story, a childlike scientist is kidnapped by pirates who ram-raid ships in their sub, then retreat to their island lair. The villains dupe the scientist into creating the terrible cannon, while a nondescript hero tries to thwart them. The story is from a lesser-known Verne book, *Facing the Flag*, though most viewers would receive it as a variant of *20,000 Leagues under the Sea* (1954), filmed by Disney a few years earlier.

Zeman's film has an underwater fight with a stop-motion squid, but it's brief. The director is far more interested in creating a cumulative dream through his *range* of critters and trick-shots, supported by Zdeněk Liška's eerily mechanical score. The loveliest effects are often the quaintest. In a lady's chamber, the shards of light coming through a window are a frozen illustration. A film-in-film interlude shows cut-out war-camels on skates. The massive explosions are realised through drawings and stage-smoke.

The mononchrome visuals are based on illustrations by Edouard Riou, Leon Bennett and other Verne artists. Zeman's next feature, *Baron Munchausen* (1961) introduced exquisite colour tinting. It's wittier and more sophisticated than *Verne*, but the brilliance of its early scenes rather deflates the rest. Zeman's numerous later features, including another Verne-esque adventure, 1967's *The Stolen Airship*, have long been unavailable in English. Surely a revival is overdue?

Fantasia
US, 1940 – 124 minutes
Ben Sharpsteen and eleven others
[Drawings with live-action. The original limited 1940 release included a fifteen-minute interval.
The film has been released in several different versions.]

Fantasia opens with Deems Taylor, better known to 1940 audiences as a radio broadcaster than a composer, walking on stage amid a tuning-up orchestra. As *Fantasia's* host, he explains that this animated feature won't tell a single story; rather, it will be a series of classical music pieces set to animation. (*Fantasia's* working title was *The Concert Feature*.) What we'll see, Taylor says,

> are the designs and pictures and stories that music inspired in the minds and imaginations of a group of artists. In other words, they are not going to be the interpretations of trained musicians … which I think is all to the good.

The film, however, is blatantly seeking musical legitimacy. Its conductor is Leopold Stokowski, a tawny-haired maestro star and proven screen property who'd appeared in the 1937 musical comedy *One Hundred Men and a Girl*, featuring Deanna Durbin. We mostly just see the great man's illumined back as he leads us into *Fantasia's* animation. The first sequence is a semi-abstract piece, set to Stokowski's symphonic rendering of Bach's 'Toccata and Fugue'. The on-screen ripples and contrails are linear simplifications of the work of Oskar Fischinger, a German avant-garde animator.

Then come dances from Tchaikovsky's 'Nutcracker Suite': flower fairies, sultry goldfish and Art Babbitt's famous nodding mushrooms (on screen for barely a minute). After that, with apologies to Stokowski, comes *Fantasia's* true icon; Mickey Mouse as Dukas's 'The Sorcerer's Apprentice', overwhelmed by his army of water-bearing broomsticks. Stravinsky's 'The Rite of Spring' takes place on an early Earth of volcanoes, evolution and dinosaurs. Then there's a cherub-strewn version of Beethoven's 'Pastoral Symphony', more on which below; and a burlesque of Ponchielli's 'Dance of the Hours', with ballerina ostriches, hippos, elephants and alligators. Damned souls caper in hellfire for a colossal Devil, to the screaming strings of Mussorgsky's 'Night on Bald Mountain'. Dawn segues into a secularised 'Ave Maria' (Schubert) where the Madonna – after much indecision on Walt's part – doesn't show.

Fantasia's critical reputation is mostly the centaurettes' fault, those half-horse, half-female fancies, disporting themselves round Mount Olympus in the Pastoral segment. In 1995, Britain's Channel 4 screened a muck-raking documentary called *Secret Lives: Walt Disney*. With admirable precision, it homed in on the centaurettes. '(*Fantasia's*) banal, often tacky imagery came as a disappointment to many,' explained the narration. 'The heads of Disneyfied American teenagers are grafted onto the bodies of centaurs … . On seeing this, (Walt) Disney was impressed. He said, "Gee, this'll make Beethoven." '

Actually, the Beethoven comment came from a story meeting prior to the animation, and no 'Gee' was transcribed. (Neal Gabler quotes the line in his Disney biography.) But such smears were part of a fight

DIRECTOR Samuel Armstrong, James Algar, Bill Roberts, Paul Satterfield, Ben Sharpsteen, David Hand, Hamilton Luske, Jim Handley, Ford Beebe, T. Hee, Norman Ferguson, Wilfred Jackson
STORY Joe Grant, Dick Huemer
ANIMATION Art Babbitt, Les Clark, Fred Moore, Bill Tytla, Wolfgang Reitherman, Ward Kimball, Eric Larson, John Lounsbery

Walt had picked himself, setting the ordinary American (that is, himself) against the stuffed shirts of the music establishment.

'We figured that if ordinary folk like ourselves could find entertainment in the visualisations of so-called classical music, so would the average audience …' Walt said after *Fantasia*'s release.

> I imagine that the twelve hundred young people in my organisation who helped make *Fantasia* are a pretty fair cross-section of average American culture. They're from the average American home with the average American advantages and upbringing. Every day I see them prove they know the difference between the real stuff and the phoney.

The populism both provoked and pre-empted a blunt response from Igor Stravinsky, the only living composer represented in *Fantasia*. He declared, 'The mass add nothing to art.' Well, *Fantasia* may not be art, though the label fits it surely more closely than 'kitsch', which reviewers wave at the film like a talisman. For what *is* clear is that, within the hand-drawn form, *Fantasia*'s scope and spectacle are matchless.

In 'The Rite of Spring', for example, we wander through space to a molten Earth where volcanoes blast like ships' funnels. From macrocosm to underbrush; the Nutcracker is a waterborne ballroom of whirling blossoms, cascades of dancing thistle-men. Gibbous legions swarm round Bald Mountain; one reviewer described them as mad sperm. Dance of the Hours' bestial ballet ends in zigzag insanity, with the 'gators riding ostriches and twirling hippos on their scales.

Walt publicly thanked Stokowski and Taylor for 'holding my head up when the water got too deep'. But doesn't Mickey command water with the stolen Sorcerer's hat? No, he only dreams he does, when it threatens to drown him (later, it drowns the whole Earth). After his omnipotent master saves the day, Everyman Mickey gives his cheesiest grin in the film's most Disney moment. But the Sorcerer cocks his brow like Walt. Is Walt him, Mickey or both? The question exercised critics, who noted that *Fantasia* was made when Walt was at the height of his hubris, and rushing into calamity (see p. 209).

The scowling Sorcerer, who conjures great butterflies into being and parts the waters like Moses, is a power sibling to Stokowski on his podium, Zeus throwing down his thunderbolts and even Chernabog, the devil of Bald Mountain, toying with the damned in his giant hands. But there are gentler magicians, more in line with the Disney we know, like the Nutcracker flower-fairy who yawns, lounges and lights up a spiderweb. Then there are the heroes without magic: the perky little mushroom, captivatingly out of step with his peers; the bold foal Pegasus, chasing a rainbow to its underwater roots; and the animal ballerinas who spoof a spoof through the sheer beauty of their dance steps. Chuck Jones mocked *Fantasia*'s hubris in his Wagnerian cartoon *What's Opera Doc?*, but Dance of the Hours had beaten him at his parodic game.

Fantasia's first wide release, bereft of its pioneering multichannel 'Fantasound', was reduced to around eighty minutes. Forty years later, a 1982 release replaced Stokowski's score with one digitally reorchestrated by Irwin Kostal. Both these apocrypha are now lost to history. The 2001 DVD retains Taylor's more verbose narration that's trimmed from most prints, though the 'restoration' overdubs him. The supposedly uncut DVD does *not* have any of the long-excised shots of the centaurettes' simpering, kinky-haired, hoof-shining black maid.

The belated sequel, *Fantasia 2000*, was the first animated feature released in the IMAX format, which would have impressed Walt more than the film. It only rises to the level of the original in its last sequence. With some irony, it's set to another Stravinsky piece, 'The Firebird'. Cleverly, the animators set *Fantasia*'s macho motifs – the Firebird is both a volcano *and* a demon – against a Nutcracker-style gentle flower-fairy. Her swelling pantheist victory convinces much more than Walt's Ave Maria.

Fantastic Mr Fox
US, 2009 – 86 minutes
Wes Anderson
[Stop-motion]

The stop-motion *Fantastic Mr Fox* adapts a British classic, Roald Dahl's tale of a fox's battle with three monstrous farmers ('Boggis, Bunce and Bean, one fat, one short and one lean'). It was animated in Britain, at London's Three Mills complex, and opened in Britain before America. Yet it's stamped by its Texan director, indie icon Wes Anderson, who never hides the film's jerky motions or transatlantic overlays.

Dahl's tale, like Starewitch's stop-motion *Le Roman de Renard**, celebrated its hero's brilliance as he steals the farmers' property from under their noses, then outdigs them when they rip up his hill with giant cranes. That's all in the film, but the 'quote-unquote Fantastic Mr Fox', voiced by George Clooney, has changed. Anderson makes him a tweed-and-corduroy American bourgeois, who frets whether anyone reads his newspaper column, or if he'll die at the same age as his father ('I'm seven non-fox years old!'), before tearing into his buttered toast. The animals – all American – play hilariously garbled baseball, listen to Disney's 'Davy Crockett' anthem and give Animal Power salutes. The humans are British Buckinghamshire – Dahl's turf – with Michael Gambon's chief villain coming over as a cross between Jeremy Clarkson and Dahl himself.

Anderson co-wrote the script with Noah Baumbach, who'd directed the family-lacerating live-action drama, *The Squid and the Whale* (2005). Their only concessions to the kids are to invent an all-purpose swear word ('cuss', with variants like 'cluster-cuss') and to drop in occasional phrases from Dahl's story, which sit oddly amid the dry indie-isms. (Dahl's colourful descriptions of the farmers, for instance, are now delivered deadpan by Bill Murray's lawyerly badger.) Pixar would have used the younger foxes as a bridge to child viewers; Anderson makes them into moody, twitchy teens. *Fantastic Mr Fox* is a 'family' film only because the main characters happen to be funny-looking animals who sometimes do cartoonish things.

But this is a particular *kind* of cartoon. Take away its soundtrack – the script, the voices and a quick-shuffle song list ranging from the Beach Boys to a banjo Jarvis Cocker – and *Fantastic Mr Fox* would be as dateless and stateless as the toy-like toons it recalls. The characters, with their finger-rippled hair, may reference Starewitch and *King Kong**, but the film is closer to Britain's *Camberwick Green* (1966), *Trumpton* (1967) and *Chigley* (1969); to France's *Le Manège enchanté* (2005); to Czechoslovakia's *The Emperor's Nightingale**; and to Rankin/Bass's *Rudolph the Red-Nosed Reindeer* (1964). If you didn't recognise *Le Manège enchanté* in that list, that's because its scripts and sensibility were reinvented in Britain as *The Magic Roundabout*.

All of these have miniatures that look like miniatures, toys looking like toys, and a small-scale domestic charm not even Pixar can simulate. (Anderson calls it 'That magical effect where you can see how it is accomplished.') Since *The Nightmare before Christmas**, stop-motion features had avoided a 'table-top' look, but *Fantastic Mr Fox*'s ruddy backgrounds feel like lumpy carpets or bedclothes. The characters walk in the stiff uprights and straight lines of action figures; the camera favours smooth

DIRECTOR Wes Anderson
PRODUCER Allison Abbate, Scott Rudin, Wes Anderson, Jeremy Dawson
STORY Wes Anderson, Noah Baumbach
SCORE Alexandre Desplat
DESIGN Felicie Haymoz, Victor Georgiev, Huy Hu, Chris Appelhans
ANIMATION Mark Gustafson, Mark Waring, Jason Stalman, Kim Keukeleire, Dan Alderson

laterals. When Mr and Mrs Fox embark on a farm-heist, there's no effort to make their movements detailed or realistic as the dolls slide from acrobatic pose to pose. Explosions look like tissue paper, and when the players get dazed or die, their glass eyes become spirals or crosses.

Critics have read all this as a cipher for Anderson's live-action treatment of actors, story and characters. Judged rather on its own terms, *Fantastic Mr Fox* is often amusing and even endearing (both qualities in Fox's hopeless opossum sidekick, voiced by Wallace Wolodarsky). Yet at the same time it's mostly unmoving. The puppet close-ups give an illusion of dramatic nuance, and sometimes more than that, but we're too aware that these brand-quirky characters are heading towards resolutions as pat and traditional as any fairytale. Maybe an enterprising dubber will appropriate Anderson's film, hire new writers and voice-actors and translate it from American-indie back into English. It worked for *The Magic Roundabout*.

Fantastic Planet
France/Czechoslovakia, 1973 – 72 minutes
René Laloux
[Drawings and cut-outs]

DIRECTOR René Laloux
PRODUCER Simon Damiani, André Valio-Cavaglione
STORY René Laloux, Roland Topor
SCORE Alain Goraguer
DESIGN Roland Topor
ANIMATION Josef Kábrt, Josef Váňa, Jindrich Bárta, Zdena Bártová, Bohumil Sedja

An exotic planet teems with outlandish monsters and vegetation. Giant blue-skinned aliens mind-meld with the cosmos. The hero's journey sees him liberate a people from their exploiters. *Fantastic Planet*'s multiple similarities to *Avatar** reflect the archetypal nature of the planetary romance. For jaded critics, the older film was a set of stale clichés back in 1973; but for children who happened on it, it was a magic introduction to science fiction.

Fantastic Planet (known more evocatively in France as *La Planète sauvage*) was directed by René Laloux (1929–2004). A Paris-born artist, his early career encompassed wood-carving, puppetry and a stint at the progressive La Borde Psychiatric Clinic, where he mustered the patients to create short films. However, in the same way that Henry Selick's direction of *The Nightmare before Christmas** would be overshadowed by the marquee name of Tim Burton, so Laloux's work on *Fantastic Planet* was eclipsed by his celebrated art designer, Roland Topor. Topor was a surrealist (or, for some, post-surrealist) author-illustrator, who first worked with Laloux on animated shorts, including *Les Escargots* (1965), a Gorey-esque fable about monstrous snails.

Such grotesqueries enliven *Planet*'s pedestrian story. On a distant world (*not* the Fantastic Planet, which only appears at the end), a race of giant, advanced blue humanoids, Draag, keep tiny pets called Oms. As the pun on *homme* suggests, the Oms are humans, brought to the Draag planet from a destroyed Earth. An Om boy, Terr, is raised by a doting Draag girl, who inadvertently lets him share her telepathic lessons. Armed with Draag wisdom, Terr escapes to find wild Om tribes eking out a bottom-of-the-food-chain living, and empowers them to fight back. As the critic Seth Giddings notes, the story has the oppressed group relying on enemy technology, like Native Americans getting rifles, in contrast to what happens in *Avatar*. (The story was based on a book by Pierre Pairault, writing as Stefan Wul.)

Much of *Planet* was animated in Prague, at the studio of the late Jiří Trnka. The entry on *The Emperor's Nightingale** quotes the animator Gene Deitch saying that Czech animation treats its figures as symbols rather than characters. That's true of *Fantastic Planet*, whose animation and expressions are rudimentary within their strong outlines. The figures are replaceable cut-outs, an approach used by the pioneer animator Quirino Cristiani (p. 32) and overseen here by Josef Kábrt. Only occasionally do we feel for the characters, as in the striking overture where Terr's terrified mother is hunted by Draag children. They smash her to the ground with their giant fingers, then pick her up and drop her. Later, there's some nicely played interaction between Terr and his Draag owner, Tiva. However, Tiva vanishes from the story once Terr escapes, whereas we might have expected some further dealing between her and her 'pet'.

Otherwise the characters are a tedious lot. *Fantastic Planet* is remembered for its flora and fauna, its delightfully nonchalant oddness. Meditating aliens sit quietly while their torsos melt like taffy, one sequence that gave the film its reputation as a trip. Some of the briefest details are the most off-kilter, like a whistling

Dali-esque ornament in Tiva's room (or is it an animal?), or the booby-trapped box that engulfs an Om. There are suggestive background shapes that grow kinkier as the film continues, and a host of walk-on monsters, though if you're rewatching the film, you may find fewer than you remembered. A cute baby lizard hatches from an egg, is licked lovingly by a passing pig-monster, and gobbled up in a blink. A chuckling tree-devil beats up birds; a fabulous dragon wolfs down humans like an anteater; and a wide plain is covered with giant intestinal tracts rearing up like snakes.

Everything is boldly rendered in a flat illustrative style with sandy colours and shadings. The endearingly retro electro-jazz soundtrack is by Alain Goraguer, and the film is further exoticised by its Gallic fashion futurism. Practically every female, Draag or human, is bare-breasted, though some mildly sexual scenes don't seem to have worried fans who saw the film as children.

More intense are the images of Draag chasing down the Oms with poison gas and killer machines helped, pointedly, by tame Oms. However, *Fantastic Planet* doesn't end with extermination, but rather with the heroes finding a new, truly trippy landscape that it would be wrong to spoil here. The ending is laughable in plot terms, as if the film-makers were suddenly told to finish *now*, but the last imaginative flourish sends you out bemused but happy.

Ferngully: The Last Rainforest
Australia, 1992 – 72 minutes
Bill Kroyer
[Drawings with CGI]

DIRECTOR Bill Kroyer
PRODUCER Wayne Young, Peter Faiman
STORY Jim Cox
DESIGN Phil Mendez, Mike Giaimo
SCORE Alan Silvestri
ANIMATION Doug Frankel, David Brewster, Kathy Zielinski, John Allan Armstrong, Crystal Klabunde

Ferngully: The Last Rainforest was Australia's most expensive production when it opened in 1992, though none of it was drawn or painted there. Most of the Aussie-financed film was animated in LA, with other units in Toronto, London, Seoul, Thailand and at Copenhagen's A. Film studio. In effect, *Ferngully* was a deliberately hidden 'import', like the Japanese cartoons brought to America in the 1960s, with nothing in the visuals or soundtrack to suggest it wasn't wholly Hollywood.

The film is easily labelled as an above-par Disney imitation, but it's a little more than that. Like France's *Le Roi et l'oiseau**, its setting is the most important character – the emerald rainforest, gleaming with misty animist light and populated by winged wood fairies. (The two art directors were Ralph Eggleston, later a top Pixar artist, and Vicky Jenson, the future co-director of *Shrek**.)

Ferngully is threatened by humans and their giant mobile logging unit, animated in CGI. However, in a narrative sleight to reassure the audience, the true villain *isn't* human, but Hexxus, a demon of destruction who uses greedy men as his pawns. (The critic Leslie Felperin noted that his name is suspiciously similar to Exxon.) The monster was co-supervised by Kathy Zielinski, whose credits range from *The Hunchback of Notre Dame** to *How to Train Your Dragon**.

The film shows the fairies' viewpoint until Crysta, the pert young heroine, accidentally shrinks a human, Zak, down to her size. A blond surfer type, Zak wind-surfs on leaves, climbs luminous stairs of tree-clinging fungus and sails a nut down a stream. They're all standard mini-adventures, but well integrated into the colourful cartoon whole. *Ferngully* has debts to Disney's *The Little Mermaid* (1989) (where another wide-eyed alien heroine falls for a human), but it also parallels Hayao Miyazaki's 1984 *Nausicaa of the Valley of the Wind*, whose characters climb and fly through a gigantic forest. In 2009, *Ferngully* had a revival of sorts, being frequently compared to James Cameron's *Avatar**.

Crysta caught flak from reviewers for being drawn as a sexualised Barbie doll (her acting is almost unbearably winsome). Few reviewers noticed, though, that her story arc is drastically different from a Disney princess. In her key moment, she realises everything the nice boy Zak told her was a lie. When she saw him in the human world, he was painting crosses on trees, which he said were to stop them from being cut down. Later, her wise-old-woman mentor shows Crysta a severed tree trunk. Crysta sees that it bears a giant red cross; then she sees *dozens* of cut trees with crosses, deforming behind her distraught flight.

Let down by her man, Crysta uses her feminine powers. The matriarch twice takes Crysta's hands and presses her towards her potential (Crysta later does the same with Zak). In the finale, Crysta plucks a seedling from a vaginal-looking pod and takes a kamikaze flight into Hexxus's red jaws. Roots burst from the monster's body, not killing it but sealing it in a wooden womb. There's a happy end for the self-sacificing Crysta, but she and the redeemed Zak *don't* pair off; the world comes first.

Ferngully has cute animals and a pop soundtrack, but the songs have at least some of the wit of contemporary Disney. (The facts of the food chain are explained through a gravelly rap number, 'If I'm Going to Eat Somebody', performed by Tone Loc.) The film-makers had the nous to employ Robin Williams as a deranged but surprisingly likeable bat, just before Disney nabbed him for Aladdin*'s Genie. However, Tim Curry is the true catch as the evil Hexxus. The pouting Rocky Horror star belts out Ferngully's sole memorably animated character, a blob of excremental sputum that liquidly inflates into a deliciously obscene, lip-smacking sludge-monster.

Finding Nemo

US, 2003 – 96 minutes
Andrew Stanton
[CGI]

In August 2002, Disney chairman Michael Eisner emailed his board about the studio's new releases. One was *Finding Nemo*, the fifth film from Disney's partner Pixar, with which Eisner had a strained relationship. 'This will be a reality check for those guys,' Eisner wrote. 'It's okay, but nowhere near as good as their previous films.'

Released the following May, *Finding Nemo* became Pixar's most successful film until *Toy Story 3* (2010), earning $865 million around the world. Yet some reviewers agreed that *Nemo* was second-hand, second-rate Pixar. The fishy leads were an odd-couple duo, like *Toy Story**'s Buzz and Woody and *Monsters, Inc.**'s Mike and Sully. Both *Monsters, Inc.* and *Finding Nemo* were also odes to good parenting, as would be Pixar's next film, *The Incredibles**.

Finding Nemo can therefore look like a formula crowd-pleaser, relying on a gorgeous undersea world that marries the delicacy of the artists' pre-production drawings, pastels and paintings to the naturalism of state-of-the-art CGI simulation. Reviewing the film in *Empire* magazine, Olly Richards noted that it was *Finding Nemo*'s 'background elements, like endless floating particles undulating as any sea creature goes by, or the constantly moving lighting refracting with the sea's surface movement, that create a believable environment'.

Surprisingly, the film-makers choose to have their loveliest moment early; a ray swoops over our heroes' home reef through rainbows of fish and coral, singing the names of different marine species in tribute to Tom Lehrer's recital of the Periodic Table ('Oh, let's name the species, the species, the species, let's name the species that live in the sea …').

But *Nemo*'s character arcs have their own elegance. The story: Marlin, an over-protective single-dad fish, is aghast when his little 'boy', Nemo, is scooped up by a human diver and borne away. Nemo is trapped in a fishtank in a Sydney dental surgery, and the characters don't meet again until the end of the film. Yet Nemo is still able to hear news of his dad's heroism, as Marlin travels thousands of miles to the rescue, which encourages Nemo in turn to escape. The same indirect causation later underpins Stanton's *WALL·E**, where the robots' adventures have an inadvertent impact on the humans.

There are beautiful visual rhymes; the image of a tiny Nemo in his egg at the film's start is reprised when Marlin embraces him at the end, and tangentially referenced when the singing ray points to a tiny bacterium containing its own inner universe. The more comic scenes are balanced between the neurotic Marlin, who can never enjoy the fleeting moment, and his amnesiac companion Dory (perfectly voiced by Ellen DeGeneres), who only *has* that moment. In the best gag, Dory and Marlin flee a maddened Aussie shark through a sunken submarine. The monster bashes a bulkhead and Dory forgetfully chirps, 'Who is it?'

Later, Dory realises she remembers more with Marlin, who's thereby shaping her identity even when he doesn't know it, a lovely metaphor for parenting. 'I look at you and … I'm home,' Dora tells Marlin near

DIRECTOR Andrew Stanton
PRODUCER Graham Walters
STORY Andrew Stanton, Bob Peterson, David Reynolds
SCORE Thomas Newman
DESIGN Ralph Eggleston, Dan Lee
ANIMATION Alan Barillaro, Mark Walsh, Carlos Baena, Bobby Beck

the end, her cartoon lips wobbling piteously. In the context of an epic sea journey, 'home' evokes Homer. Marlin battles through monsters and dangers, but just wants to get himself and Nemo back to his reef. There's an especially Homeric moment when Marlin tells the story of his adventures while riding a surfer sea turtle (voiced by Stanton).

Nemo's picaresque story also evokes Disney's The Jungle Book*, with Marlin and Dory replacing Bagheera and Baloo. In Finding Nemo, though, the child *can* fend for himself in the wild, and it's his dad's job to inspire him. Unfortunately, Nemo's bids to escape his fishtank are less interesting than Marlin's journey, diluting it as the action cuts back and forth. The annotated DVD commentary mentions a deleted twist for Nemo's story in which a tough-sounding fish, voiced by Willem Dafoe, turns out to be a hollow fraud (and, therefore, the opposite of Marlin). While that version might still not have worked, it reflects the film-makers' struggle with a twin-track narrative too reminiscent of TV.

It didn't matter. Finding Nemo became Pixar's first film to win a Best Animated Feature Oscar (Monsters, Inc. had lost to Shrek* the previous year). Two days after the nomination, Pixar's owner Steve Jobs announced that Pixar was breaking up with Disney. There would be a reconciliation, but only after Michael Eisner – the man who said Finding Nemo would be Pixar's 'reality check' – was history.

Fritz the Cat
US, 1972 – 78 minutes
Ralph Bakshi
[Drawings, with brief live-action]

DIRECTOR/STORY Ralph Bakshi
PRODUCER Steve Krantz
SCORE Ed Bogas, Ray Shanklin, B. B. King
ANIMATION John Gentilella, Martin B. Taras, Lawrence Riley, Clifford Auguston, Norm McCabe

Fritz the Cat, star of underground comics and America's first truly X-rated cartoon feature, was murdered in 1972 by way of an ice-pick to the head. It was the kind of killing that *Fritz*'s *enfant terrible* director Ralph Bakshi would have presented in luridly aestheticised cartoon detail. In fact, though, Fritz was killed in protest at Bakshi's film. Robert Crumb, the cat's creator, had seen Bakshi's take on his *Fritz* strip and hated it, though his complaint that the film was 'more twisted than my stuff' might be taken as a compliment by fans of Crumb's gnarlier work. Crumb trepanned Fritz in a strip called, with due irony, 'Superstar'.

Animation's most pugnacious and divisive figure, Bakshi has been hailed as its greatest visionary, and dismissed as a maker of museum-piece schlock. Many viewers, especially in Britain, only know Bakshi's fantasy films – *Wizards* (1977), the animated *The Lord of the Rings* (1978) and *Fire and Ice* (1983) – which increasingly used rotoscoping, or disguised live-action. (See also *American Pop**.) However, these films came after Bakshi's extraordinary trio of personal, X-rated features, of which *Fritz* is the only one on British DVD. They caricature New York, its energy and violence, and the racial sectarianism under the melting-pot homilies. (Bakshi himself was a working-class Jew from Brownsville, central Brooklyn.) In *Fritz*, US bomber planes napalm Harlem into the Stone Age, cheered on by those well-known white supremacists, Mickey and Donald.

Bakshi broke away from a Disney orthodoxy that had been marginalised in the cinema by *Easy Rider* (1969) and *Bonnie and Clyde* (1967). In another way, though, he was a cartoon classicist, insisting on the full-frame character animation that was being killed by TV production lines. *Fritz*'s urban backgrounds – chiefly drawn by Ira Turek and painted by Johnnie Vita – are presented with skewed perspectives, crass black lines and a sick cauldron of watercolours. On the soundtrack, Bakshi incorporates taped voxpops from streets and bars, set to gross bits of business. The opening scene has three construction workers (drawn, like all *Fritz*'s characters, as unkemptly shaded toon animals) griping about the promiscuous students undermining the 'bourgeois American-type society family'. While they argue, one pisses a stream down to the street as the titles roll. It's a fair warning of Bakshi's approach – gross and confrontational – though British viewers may be reminded of the genteel animal defecation in Nick Park's voxpop *Creature Comforts* (1989).

Fritz is one of the student decadents: horny, phoney, stupid but innocent. Reviewers compared him to Voltaire's Candide, even Disney's *Pinocchio**, which Bakshi loved as a child. We first meet Fritz as a happy hedonist, duping three airhead girls into a bathtub zoo orgy that's more '*Carry On*' than *Deep Throat*. (Fritz's deft untangling of his harem's legs as they dangle over the bathside is priceless, animated by Manny Perez). The dialogue is 60s-fruity: 'I ain't no jive-ass black nigger, honey!' declares a gay black crow, mincing away. Fritz's adventures telescope the decade, as he triggers a race riot that turns Harlem into Vietnam, then hits the desert and runs into Manson-esque sado-terrorists. Bakshi originally meant to

BLACK INK FILMS LTD.
Present
"FRITZ THE CAT".'x'
A STEVE KRANTZ Production—
based upon the characters
created by R. CRUMB
Screenplay by RALPH BAKSHI
Directed by RALPH BAKSHI
Produced by STEVE KRANTZ

end the film with Fritz recruited as the terrorists' stooge and blown to bits by their dynamite ('Far out …' Fritz says as the fuse burns down). But the director was persuaded to put in a cop-out epilogue, giving Fritz cartoon powers of survival that the film had rejected until then.

If Fritz had died, not only would the film have had more integrity, it would have blunted Crumb's revenge (so what if he killed Fritz too?). It would also have precluded the unwatchably boring sequel, *The Nine Lives of Fritz the Cat*, directed by Robert Taylor. Bakshi had no part in that, going on instead to *Heavy Traffic* (1973) and *Coonskin* (1975, released to video as *Street Fight*). More personal than *Fritz*, these films continue to present New York's abject worlds through sometimes remarkable animation. In *Coonskin*, a quack black revolutionary reverend strips obesely naked, prancing round like a *Fantasia** hippo (animated by ex-Disney artist Ambrozi Paliwoda).

Embracing mixed media, Bakshi uses live-action film to casually link or background the drawings, while he fills time-outs with jerkily moving storyboards.

While making *Fritz*, Bakshi said the idea of 'grown men sitting in cubicles drawing butterflies floating over a field of flowers, while American planes are dropping bombs in Vietnam and kids are marching in the streets, is ludicrous'. As of writing, he continues to mock square liberalism, berating white viewers disturbed by his *ironic* black stereotypes as idiots and closet racists. His rhetoric is reflected in one of his most bitingly powerful images; a live-action Scatman Crothers singing Bakshi's 'Ahm a Niggerman', in *Coonskin*. Beyond that, though, Bakshi's cartoon vision is often pitifully stretched, a morass of bloody slapstick, sex and grotesquerie. Quentin Tarantino is a vocal fan, and animation needs these incendiaries. But please, can the next Bakshi be *better*?

Ghost in the Shell 2: Innocence
Japan, 2004 – 99 minutes
Mamoru Oshii
[Drawings/CGI]

Dolls, dogs, gods, children and their relationships with neurotically self-conscious humanity come under philosophical investigation in Mamoru Oshii's sequel to his film, *Ghost in the Shell*, made a decade earlier. Rendered in a blend of drawn and computer animation, the sequel's first half looks like a sleekly beautiful variant on the future-noir aesthetic of *Blade Runner* (1982), with 1950s cars and dingy alleys overshadowed by sterile techno-splendour.

However, *Ghost in the Shell 2: Innocence* could be comfortably double-billed with Richard Linklater's animated journey of ideas, *Waking Life* (2001) (see p. 177). Its later scenes explore byways dreamier than *Spirited Away**, as its subdued heroes loop through the Chinese-doll geometry of a time-warping crystal palace, and later plunge into a steel Tartarus of dead-eyed killer mannequins.

The protagonists drop aphorisms and quotations (Descartes, Shelley, Milton and the Old Testament are just the start), as readily as Disney characters once burst into song. Critic Steven T. Brown sees a nod to the citation-heavy work of Jean-Luc Godard, and notes the quotations reflect our 'always already mediated thoughts and intentions'. In *Innocence*, humans are puppets of cerebral, civilising frameworks, which download into our constructed minds as easily as the film's protagonists download into artificial bodies.

The *Ghost in the Shell* franchise began as a strip by the artist Masamune Shirow (the pen-name of Masanori Ota). Shirow envisioned a future in which people inhabit mass-produced cyborg bodies, while computer networks extend virtual human senses. The heroes of *Ghost in the Shell* are detectives and public servants; Oshii stresses they're also philosophers. As in his other films, the protagonists' musings are expounded in monologues, dialogues and wordless reveries. A transcendent carnival of man-made gods on giant boats counterpoints a canal interlude in the first *Ghost*, when Oshii used water, mud and mannequins to convey a world of disposable, decaying mortals, transfigured suddenly by rain.

The first film was made in response to the world success of *Akira** and backed by Britain's Manga Entertainment. Its imagery influenced *The Matrix* (1999); most obviously, *Ghost*'s glowering, masculine heroine Kusanagi was homaged in *The Matrix*'s Trinity character, played by Carrie-Ann Moss. This may have encouraged DreamWorks to release Oshii's sequel to US cinemas, though even Mitsuhisa Ishikawa, the president of the studio Production I. G, admitted that the second *Ghost* was too cryptic for the mass market.

The main protagonist this time is Kusanagi's hulking cyborg comrade, Batou. (Kusanagi had found a higher destiny at the first film's climax, though she has a pervasive influence on the sequel's action, and returns in person at the end.) The setting is a luxuriant world of grandiose carnivals, golden oceans of communications towers and pungent skyscapes of brown-red. Oshii retains the spartan character animation

DIRECTOR/STORY Mamoru Oshii
PRODUCER Mitsuhisa Ishikawa, Toshio Suzuki
SCORE Kenji Kawai
DESIGN Yohei Taneda, Hiroyuki Okiura
ANIMATION Kazuchika Kise, Tetsuya Nishio, Hiroyuki Okiura, Toshihiko Nishikubo, Naoko Kusumi

from his earlier films, his characters often freezing into near or total immobility, 'animated' only by flickering light, before bursting into action. Typically for Oshii, these action scenes are strictly rationed. However, he makes a dry joke of laboriously setting up his heroes for a fine-balanced meeting with yakuza gangsters, then ploughing straight into shoot-em-up carnage without a pause.

The story sees Batou investigating killer sex-dolls, but the only erotic moment has a ghostly geisha droid begging 'Help me', while ripping out her robot heart. (The scene is based on an illustration by the German artist Hans Bellmer, whose doll imagery pervades the film.) Oshii's cerebral elaborations on the plot – based on a chapter of Shirow's original manga strip – mean we've almost forgotten the mystery by the time it's wrapped up, with a suggestion that we should have cared more for the dolls than the humans all along. It's the dolls, after all, which are forced from the uncanny into the horrors of anthropomorphism.

Dispensing with his usual writing partner, Kazunori Ito, Oshii focuses on his own mouthpiece interlocutors, including a languid chain-smoking woman coroner called Haraway (a nod to Donna Haraway, author of *A Cyborg Manifesto*) who asks why humans are obsessed with recreating themselves, and a mad hacker in the crystal castle who's so enamoured with soulless dolls that he becomes one. But the investigators in *Innocence* look most human beside what Oshii presents as unself-conscious Others: a rookie cop's little girl, Batou's beloved basset hound.

Beyond the cinema *Ghost in the Shell*s, Production I. G made a lavish alternative version of Shirow's comic for TV, handily catering for viewers who disliked Oshii's art-house approach (though many fans enjoyed both). *Ghost in the Shell Stand Alone Complex* had the same lead voice-actors as the films, but a separate continuity and a different director, Kenji Kamiyama. A TV-movie sequel followed, subtitled *Solid State Society*.

The Girl Who Leapt through Time
Japan, 2006 – 98 minutes
Mamoru Hosoda
[Drawings with CGI]

In the live-action *Groundhog Day* (1993), Bill Murray's antihero is trapped in an endlessly repeating twenty-four hours. He tries seducing a woman, courting her over and again to correct every *faux pas* and get her into bed. He gets his face slapped umpteen times, but he never gets the girl (until he stops trying).

The charming Japanese film *The Girl Who Leapt through Time*, directed by Mamoru Hosoda and animated by Tokyo's Madhouse studio, cleverly inverts this sequence. The protagonists are a teen boy and girl who have an easy, jocular friendship. One drowsy evening, the boy gives the girl a lift on his bicycle and, out of the blue, asks if they might date. The girl is horribly embarrassed. Because she's a time-traveller, she resets the scene again and again, trying to steer the conversation away from the dreadful subject. But the boy keeps asking her out, and her trans-temporal meddling only spoils their friendship.

Romantic comedies with desperately shy youngsters are two-a-penny in Japanese cartoons, but *The Girl Who Leapt through Time* has more to say than most. Its effervescent heroine, Makoto, learns she can time-travel when she magically reverses a terrible accident (and a spectacular one at that; her bike crashes into the barrier of a railway crossing, flinging her into the path of an oncoming train!). Naturally, Makoto treats her new ability as a wonderful superpower to make life easier. In the film's funniest scenes, she aces school tests and burns through marathon karaoke sessions. However, Makoto belatedly starts to see that her 'time-leaping' is having frightening butterfly effects on her friends, including the two boys she most cares about. Perhaps too late, she realises no one can set the clock back forever.

Hosoda's film blends witty comedy, can-do optimism, wistful yearning, romantic obsession (another character crosses oceans of time just to see a painting) and traumatic tragedy (but with time-travel there's always the chance of a reset). The airy pastels and clean lines recall the 1960s flashbacks in Isao Takahata's *Only Yesterday**. The lanky-limbed Makoto was designed by Yoshiyuki Sadamoto, creator of some of anime's most famous poster-girls, including *Neon Genesis Evangelion**'s Rei.

The character animation can be broad and rough, especially in some off-putting shots of Makoto laughing, but the hand-drawn motion is emphatically energised. Makoto time-travels by performing mighty, stone-skipping leaps on water, an athlete's answer to the charging DeLorean in *Back to the Future* (1985). In the vivid climax, drawn by Ryochimo Sawa, the girl sprints against an indifferently travelling 'camera', pummelling her way heroically from one side of the frame to the other.

Makoto's running illustrates the moral of 'Time waits for no one', written in English on a blackboard, as she embraces the future with courage and hope; a future that's expressed in unformed cloudscapes bubbling up in perfect blue anime skies. However, the director is canny, sometimes slowing the school scenes down to romanticised reveries and returning again and again to Makoto's baseball practices with her friends, letting us share her illusion that such things never change. Like much anime, *The Girl Who*

DIRECTOR Mamoru Hosoda
PRODUCER Takashi Watanabe, Yuichiro Sato
STORY Satoko Okudera
SCORE Kiyoshi Yoshida
DESIGN Yoshiyuki Sadamoto
ANIMATION Hiroyuki Aoyama, Chiaki Kubota, Shinji Ishihama, Aiko Wakatsuki, Akira Takata

Leapt through Time treats high school as Lewis Carroll treated childhood: 'Ever drifting down the dream/ Lingering in the golden gleam.'

Although it's not necessary to know the background to enjoy the film, it's a sequel to a popular 1960s story, written by Yasutaka Tsutsui. (Tsutsui's later novel, *Paprika*, was adapted as a Madhouse anime film by Satoshi Kon; see p. 212.) In Hosoda's film, Makoto confides in an elegant aunt, who, unknown to her, was the time-travelling teenager in Tsutsui's original. The point would be picked up by older viewers who knew Tsutsui's tale or one of its many live-action Japanese adaptations, such as the 1983 film, *The Little Girl Who Conquered Time*.

Grave of the Fireflies
Japan, 1988 – 90 minutes
Isao Takahata
[Drawings]

Near *Grave of the Fireflies'* ending, after the main character and the audience have both had their hearts broken, a smiling man says, 'Beautiful day, in spite of it all.' Isao Takahata's film, about two young children living and dying in wartime Japan, mediates between beauty and tragedy. Nature's loveliness is lyrically depicted, as we would expect from Ghibli, the studio which Takahata founded with Hayao Miyazaki. Short-lived fireflies serve as metaphors for the children, replacing cherry blossoms as representations of exquisite mortality. Provocatively, *Grave* finds beauty in war, suffering, even dying children. It intoxicates the protagonist Seita, a boy whose closest relationship is with his starving infant sister, and who is so socially alienated that he cheers wildly as Japan burns.

Grave's first scene shows Seita himself starving in a station, watched by his ghost ('This is the night I died'). Even the spirit world is shaped by war. The ghost has the blood-red glow of an air raid as it takes us back in time and into the mortal Seita's shoes. Aged fourteen, Seita must protect his adorable four-year-old sister, Setsuko. He straps her to his back and runs a gauntlet of exploding buildings as his city, Kobe, is razed by American B-29s. The opening may remind youngsters of video games; the protagonist first dies, then is resurrected into peril.

Takahata, though, saw war first-hand. *Grave's* opening reflects his nightmare experience as a ten-year-old boy, running through a blazing town. Seeking to communicate the war to younger viewers, Takahata chose a novel by Akiyuki Nosaka (itself based on Nosaka's war experiences, including the loss of his infant sister). Nosaka's character Seita can't endure the traumas of war. After his mother perishes, he stays with an aunt who scolds him for his laziness, when he just wants to be with Setsuko, secure in his role as big brother. Eventually, Seita takes Setsuko away to an abandoned shelter by a lake, where they live free and hungry.

At first, we share their hopes; if the first scenes suggested a video game, the children's home-making evokes *Swallows and Amazons*. But this is no holiday. Setsuko becomes malnourished and wastes away, though her besotted brother, in Nosaka's words, 'has no choice but to see her as becoming even more beautiful'. Food and sweets become central motifs; Setsuko has a tin of fruit drops which slowly run out. Later, as she's dying, Seita tries to steal food, but is finally reduced to hand-feeding her ice-cubes, the gestures precious and pathetic. At the last, he fills the tin with Setsuko's cremated ashes.

Long before *Grave* was made, Takahata's colleague Miyazaki remarked that Japanese teenagers read *The Diary of Anne Frank* out of perverse envy for Anne's situation. 'They may wish that they, too, could live life to the fullest amidst such tension, in such an extreme environment.' *Grave* is full of intense experiences. Seita sluices his face with water from a burst pipe; Setsuko capers in a cloud of fireflies; the children shrink terrified from a rain of incendiaries. In one extraordinary tableau, upsetting yet overtly distanced, Setsuko hunches on the ground, weeping, while Seita does endless gym flips over a pull-up bar, desperate to distract

DIRECTOR/STORY Isao Takahata
PRODUCER Toru Hara
SCORE Michio Mamiya
DESIGN Yoshifumi Kondo
ANIMATION Yoshifumi Kondo, Megumi Kagawa, Kitaro Kosaka, Hideaki Anno

her emotions and displace his own. As the critic Ed Hooks notes, Seita's acrobatics are a shout: 'No! I will not die!' In a sudden cut, the children are abstracted against near-blank white space, the image reduced to its graphical basics.

Grave closely matches Miyazaki's infinitely happier My Neighbour Totoro*, with which it was double-billed in Japan, though Takahata said audiences who saw Totoro first did not want to watch Grave to the end. Both films portray acutely observed children, who are drawn together by missing parents, while taking solace from nature. (There's even a shared moment in each where a girl accidentally squishes a bug.) In some ways, though, Grave is thematically closer to Miyazaki's later Spirited Away*, where a spoiled modern child must cope with old-fashioned hardship.

Takahata saw Seita as a modern-style boy, unable to endure in a hard time. He hoped youngsters would reflect on the character's catastrophic mistakes that kill him and his sister. Instead, as Takahata wryly admitted, the audience just felt sorry for the children, and Grave became famed as one of the most emotionally devastating films ever. In 2005, a live-action remake on Japanese TV sidestepped the problem by asking viewers to judge an adult instead of a child. The film foregrounds the character of the harsh aunt who, we now see, must choose between saving Seita and Setsuko or her own children.

Happy Feet
US/Australia, 2006 – 108 minutes
George Miller
[CGI]

Happy Feet's basic tale of a dancing penguin, voiced by Elijah Wood, who can't conform to the standards of his singing peers, could have been told in cartoons at any time in the last seventy-five years. Indeed, its themes aren't far from a 1936 Tex Avery cartoon, *I Love to Singa*, a *Jazz Singer* spoof about an owl who insists on singing jazz to the horror of his parents. (The cartoon is included on the US DVD of the film.)

Yet *Happy Feet* is the first Hollywood animated feature to evoke the feeling of a live-action spectacular throughout its running time. Cartoon films routinely pastiche or parody live-action cinema in individual set pieces, and *The Incredibles** director Brad Bird upped the ante in sophisticated camerawork. Here, however, George Miller, the Australian live-action director of *Babe* (1995) and *Mad Max* (1979), goes all out to create a brassy film style that's equal parts Peter Jackson and Cecil B. DeMille. The film is packed with wildly spinning camerawork and ice-architecture of biblical proportions, as a penguin cast of thousands dance against vast Antarctic backgrounds. Even the more familiar CGI spectacles are ramped up beyond anything we've seen before, from a stupendous avalanche to the hero Mumble's dive from a thousand-foot cliff.

The film needs these assets to overcome its shortcomings. Even the first scenes may put some viewers off the picture, as we're thrust into the midst of CGI penguins mouthing rock and pop numbers in a kitsch parody of *Moulin Rouge* (2001). The penguin dance sequences are more palatable – motion-captured, with Mumble's moves performed by dancer Savion Glover – but they're still a cute novelty that lose much of their force on the small screen. Far from competing with humans, the birds' ungainly, robotically regimented steps can't compare with *Mary Poppins*'s hoofing penguins forty years earlier.

There's only a broad attempt to differentiate *Happy Feet*'s clone-like birds, and no serious effort to make the voices inhabit the CGI characters. (In those ways, the film scores below a rival penguin animation, Sony's breezy *Surf's Up,* 2007.) The voice-actors are subordinate to the visuals, though this is an advantage with Robin Williams, playing dual roles as a Latino penguin and a fake guru channelling Barry White, who's funny without stealing the film. The characters are functional more than memorable, though Williams's guru, called Lovelace, is shown to have a choking problem – a startlingly filthy film in-joke.

The script, though, is pleasingly clever. Mumble's idiosyncratic dancing is presented as a metaphor for communication, which he uses romantically to woo his sweetheart, Riverdance-style, before embarking on a quest to contact the aliens threatening his world (us). In the US, some conservative pundits claimed the film was propaganda, anti-religion, pro-environment *and* pro-gay, the last because misfit Mumble's 'deviant' behaviour is finally accepted by his peers. Most viewers, though, will find *Happy Feet* no more subversive than Disney's *Dumbo**.

DIRECTOR George Miller
PRODUCER Doug Mitchell, George Miller
STORY George Miller, John Collee, Judy Morris, Warren Coleman
SCORE John Powell
DESIGN Mark Sexton
ANIMATION Daniel Jeannette, Stuart Lowder, Craig Baxter, Brendan Body, Miguel Fuertes, Tim Gibson, Victoria Livingstone

A fairer criticism is Miller's reliance on intensely scary scenes involving giant toothy monsters (seals, killer whales), not to mention driving Mumble into an unhinged, head-banging fit of despair near the end. All this would be justified if it deepened or supported the characters; classic Disney went as far. In *Happy Feet*, though, it feels cruelly gratuitous, for all the flair of the scenes themselves. But they're of a piece with what's an eccentric, overblown, enjoyably dizzying experience of a film.

Hoppity Goes to Town
US, 1941 – 78 minutes
Dave Fleischer
[Drawings (and live-action miniatures)]
[Originally released as *Mr Bug Goes to Town*]

Hoppity Goes to Town was the second non-Disney Hollywood cartoon feature, following *Gulliver's Travels* (1939). Both films were made by the Fleischer studio, today remembered more for its Betty Boops and Popeyes, and for creating more jazzy, sultry cartoon lands than Disney would countenance. By the time of the features, though, the studio's spice and strangeness – especially its tendency to turn incidental props into pliable cartoon critters – had been toned down. Perhaps such worlds couldn't have sustained a feature, though it would have been fascinating had Fleischer tried.

Gulliver and *Hoppity* were made in Miami, but *Hoppity* is set in New York, where Fleischer shaped its identity. The cartoon city is all sleek art-deco structures and rotoscoped humans, as in Fleischer's *Superman* cartoons. The publicity made much of the scale Manhattan model which appears under *Hoppity*'s titles. Taking four months to build in distorted perspective, it was an obvious riposte to Disney's extravagant multiplane effects in *Pinocchio**. It is, indeed, impressive, in a film all about different-scaled spaces.

The main setting is the grass-level home of an insect community, which is threatened by humans tramping through the neighbourhood. The insects are traditionally cartooned Jiminy Crickets. There are various 'types': a dowager ladybug, a bee-girl ingénue and a corrupt capitalist beetle. Hoppity himself is a blandly amiable grasshopper, given to gee-whizz exclamations where maturity would have suited. He sets out to solve his neighbours' problems, which are complicated by the bad beetle's designs on the girl.

However, one of the film's interesting points is that its villain is a side-show. Not only is he comically vain and cowardly, his actions bring human developers down on the insects' land, at which point he's as hapless as everyone else. But the insects don't hide from the human world; rather, they run intrepidly in and out of its concrete cracks. In the finale, they ascend a skyscraper as it's cemented and bolted together. Still epic and exhilarating, the sequence shows *construction* as a force of nature in the home of modern high-rise. The end shows the humans as bugs themselves, a trace of the social comment erased from Fleischer's *Gulliver's Travels*.

A parallel subplot about an urbane human songwriter and his wife, living in a dinky brownstone threatened by developers, foreshadows *Up** and *One Hundred and One Dalmatians**. *Hoppity*'s closest descendant, though, is DreamWorks' *Antz**, and DreamWorks animation generally, which is often sold as quasi-live-action. 'I know that the feature cartoon is ready to compete seriously with live-actor (sic) movies,' Dave Fleischer said. 'We can tell adult stories now with our hand-drawn actors equally as well as the live-actor films can.' To anyone else, though, *Hoppity* is plainly a kids' cartoon with sub-Disney characters but an unusually imaginative plot.

'Play the latest movie game,' teased the posters. 'Is Hoppity Bob Hope? Is Honey [Hoppity's bee love interest] Madeleine Carroll? How many of your favourite stars can you find?' Today the characters would be

DIRECTOR Dave Fleischer
PRODUCER Dave Fleischer
STORY Dave Fleischer, Dan Gordon, Ted Pierce, Isadore Sparber
SCORE Hoagy Carmichael, Frank Loesser, Leigh Harline
ANIMATION Willard Bowsky, Myron Waldman, Thomas Johnson, David Tendlar, James Culhane

voiced by their live-action equivalents, rather than by the likes of Jack 'Popeye' Mercer and Pinto 'Goofy' Colvig (playing a snail version of his *Snow White** character, Grumpy). Star voices could have livened *Hoppity*'s unmemorable cast, though C. Bagley Beetle and his henchmen provide plentiful gags. The henchmen are given to effeminate clowning, to the degree that it's now impossible *not* to read them as gay.

Hoppity was made in the Fleischer studio's dying days, when the brothers Max and Dave were estranged to the point of loathing. By the film's general release in 1942, they were gone, terminated by their creditors, Paramount. *Hoppity*'s trade screening was on 4 December 1941, three days before Pearl Harbor. It's often said that the war killed the film, though cartoon historian G. Michael Dobbs argues that Paramount buried *Hoppity* in a publicity-starved release to stop Max ever reclaiming his studio.

Poignantly, the film has a couple of old-style 'Fleischeresque' moments where objects seem to come alive. A giant human glove flexes its fingers during a fight; a battery grins and spins before burning out. A 'Chinaman' impression and a blackface gag are more startling, not for their presence in a 1940s cartoon (Disney's *Fantasia** was more offensive), but because no distributor troubled to excise them in later years.

How to Train Your Dragon

US, 2010 – 98 minutes
Chris Sanders, Dean DeBlois
[CGI]

The dragon doesn't speak, to begin with. To misquote a famous fairytale, that must be understood, or nothing wonderful could come from the story that *Lilo and Stitch** directors Chris Sanders and Dean DeBlois proceed to tell. Animals, of course, usually talk in cartoons, and dragons often talk in fantasies (including the children's books by Cressida Cowell on which this film is loosely based). Tolkien's evil Smaug was grandly loquacious in *The Hobbit*. 'My armour is like tenfold shields, my teeth are swords, my claws spears, the shock of my tail a thunderbolt, my wings a hurricane, and my breath death!' DreamWorks' film, though, is a strange beast; a toon animal tale told from a human viewpoint.

After *Lilo*, co-director Chris Sanders had developed a Disney CGI film, *American Dog*, whose early artwork suggested an even quirkier piece. But when Pixar's John Lasseter came to Disney, he had 'creative differences' with Sanders, who left for DreamWorks in 2007. Sanders's supporters accused Lasseter of acting with the executive mentality he'd condemned in Disney. During a Q&A at London's BFI Southbank, Lasseter claimed Sanders's vision 'was a little more out there than what we all felt (*American Dog*) could and should be'. (Lasseter cited Pixar's *Toy Story 2* (1992) and *Ratatouille* (2007) as precedents; both needed makeovers and new directors.) Without Sanders and his kooky designs, *American Dog* became *Bolt* (2008).

Ironically, Jeffrey Katzenberg at DreamWorks brought Sanders and DeBlois onto *Dragon* to change up a whimsical story into a more mainstream, high-stakes adventure. In the film, Jay Baruchel voices Hiccup; the name suggests broad comedy, but the story is reminiscent of the humorous writer Terry Pratchett, who rarely lets his corny jokes get in the way of straight plots. Hiccup is a gangly wimp in a hardy Viking island community ('Twelve days north of Hopeless and a few degrees south of Freezing to Death'), blitzed regularly by dragons. CGI cartoons often hit the ground running, but *Dragon*'s opening night-raid is especially enjoyable. The shaggy-haired, horned-helmeted Vikings thump scaly sheep-snatchers in a blend of *Asterix the Gaul* (1967) and a fireworks display.

Despite his village-runt status, Hiccup wants to get involved as much as we do, and use his patent projectile to down a Night Fury, the stealth bomber of dragondom. Miraculously, he succeeds, but no one else sees or believes him. When Hiccup finds the injured Fury, it's not much bigger than he is, a sleek black reptile more like a mammal, with a round snout, quizzical expression and great cat-eyes. It is, in fact, a gracefully feline answer to the 'bad dog' Stitch in *Lilo and Stitch*. The lad tries screwing himself up to kill it, but can't; his inarticulate emotions are well conveyed. It's only later he realises he was stopped by the power of anthropomorphism; he saw his fear reflected in the creature. He cares for the dragon (named Toothless), who's grounded by its damaged tail, and helps it fly again. The sky-topping, free-falling flights are thrilling and majestic, building on Disney's otherwise missable *The Rescuers Down Under* (1990, see p. 169), where a boy rode a great eagle.

DIRECTOR Chris Sanders, Dean DeBlois

PRODUCER Bonnie Arnold

STORY Chris Sanders, Dean DeBlois, William Davies

SCORE John Powell

DESIGN Katy Altieri

ANIMATION Simon Otto, Gabe Hordos, Fabio Lignini, Cassidy Curtis, Steven Hornby, Kristof Serrand

Dragon has shades of *Lilo and Stitch* and *The Iron Giant**, but with some changes. Toothless is a natural animal, and Hiccup, though still a boy, approaches it more as an adult than an idealistic child. Superficially at least, the two are drawn together by curiosity and circumstance. Hiccup realises that Toothless overturns the Vikings' accumulated wisdom, and Toothless (in an ingenious scene) tests the boy's intelligence by scratching a pattern in the earth for him to navigate. Their scenes charm without milking sentiment; that's left to the human story of Hiccup and his father.

Yes, this is yet another toon tale of estranged single dads and sons. Hiccup's father (voiced by *300*'s Gerard Butler) is the Viking chief, who despairs of Hiccup carrying his people's legacy. Neither the human nor animal stories have great poignancy, but they make good complements, especially when Hiccup is communicating better with Toothless than his dad. The most on-the-nose moment has Hiccup tell another dragon, 'I'm not one of them' (the Vikings) before his shocked patriarch. Of course, the film ends in happy harmony between the characters and species. But it's made less glib by Hiccup not surviving the climactic conflict (a cloud battle with a *bad* dragon) intact. It's a real surprise and maybe the most honest thing in the film.

The Hunchback of Notre Dame
US, 1996 – 90 minutes
Kirk Wise, Gary Trousdale
[Drawings with CGI]

At one point in Disney's *The Hunchback of Notre Dame*, the rough-hewn hero is confronted by a child with no grown-up prejudices. In an echo of *Frankenstein* (1931), the little girl touches the hunchback's strange face without fear or revulsion. Disney's strange-shaped *Hunchback* asks for similar tolerance from viewers. Kids will wonder why the villain behaves so oddly towards the woman he wants to kill, inhaling the scent of her hair or dreaming of her flaming ghost rising from his fireplace. Grown-ups – especially those who've read Victor Hugo – must contend with a hunchback who looks like, as one reviewer put it, 'a cute, dorsally challenged Mickey Rooney'. This Quasimodo croons with the voice of *Amadeus*'s Tom Hulce, and is first seen helping a fledgeling bird fly, while a gargoyle comes to life and spits out the bird's nest. Some viewers will share the gag reflex.

In the mid-1990s, cartoon whimsy – and yes, the *Hunchback* gargoyles wisecrack and sing – started to feel incongruous in features front-loaded with heavy subjects. (The ultimate example of the trend was DreamWorks' *The Prince of Egypt**.) *Hunchback* was directed by Kirk Wise and Gary Trousdale, who'd done much to update the Disney brand with *Beauty and the Beast**. 'We've got to keep going and not keep making *Dumbo** forever,' Wise said.

The start of *Beauty and the Beast* had lifted the fairytale with a fastidiously handsome Disney castle and dignified narration by David Ogden Stiers. *Hunchback* starts with the towers of Notre Dame bestriding the clouds. In an operatic prologue, produced at Disney's Paris studio, the evil Judge Frollo (Tony Jay) longs 'to purge the world of vice and sin'. He pursues a gypsy woman to her death on Notre Dame's steps (a bloodless but powerful scene), then recoils from her swaddled child. He's about to 'send it back to hell', when Stiers intervenes as the Archdeacon, singing, 'You never can run from nor hide what you've done from/ the eyes, the very eyes of Notre Dame.'

The fussy lyrics proclaim the loss of *Beauty*'s songwriter Howard Ashman, replaced by Stephen Schwartz (*Wicked*). Alan Menken returns as musician with a hard-to-digest score, pompous but sometimes magnificent. In Hugo's novel, Frollo *was* the Archdeacon, adopting Quasimodo out of compassion, but his fall from good to evil was too much for Disney. Still, the new Frollo is startling, a proto-Nazi with bony fingers and a parchment face who smashes an ant colony to show how he'll deal with the city's gypsies. He's also a wicked stepfather, demeaning Quasimodo in duet ('You are deformed/I am deformed/and you are ugly/and I am ugly …').

His undoing is the gypsy Esmeralda (smokily voiced by Demi Moore), whose exotic dancing feels like Jessica Rabbit without the caricature, though it's technically impressive. It was animated by Ann-Marie Bardwell, who'd supervised the heroine in Canada's *Rock & Rule** many years earlier. Frollo's agonies of operatically strangled lust were drawn by another woman, the veteran Kathy Zielinski (p. 71)

Rather than the book, *Hunchback* remakes the 1939 film which had Charles Laughton as Quasimodo, a secular villain and a happy ending. It also had a scene where Maureen O'Hara's Esmeralda prays for her

DIRECTOR Kirk Wise, Gary Trousdale
PRODUCER Don Hahn
STORY Kevin Harkey, Gaetan Brizzi, Tab Murphy, Irene Mecchi
SCORE Alan Menken
DESIGN Anne-Marie Bardwell, Marek Buchwald, Joe Grant
ANIMATION James Baxter, Tony Fucile, Kathy Zielinski, Russ Edmonds

people, in counterpoint to the greedy parishioners of Notre Dame. Disney expands this into another song ('God Help the Outlaws', sung by Heidi Mollenhauer), which makes good use of the title setting, with Esmeralda illumined by candles and stained glass.

Quasimodo scrambles through spaces between stone and wood, Gothic shadows and saturated sunsets, though the directors claim they were most interested in the grand spectacles. The pyromaniac Frollo sets Paris ablaze, and Quasimodo sweeps Esmeralda up to Notre Dame's battlements, crying 'Sanctuary!' to crowds of Peter Jackson proportions. But even the famous images can feel weirdly redefined, thanks to the teen-romance elements in this version.

Quasimodo becomes an ugly-duckling adolescent; even when he's tied down and pelted with vegetables, it feels like a medieval take on Sissy Spacek's prom nightmare in *Carrie* (1976).

In *The Animated Movie Guide*, Martin Goodman argues, 'One can almost feel the creators yearning to make a more mature version (of the story).' The directors' own comments seem to deny this, while producer Don Hahn claims that *Hunchback* had little executive interference. However, the film's ending was, uniquely, made more downbeat in a Disney stage musical that ran in Berlin as *Der Glöckner von Notre Dame*. Though softer than the book, it countenances tragedy; Esmeralda dies in the hunchback's arms.

Ice Age
US, 2002 – 81 minutes
Chris Wedge
[CGI]

Ice Age's limits are shown up most eloquently by one of its predecessors. In 1998, director Chris Wedge released the haunting seven-minute film, *Bunny*, a strange CGI fantasy about ageing and bereavement, long before Pixar's *Up** risked such themes. Wedge acknowledges that *Ice Age*, his feature four years later, was far less personal.

> If the American audience was more like the French, then our films might be able to be a bit darker … . One big question is, is it important to make an animated film accessible to children? That may be what divides a big animated movie from a small one.

Wedge was a player in CGI's prehistory, working on Disney's *Tron* (1982) back when computer commands were entered on IBM punchcards. When I interviewed him after *Ice Age*, he admitted missing the time when Blue Sky, the studio he co-founded, was smaller and more independent, making roaches for *Joe's Apartment* (1996) and a penguin for *Fight Club* (1999). In 1999, Blue Sky became wholly owned by Fox. Wedge says that otherwise, the studio might not have survived.

> The commercials and effects work was running dry, and we couldn't have sustained ourselves or grown the company. If I had made (*Ice Age*) by myself, it might have been more abstract and much less successful. When you have your face in your work, you sometimes need someone looking over your shoulder to say, 'What do you mean by that?' Then you realise you haven't made your intentions clear enough.

Directed by Wedge, with co-director Carlos Saldanha, *Ice Age* is a prehistoric road-trip, following the course of two older cartoons, Don Bluth's *The Land before Time* (1988) and Disney's CGI *Dinosaur* (2000). Both used talking dinosaurs, but *Ice Age* varies things a little with Manfred the woolly mammoth, Sid the bipedal sloth and Diego the sabre-toothed tiger (voiced by Ray Romano, John Leguizamo and Denis Leary). The bachelor trio find a lost human baby in the wilderness and must return it to its species, though *we* know one of the three is a traitor. Like Japan's *Tokyo Godfathers**, *Ice Age* reprises John Ford's *3 Godfathers* 1948), *3 Men and a Baby* (1987) and other variants of a story dating to the silents.

Smart and breezy, *Ice Age* almost completely lacks the split-level humour or referential knowingness of *Toy Story** and *Shrek**. Its characters don't parody office staff or Disney figures. Instead, they're anthropomorphised by default in a cartoon where humans are blocky primitives who (the tiger Diego points out) *can't talk*. In place of *Toy Story*'s alpha-male duels, *Ice Age*'s characters mostly annoy each other, with Leguizamo's Sid as the chief irritant, winning us over with his bloody-minded persistence. (Manfred to Sid: 'Isn't there someone else you can annoy? Friends, family, poisonous reptiles?')

DIRECTOR Chris Wedge
PRODUCER Lori Forte
STORY Michael J. Wilson, Peter Ackerman, Michael Berg
SCORE David Newman
DESIGN Peter DeSève, Peter Clarke, Brian McEntee
ANIMATION James Bresnahan, Michael Thurmeier, Nina Befaro, Floyd Bishop Jr

In fact, the film's really about Manfred, who brings in some of *Bunny*'s melancholy between the crazy dodos, lava traps and disappointingly ordinary villains. *Ice Age* boldly builds to a tragic revelation, that the solitary Manfred lost his mammoth mate and calf to humans. The scene is shown gracefully and touchingly in a set of moving cave paintings, with Manfred's expressions confined to his eyes and shaggy forehead. (Watch when he clasps the human child to him with his trunk.)

Not only is the scene better than a showily stylised flashback in DreamWorks' *The Prince of Egypt**, but *Ice Age*'s opening is sharper and funnier than any of Pixar's shorts to date, with a hysterical sabre-toothed 'Scrat' squirrel harried by a high-speed glacier. Created in the storyboard, this sequence did double duty as the cinema trailer. Wisely, the Scrat – hilariously voiced by Wedge – is threaded through the story much like the mice in Disney's *Cinderella*, though nothing matches his opening scene.

Ice Age's sequels, *Ice Age: The Meltdown* (2006) and the 3D *Ice Age: Dawn of the Dinosaurs* (2009) were less rewarding, despite their ballooning world box office. At least they provide closure for Manfred, who finds a new family by the end of part three.

Idiots and Angels
US, 2008 – 78 minutes
Bill Plympton
[Drawings]

DIRECTOR/STORY/ANIMATION Bill Plympton
PRODUCER Biljana Labovic
SCORE Nicole Renaud, Corey A. Jackson, Tom Waits

When Bill Plympton was in high school in Portland, Oregon, his grocery job included making deliveries – soda, cigarettes – to the local dive bar.

> It was like a church, almost religious, very spiritual, because it was so *dark*. The only light that came in was through a little window on the door. The cigarette smoke permeated the air. I thought, what a wonderful, mysterious kind of atmosphere.

This schoolboy impression found its way into Plympton's animated feature, *Idiots and Angels*. Entirely hand-drawn by Plympton, it's a grotesque but surprisingly moral fable about a bar, an idiot, a miracle and the lunacy that ensues. The wordless film has a soundtrack of laughs, shouts and screeches, plus music from Tom Waits and chanteuse singer Nicole Renaud. It's an adult animation, but its slapstick cruelty makes it feel like a gross Roald Dahl or 'Looney Tune', interpreted by *New Yorker* artists. Plympton himself spent fifteen years as an illustrator and print cartoonist, contributing to *Village Voice* and *Vanity Fair*, but earning more from sex mags. In *Idiots and Angels*, the sexual slapstick veers into disturbing abuse, risky in such a male film.

Plympton first broke into animated pop culture with the Oscar-nominated *Your Face* (1987), a 'low-budget, three-minute bit of whimsy' where the face of a singer twists, scrunches and explodes. British viewers may remember Plympton's head-twisting 90s ads, such as 'The Best Thing about Nik Naks', while MTV raised his profile in America. He was invited to Disney – a studio he admires – with the offer of a huge salary without autonomy. 'They could have put me on some stupid TV show like *Duck Tales*,' says Plympton, who turned it down. Years later, he learned Disney had wanted him for *Aladdin**'s Genie.

Plympton is now a mainstay of the festival circuit, where he secures distribution for his self-funded films, making one or two shorts a year. Plympton also makes an animated *feature* every three or four years, drawing each frame himself. His first was 1992's *The Tune*; *Idiots and Angels* is his sixth (counting *Mondo Plympton*, 1997, a collection of his shorts). Plympton can produce up to 100 drawings a day, 'if it's an easy scene, with not a lot of details or backgrounds'. He does a new picture each three or four frames; *Idiots and Angels* needed 25,000.

Each picture is a jaunty pencil sketch, its personality underpinning the freehand shading and simplicity. There are clouds with weeping faces, lines of lollipop trees and herds of appealingly fat cars. Angles and distances warp; the murky bar takes on Wild West dimensions. Faces are meaty and stretchable, without Disney glamour. The characters themselves are ciphers (Plympton calls them his puppets), like bystanders in a newspaper cartoon.

Idiots and Angels' anti-hero is an out-of-the-suitcase gun-seller, but mostly a barfly with horny fantasies and a short fuse. He blows phallic smoke-cones, snarls like the Hulk and lights a touchpaper to

the petrol tank of a driver who takes his space. (His victim's frantic dash and immolation are pure 'Looney Tunes'.) But Angel is mortified to find wings on his back, mocking his manhood and reducing the bar's denizens to hysterics. He frantically tries killing the wings, even himself, but the wings ruthlessly hijack him into doing good.

There are echoes of *Groundhog Day* (1993): the dry comedy of the hero's hellish frustrations, his life's grinding rhythm as he gets up each morning, showers, then drives to the bar for another bout of strangeness. Plympton's textured pencilwork recalls British animator Joanna Quinn and her raucous XL heroine Beryl (introduced in the short *Girl's Night Out*, 1986). Plympton concedes he may have borrowed from Quinn; *Idiots* features a fat woman character who dreams she's a tassel-spinning Venus.

Other images, though, could only be Plympton's. A man slithers up a beautiful nude blonde; a tear is pushed back into an eye-socket; someone is shot and we see an anatomically fastidious bullet-enters-heart. The dénouement involves the shocked villain giving birth (though it's presented as a miracle rather than an *Alien* monstrosity) and a happy-ending dick gag. We're left, not quite cynically, to work the gender politics out for ourselves.

What comes through strongest, though, is the melancholy fable of wings that exist only for good, lifting us into the clouds even as we fight little wars to destroy or control them. When Angel 'kills' the wings, in a gory but restrained scene (for Plympton), we're sorrier for the feathers than for any of the humans. Plympton's next project will tackle another downer; it's a 'tainted-love' story through female eyes, called *Cheatin'*.

The Illusionist
UK/France, 2010 – 85 minutes
Sylvain Chomet
[Drawings (with brief live-action and CGI)]

The Illusionist is a film about journeys and motion that happen mostly in one place, the Edinburgh of 1959. Its long wide takes mimic the work of its subject and inspiration, the French comedian Jacques Tati, who wrote the script upon which the film is based. There's a little of the pawky humour of *Belleville Rendez-Vous**, director Sylvain Chomet's previous film, but too rarefied this time to satisfy all *Belleville*'s fans. Even the actual jokes tend to sigh away. 'I've eschewed black humour for Tati's innate poetry,' Chomet said. As animation, *The Illusionist* feels as close, or closer, in spirit to Jiří Trnka's stop-motion *A Midsummer Night's Dream**. In their mostly wordless films, Chomet and Trnka continue the silent-comedy tradition of dignifying unruly motion, without the pratfalls of *WALL·E**.

Belleville Rendez-Vous contained around 1,300 shots; *The Illusionist* has just 400. Quite a few of them show the title character, a struggling stage magician, in transit on ferries, boats and trains as he wanders from Paris via London into the misty mysteries of Scotland. Both the landscapes and vehicles are more majestic than those in the bathetic *Belleville*, though Chomet often lets the far backgrounds dissipate into sketched lines. It's as if a John Ford film had met the modernist graphics of Disney's *One Hundred and One Dalmatians**, which Chomet cites as an inspiration.

Most of the time, we watch the characters' own motions in lengthy, low-key scenes, and especially the motions of the magician, Tatischeff. One doesn't need to know that Tatischeff is modelled on Jacques Tati (Tatischeff was his full name) to be struck by his screen presence. Everything about him seems a third too big, especially his huge hands and feet, his swinging arms and braced elbows. He strives for elegance but must settle for charmingly affected dignity. Given that his whole manner suggests repression and vulnerability, it would have been fascinating to see him paired up with the steely Madame Souza from *Belleville*.

The Illusionist, though, links him with Alice, an impressionable ingénue from the Hebrides, which Tatischeff visits just as their inhabitants get their first electricity. Like Tatischeff, Alice is gawky, gauche and charming. Her face seldom changes drastically, yet it and her motions convey a brook-like flow of surprise, curiosity and delight, while Tatischeff is all urgent unease. Captivated by Tatischeff's act, Alice invites herself along with him; they accept each other instinctively as father and daughter.

They reach Edinburgh, where Alice is beguiled anew by the city lights and shop displays, and becomes an avid window-shopper. But Edinburgh is too rich to be commodified. Chomet glories in its steep streets, its tall buildings and piled landscape that lour or transcend depending on the ever-changing clouds and light. The director compared the experience of Edinburgh's turbulent weather to that of a journey aboard a moving city.

Insofar as *The Illusionist* is a fable, it seems to concern the necessary (or at least useful) illusions of growing up: the pretty dresses and flashing lights which entrance Alice, or the prettier boy pop singers who draw

DIRECTOR/DESIGN Sylvain Chomet
PRODUCER Bob Last, Sally Chomet
STORY Jacques Tati, Sylvain Chomet
SCORE Sylvain Chomet, Malcolm Ross
ANIMATION Laurent Kircher, Thierry Torres Rubio, Nick Debray, Charlotte Walton

screaming crowds of girl fans. Tatischeff, of course, embodies illusion in its pure state, even if his own style of magic has fallen out of fashion. When he fails on the Edinburgh stage, he ends up inside a shop display himself, flourishing ladies' garments instead of white rabbits. (His own rabbit is a pugilist brute.) He's luckier than his cast-off neighbours; a clown about to hang himself, a ventriloquist whose puppet is his soul he must pawn.

The Illusionist plots Tatischeff's own downward fortunes, even as he raises Alice up from a duck-footed waif to a fair lady, bestowing her with coats and shoes (she thinks by magic) till her handsome swain appears. Even the lovers' first kiss occurs before shop-window mannequins. It's a reverse of Miyazaki's *Kiki's Delivery Service**, another animation about coming to the big city. Miyazaki's Kiki *wants* the pretty clothes she sees in shop windows, rather than her dowdy witch's attire, but in the end she sees other girls copying *her*. In *The Illusionist*, the outsider Tatischeff helps Alice through conformity as part of a healthy growing process, before leaving her with an anti-spell to break the bond. 'Magicians,' he warns her (in writing, not speech), 'do not exist.'

Yet they will still be needed, as long as there are children. We see two younger Alices in the later scenes, one eyeing 'our' Alice's new finery, the other – a child on a train – ready to be enchanted in her turn by Tatischeff's magic, if only he had magic left in him. They put a cyclical spin on the film's beguilingly crowded world, where our eyes frequently wander from Alice and Tatischeff to the snapshot background extras, individuated as humanely as those in Masaaki Yuasa's *Mind Game**. At the end, Chomet breaks his own austere styling with a couple of liberated camera shots, including a victory roll around Edinburgh, before ceremonially dousing the city lights. The enduring world, the individual's passing, *The Illusionist* gives them both their place.

The Incredibles
US, 2004 – 110 minutes
Brad Bird
[CGI]

Early on in *The Incredibles*, the downtrodden protagonist, Bob (whom *we* know was once a Herculean superhero, Mr Incredible), is called before a tyrannical middle-manager in a drab insurance office. The pint-sized boss's pointing and pacing are simultaneously exaggerated and shrunk down; he looks like a puppet from the satirical British TV series, *Spitting Image* (1984–96). 'A company is like an enormous clock,' he squeakily intones, Bob parroting him resignedly. 'It only works if all the cogs mesh together …'.

The scene reflects the career of director Brad Bird. 'In my first animation job, I worked under a director who underestimated a lot of people, and hobbled them with low expectations,' Bird said. In another interview, he put his frustration in *Incredibles* terms: 'The superhero can do all these marvellous things, but no one wants him to.' Bird was presented by Pixar as a strong-willed outsider, an auteur to challenge the bureaucrats. It helped that Bird had been classmates with John Lasseter, Pixar's co-founder, at the animation school CalArts. Since then, Bird had proved himself through an acclaimed cartoon feature, *The Iron Giant**, released by Warner Bros. (see the next entry).

Bird's Iron Giant dreamed of being Superman. Bob in *The Incredibles was* Superman, or the film's close equivalent. But he's now consigned to middle-aged mundanity, unable to connect with his wife and kids, who all have superpowers. As Ken Gillam and Shannon R. Wooden noted in a paper on Pixar's post-princess protagonists, *The Incredibles* extends the process of male emasculation begun in *Toy Story**. Spaceman Buzz was put in a dress, superhero Bob is plonked in an itty-bitty office cubicle. Meanwhile, his nemesis Syndrome is an embittered fanboy ('I'm geeking out!'), twisted decades ago when Bob rejected his pleas to be a sidekick. The backstory makes Syndrome an evil twin to the Iron Giant, who *did* get elevated to super-status.

The Incredibles matches Pixar's already sophisticated themes to a retro-modern clean-line aesthetic ('I used to design for *gods*!' snaps fearsome fashionista Edna Mole, voiced by Bird himself), romantic badinage ('Whatever happened to ladies first?'; 'Whatever happened to equal treatment?') and witty suggestion ('Is this … rubble?,' asks Bob's wife Helen, catching Bob sneaking into their house at night). The family values don't preclude playful innuendo. Witness Bob entering an egg-shaped capsule with a platinum blonde femme fatale, before they're drawn together down a tubular tunnel.

Pixar's first film to foreground CGI humans, *The Incredibles* has definitively stylised players, contrasting with those in the first two *Shrek*s* (which predated *The Incredibles*) and *The Polar Express** (which came out five days later). The viewer responds to Pixar's proudly smooth-skinned constructs as real, and yet they can cause a kind of double vision in the midst of dramatic scenes. We suddenly notice *how* caricatured these 'humans' look, without the countervailing relief of a non-human lead (as in *Ratatouille*, 2007, *WALL·E** or Disney's *Bolt*, 2008). The experience certainly *feels* akin to the uncanny disconnect that Pixar fans – and Bird himself – use to hammer less cartoony characters (p. 157).

DIRECTOR/STORY Brad Bird
PRODUCER John Walker
SCORE Michael Giacchino
DESIGN Tony Fucile, Teddy Newton, Lou Romano
ANIMATION Steven Clay Hunter, Alan Barillaro, Carlos Baena, Bobby Beck, Michael Bernstein

Mostly, though, *The Incredibles'* characters pull us into their human and superhuman worlds. In one scene, Bob is shown lying to Helen, telling her he's going to a business conference. His face acting is supple and enjoyable. But the sympathetic affect pays off in the *next* scene, as Bob talks secretly on a phone, carrying the presence of an ageing man desperate to regain his glory years. A reverse principle holds in Bob's lone fight with a spherical robot on a volcanic island. It's thrilling because it stresses the metallic foe's baleful otherness *à la* classic stop-motion titans: Talos in *Jason and the Argonauts* (1963), the ED-209 in *Robocop* (1987). By the time we get to Bob's son Dash, racing furiously against flying machines and having the time of his life, the scene can't help but feel generic (resembling one in *Return of the*

Jedi, 1983), despite Bird's integrity in using action to advance character.

In *The Incredibles*, Bob rails against social mediocrity, a point leapt on by critics and fans excited by a cartoon with political substance. However, Bird called such analysis 'Ayn Rand nonsense' (referring to the author of *Atlas Shrugged*) and undercuts Bob's sentiments by his portrayal as a competitive dad, pathetically trying to live through his son. While Bob moans about the superfast Dash not being able to run in a school race, Helen stretches to her elastic height, towers over him and yells, 'This is not *about you*!' Perhaps in the end, the moral is just what an inarticulate teen boy observes in the last scene: 'Different is great!' Even if those cogs don't quite mesh any more.

The Iron Giant
US, 1999 – 86 minutes
Brad Bird
[Drawings with CGI]

In *The Iron Giant*, a robot from space meets a young boy in a 1950s Maine dressed in Fall reds and browns. The season reflected the decline of hand-drawn features when the film opened in 1999, four years after *Toy Story**. (Even Disney's 'hit' musical *Tarzan*, released a few weeks later, was fatally expensive.) *The Iron Giant* was produced by what its own director, Brad Bird, called the dysfunctional animation unit at Warner Bros., whose most recent film had been the awful *The Magic Sword: Quest for Camelot* (1998).

Bird had a low budget, a breakneck schedule and independence in Hollywood terms (though executives pestered him for changes, such as contemporising the setting). As a teen, Bird had studied under Milt Kahl, one of Disney's elite 'Nine Old Men' animators. Later, he became an executive consultant on toon sitcoms, including 180 *Simpsons* episodes. Yet Bird wanted *The Iron Giant* to have the rhythm and emotions of classic Disney, ditching the Broadway musical turns of the rebranded studio and its imitators.

Loosely inspired by a declamatory children's story by British poet Ted Hughes, *The Iron Giant* has no songs, sidekicks or virtual three dimensions. (The look is cosily flattened while never graphically flat.) It's one of relatively few cartoon features to have an engaging boy hero (Hogarth), voiced by twelve-year-old Eli Marienthal, whose first appearance is accompanied by ebullient strings as he freewheels into town on his bike. He's effectively Peter from *Peter and the Wolf*, ready at the first sign of alien invaders to scamper into gnarled and fanged woods. Some bathroom humour reminds us this is a 90s film (Hogarth gleefully spikes an enemy's milkshake with a laxative), but even this reflects Bird's fond complicity with his hero.

In Disney's *Beauty and the Beast**, Belle knows she's in a fairytale because she reads books. Hogarth knows he's in a sci-fi film because he watches schlocky monster flicks, cackling '*You're gonna get it!*' at the cardboard victims. He's one of the most effusive characters to appear in a cartoon feature, though there's a telling moment when we see his energy wear down his self-possessed widowed mother, voiced by Jennifer Aniston. Occasionally Hogarth's animation can't match Marienthal's voice-performance, as in a touching but over-stagey scene where he tells the giant about death and immortality. The climax, though, is movingly underplayed, as Hogarth realises there's nothing he can do but let events take their course – perhaps a first in a Hollywood cartoon feature.

The titular giant, animated in well-integrated CGI, was conceived as a gun with a soul, a war machine who grows a heart by meeting Hogarth. The 'monster-from-space' motif homages 1950s sci-fi; a more recent precedent was *Terminator 2: Judgment Day* (1991), where a hulking cyborg Schwarzenegger is humanised by a young boy. There's a similar storyline – though with a girl – in the last chapters of Hayao Miyazaki's epic comic-strip version of *Nausicaa of the Valley of the Wind* (see p. 167). Bird's giant is clunky and overbuilt, all dull bolted metal, but beautifully voiced by a gravelly Vin Diesel, who conveys the innocence of Dumbo and the pathos of Boris Karloff.

DIRECTOR Brad Bird
PRODUCER Allison Abbate, Des McAnuff
STORY Brad Bird, Tim McCanlies, Andy Brent Forrester
SCORE Michael Kamen
DESIGN Mark Whiting, Ray Aragon, Victor J. Haboush, Lou Romano
ANIMATION Tony Fucile, Richard Baneham, Grace Blanco, Richard Bazley, Bob Davies

The character's strong emotions shame Pixar's later metal characters in *Cars* (2006) and *WALL·E**. Ed Hooks, who teaches acting for animators, picks out a sequence of broad but convincing pantomime as the giant tries frantically to dispose of a blaring car in a junkyard, his quickfire expressions and motions adding up to humanity. When the giant flies into space at the end of the film, he suggests a square-jawed comic hero (his last word is 'Superman …'), but his tranquil expression conveys the softness of flesh and blood.

The villain is a false father figure, the FBI investigator Kent (voiced by Christopher MacDonald). The character looks like a buffoonish parody of Basil Rathbone and was designed as a spoof of the American dad. The film becomes a suspense thriller, including a fine sequence where a sleepless Hogarth and Kent watch each other from shadowed rooms, the camera briefly panning from the smirking Kent to a photo of Hogarth's late father. Fortunately, Hogarth finds an alternative dad, a beatnik scrap-artist (voiced by Harry Connick, Jr), whose cool poise makes for delightful comedy when his character meets the giant.

Hogarth believes that souls don't die, and on repeat viewings a strange interpretation of the film suggests itself. Bird wanted to depict the giant's origins in a deleted scene where his electric dreams are broadcast on TV, showing robot conquerors storming from world to world. Yet in a film whose Oedipal conflicts evoke *Hamlet* more than *The Lion King** ever did, what if the giant's soul came from elsewhere; what if he was infused with the ghost of Hogarth's *real* father?

Ivan and His Magic Pony

USSR, 1947, remade 1975 – 55 minutes (1947), 70 minutes (1975)
Ivan Ivanov-Vano
[Drawings]

Russia's first animated feature was *The New Gulliver* (1935), two years before Disney's *Snow White** and four before the Fleischers' *Gulliver's Travels*. Directed by Aleksandr Ptsushko, the film set a real boy amid stop-motion puppets, and turned Swift's story into a salutary Communist fable. The hero dreams himself into Lilliput and supports a workers' revolt against their bourgeois rulers.

At the same time, Russian industry was taking lessons from its enemy. With Disney's assembly line as a model, Russia's cottage-industry cartoon studios were merged into a state body, Soyuzmultfilm in Moscow. In its early years, the film-makers were pressed to emulate Disney in technique and content. They included Ivan Ivanov-Vano, who'd worked in animation since 1923 and was ready to adapt. His 1938 short, 'The Little Liar', starred an imitation of Donald Duck, though the animator who drew it, Fyodor Khitruk, called it unsuccessful. (Khitruk himself later created a series of graphically brilliant *Winnie the Pooh* cartoons, light-years removed from the Disney versions.)

Ivanov-Vano's *Ivan and His Magic Pony*, produced by Soyuzmultfilm, is a children's fairytale, with songs and a canny cartoon animal. However, unlike 'The Little Liar', the film has few debts to Disney. Rather, it's closely based on a nineteenth-century narrative poem, attributed (not without controversy) to Pyotr Yershov. In the story, a foolish but spirited peasant boy, Ivan, tames a wild flying horse. The animal gives him a humpbacked pony, as buoyant as Ivan himself, to guide the lad through adventures with phoenixes, a giant ship-eating fish and an unearthly maiden. For Anglophone viewers, the pony echoes 'Puss in Boots', while the boy performs Herculean tasks for a greedy Tsar.

The film – variously called *The Magic Pony*, *The Magic Horse* or *The Little Humpbacked Horse* – is homely in the best way, a colourful moving-picture book. Its compositions and flowing motions are so pleasurably legible that they more than compensate for the lack of Disney 'life'. The palette swings between the chill blue skies and white walls of the Tsar's capital and the brightly streaming flames and manes of the firebirds and horses. Ivan and the pony's spirited prancing are never irksomely cute, their pairing somewhere between idealised pals and parent and child. The talking pony saves Ivan from all his scrapes, while the magic princess (snared by Ivan) leads the besotted Tsar to a fool's doom in a tartly ruthless ending.

The original cartoon appeared in 1947, later playing in America dubbed and subtitled. By the 1970s, the print was apparently past restoration. Ivanov-Vano, then in his seventies himself, directed a reconstruction from scratch. In live-action terms, it's a 'shot-by-shot' remake, keeping the flow of the scenes and business intact, while changing all the specifics of drawings and movement. The big change – and an easy way to tell the two versions apart – is that the remake adds an episode that wasn't in the first film, where Ivan enlists a huge cursed fish to find a lost ring.

1975 version:
DIRECTOR Ivan Ivanov-Vano, Boris Butakov
PRODUCER Fedor Ivanov
SCORE V. Oransky, V. Vassilyev
ANIMATION Valentin Kushnerev, Viktor Shevkov, Oleg Safronov, Nikolai Fedorov, Marina Rogova

It's the remake that can be found in second-hand US dubs (for example, on the 'Stories from my Childhood' DVD series released by Films by Jove). However, the original film was restored in 2004 and released on Russian DVD. Viewing them together is a strange double vision, like watching the Spanish *Dracula* made in tandem with the Bela Lugosi classic (1931), or leafing through the multiple versions of Hergé's *Tintin* strips. The animation and action when Ivan tames the wild flying stallion (drawn by Nikolai Federov) is far more exciting in the original film. However, a scene where the Tsar is scrubbed in a bathhouse gains exuberance in the remake, while the long-necked

dancing phoenixes are more elegantly fantastic … and so the changes run from scene to scene, down to nuances in presence and staging.

But the two versions prompt a troubling thought, taking us back to Disney. What if one of that studio's great films – *Snow White*, or *One Hundred and One Dalmatians** – was redrawn the same way as *Ivan and His Magic Pony*, matching the broad action without the genius? A 'Grumpy' without Bill Tytla's sourness; a 'Cruella De Vil' without the obnoxious slinkiness instilled by Marc Davis. Would children enjoy it less? Would adults, with their faded memories of the original, spot the difference? Is animation truly an invisible art?

The Jungle Book
US, 1967 – 75 minutes
Wolfgang Reitherman
[Drawings]

DIRECTOR Wolfgang Reitherman
STORY Larry Clemmons, Ralph Wright, Ken Anderson, Vance Gerry
SCORE George Bruns
DESIGN Al Dempster Animation: Milt Kahl, Ollie Johnston, Frank Thomas, John Lounsbery

'That looks good … hopping up and down now … wiggling his fanny …'. In charming archive footage, *The Jungle Book* animators Frank Thomas and Ollie Johnston pore through a sequence of Thomas's drawings, featuring the bear character Baloo. As Thomas lets his drawings fall, flipbook fashion, his friend mimics the bear's swinging; a balding fifty-something man in short-sleeved shirt and glasses, who's so spontaneously caught up in the motion that he's moved to dance.

The Jungle Book was the last cartoon feature supervised by Walt Disney, who died ten months before its release in October 1967. Some commentators see Walt's input as perfunctory, though the 2007 DVD presses the case that he drove the film. A hit on its first release, *The Jungle Book* remains one of the most fondly regarded Disneys among non-cartoon fans. One need only hum a few notes from the breezy 'Bare Necessities' (sung by Phil Harris's Baloo, who dominates the film), to draw smiles from any crowd.

More serious-minded commentators, though, often take the part of the disapproving panther Bagheera. Leonard Maltin called *The Jungle Book* 'one of the most forgettable' of Disney's films. Michael Barrier deemed it one of the worst. Even John Grant, who defends the film, complains that its story 'meanders a little aimlessly; one keeps waiting for something really boggling to happen, but it never quite does'.

As with other Disney adaptations, one can mourn the lost opportunities in the source material. For example, Rudyard Kipling's book features a lyrical, dazzling description of the jungle boy Mowgli being captured by monkeys and swung with them through the treetops. In the film, this is reduced to a few throwaway shots while the artists serve up slapstick for Baloo and the monkeys, exposing the mechanics of the Disney formula even more nakedly than the recycled animation. When the characters snatch Mowgli from each other after 'I Wanna Be Like You', their manic motions are taken from Rat, Mole and the weasels in a 1949 Disney feature, *The Adventures of Ichabod and Mr Toad*.

Yet *The Jungle Book* has wit with its rough and tumble. The military elephant Colonel Hathi inspects one of his troops and tuts, 'A dusty muzzle … . Soldier, remember in battle a trunk can save your life.' His comically grave pachyderm face, drawn by John Lounsbery, is a mass of pompous lines, a stylistic holdover from *One Hundred and One Dalmatians**. The girlish sibilants of Sterling Holloway, voicing Kaa, are matched in the snake's curling and coiling. Louis Prima's performance is punctuated by the oversized arms of ape king Louie, giving his trumpeting mass and meat. The villainous Shere Khan (drawn by Milt Kahl) has only to turn away from the camera, letting George Sanders's silky tones complement his rippling stripes. 'And now for my rendezvous with the little lost mancub …'.

The mancub himself shows little sign of his feral upbringing, being malleable or pigheaded as the story demands. Yet there's a pathos to the repeated scenes of him wandering purposeless through the jungle, oblivious to its beauty, amid the melancholia of George Bruns's music, Walter Sheet's orchestration and the

jungle backdrops styled by Al Dempster, which tend towards *Bambi*'s watercolour impressionism. It's these elements, between and behind the fun, that give the film its form.

Even young viewers see how dull Mowgli is, which in turn highlights the grown-up, parental, perspective of Bagheera. The panther frames the film in his opening voice-over, and later argues Baloo (who wants to adopt Mowgli) into giving up the boy in an unshowy and sensitive scene. Baloo and Bagheera foreshadow the odd-couple duos in Pixar films; their parental responsibilities especially anticipate *Monsters, Inc**.

Of course, kids will lose interest in Mowgli, as soon as he's 'twitterpated' (to use *Bambi*'s phrase for seduction) by a village girl and heads into manhood – a fact that Kipling appreciated, dismissing Mowgli's married life as a story for grown-ups. Johnston's animation of the scene suggests romance, even sexuality, but Mowgli's final expression is a goofy grin, deflating the moment even before Baloo's deadpan 'He's hooked!' No matter; we turn and head back into the jungle with Baloo and Bagheera, back to the dancing and singing.

Kiki's Delivery Service
Japan, 1989 – 102 minutes
Hayao Miyazaki
[Drawings]

Kiki's Delivery Service starts with a girl lying in a meadow, her hair and clothes rippling breezily, clouds scudding in the sky. It's stillness of a kind familiar in director Hayao Miyazaki's work (you can find equivalent 'at rest' moments in most of his films, even in his manic action début, *The Castle of Cagliostro*, 1979). In a moment, thirteen-year-old Kiki will realise it's time to leave, to fly away on her witch's broom and live independently in a place of her choosing. But to soar means to lose the equilibrium of the meadow; will she ever regain the ground?

Miyazaki's fifth film, *Kiki* was his first to be released by Disney in the 1990s, when Japanese animation was still fairly cultish in America. If Disney had released *Kiki* without its credits, many of the audience might have thought it was American, following Disney's lead if not its style. Kiki's talking cat Jiji ('jee-jee') is the kind of comic sidekick we expect from Disney, though he upstages the protagonist far less than *Cinderella**'s mice or *Mermaid*'s Jamaican crab (1989). It's rather fitting that Jiji spends a while pretending he's a soft toy, the traditional destiny for Disney sidekicks.

Kiki's environment is a foreigner's imagined Europe, down to the mossy family home at the start of the film. The city where she settles is a travel-brochure mash-up, modelled on Stockholm and Visby in Sweden, with bits of San Francisco thrown in. In Japan, it might have reminded viewers of another drawn city, the nineteenth-century Genoa depicted extensively in a 1976 TV cartoon, *From the Apennines to the Andes* (aka *Marco*). Miyazaki handled the scene design and layout in the series, directed by Isao Takahata.

Like Miyazaki's previous *My Neighbour Totoro**, *Kiki* lacks a villain, a love interest or a physical conflict (until the disaster-film ending). At first, it hardly registers. We push forward with Kiki as she hugs her parents goodbye and flies into her new wide world. The background artists lay down her tracks with each new forest and town on her flight path. Like *Totoro*, and even parts of *Grave of the Fireflies**, *Kiki* is a holiday in animated form. The girl is drenched in a downpour and rides a train hobo-style, meeting some surprised cows.

The city, called Koriko or Corico, is magnificent. We fly over gables and chimney-pots to the ringing of bells, and then down into the bustle. Kiki's arrival recalls a famous multiplane scene in Disney's *Pinocchio** which showed the waking of a village. Indeed, Miyazaki makes use of multiplane processing to deepen his city's perspective.

But the first things that happen to Kiki in town are that she nearly hits a bus and gets dressed down by a policeman. No one seems interested in Kiki's great adventure; only a boy her own age, and she's *trying* to be grown-up. Kiki doesn't know what to do next, so nor do we. There's no villain to fight, as in a Disney cartoon, and no go-getting guide like Jiminy Cricket or Timothy Mouse. Jiji can't help; as Miyazaki himself

DIRECTOR/PRODUCER/STORY
Hayao Miyazaki
SCORE Joe Hisaishi
DESIGN Katsuya Kondo
ANIMATION Shinji Otsuka, Katsuya Kondo, Yoshifumi Kondo, Yoshinori Kanada, Makiko Futaki, Masako Shinohara

put it, he's really just part of the immature Kiki, which is why Disney's dubbed version was wrong to give him the sardonic adult tones of *The Simpsons'* Phil Hartman.

After an uncertain period that's rare for a cartoon – Jiji even suggests they just give up and go on travelling – Kiki decides to open a flying delivery business. Apart from facilitating meetings and adventures, she's orienting herself in a city of strangers, from the pregnant baker's owner who puts her up in her attic, to the gauche boy who wants to befriend her. As in *Totoro*, Miyazaki's close sympathy with Kiki's viewpoint is accompanied by subtle observations. He's especially interested in how Kiki behaves differently towards parents, other grown-ups and her own teen age group – in whose company, of course, she confuses herself. Then she suddenly loses her flying powers, for no clear reason, though it coincides with her new uncertainties about who she is. (Though it's not just Miyazaki teenagers who have a faltering sense of identity; the ten-year-old Chihiro in *Spirited Away** is the same.)

Finally, Kiki *does* get a guide, a bohemian female artist who draws crows in the woods, as free as Kiki wants to be. Unlike Jiji, the artist Ursula is an older Kiki, a point played up in the Japanese version where the same actress (Minami Takayama) voices both girls. Miyazaki gives them a sleepover heart-to-heart, discussing the difference between having and possessing a talent (making it yours). The director drops in some comments of his own; Ursula tells a shocked Kiki that she looks most beautiful when she's troubled. There follows an excitingly contrived action climax, and an uproarious feel-good ending, but the end-credits coda reminds us what's *Kiki*'s about; making a place for yourself on the ground even while you soar sky-high.

King Kong

US, 1933 – 100 minutes
Merian C. Cooper, Ernest B. Schoedsack
[Live-action with stop-motion]

DIRECTOR/PRODUCER Merian C. Cooper, Ernest B. Schoedsack
STORY Ruth Rose, James Creelman
SCORE Max Steiner
ANIMATION Willis O'Brien

King Kong isn't often called an animated film, despite its abundance of stop-motion monsters. However, it was unquestionably the first feature to have an animated *star*. 'Did you ever hear of … *Kong*?' asks Robert Armstrong's reckless explorer with a showman's timing. Kong is Skull Island's gorilla god, who snatches a hapless girl (Fay Wray) back to a mountain that's more castle than lair. The girl lays him low. Kong is captured and brought to New York, 'a show to gratify your curiosity', as Armstrong boasts. Roaring defiance, Kong breaks free. Reclaiming his bride, he climbs the Empire State Building to the top of the world, but not *his* world. At last, he falls to fighter planes, caricatures of nature he can't comprehend.

Kong's entrance was a screen legend back when cartoons were *little* amusements (Disney's 1933 hit was *The Three Little Pigs*). Emerging as a brutish shadow, Kong snaps trees, roars as if there were lions in his chest, and gazes down, beetle brows twitching, at the toy-like Wray. She's tethered between sacrificial stones, writhing and screaming with a sexuality predating the Hays Code. Kong grins a terrible fanged grin; a live-action grin, as any casual viewer can see. As an effect, Kong switches between animator Willis O'Brien's stop-motion puppet homunculus and a full-scale mecha-head leaning in for a close-up. Co-director Ernest B. Schoedsack knew the value of such money shots. For 1927's *Chang*, he'd filmed a wild tiger shimmying up a tree and gaping its jaws to eat him for real.

Even now, when Kong's every jerk and join is manifest on screen, they only reinforce his solid vitality. In tune with the emerging aesthetics of Hollywood cartoons, the film distends reality, driven by its central contact between the fantasy monster and the human girl. Fay Wray struggles in Kong's life-sized mechanical hand, projected behind the stop-motion puppet, as Kong tickles her and Max Steiner's score quivers to the coochie coo. Kong shreds her clothes, lifting them to his waggling nostrils. '[The censors] took it out because they thought it was too risqué,' recalled co-director Merian C. Cooper. 'All I did was make audiences from 6 to 60 laugh.'

In 1933, no one knew how Kong was done. *Modern Mechanics and Inventions* claimed he was a man in a monkey suit. Now, monsterphiles and stop-motion Frankensteins can get the whole story in magazines, picture-books and DVD extras, including a two-and-a-half-hour documentary on the R1 special edition. Kong bristles because O'Brien wrangled the puppet twenty-four frames a second, his handprints immortalised in Kong's hair. The Doré-inspired jungles of Skull Island were created by a camera shooting though painted glass and miniatures, much as Disney used layered paintings in his multiplane camera. Kong's fight with a T-Rex took seven weeks to animate, and was informed by O'Brien's prize-fighting background. The point was picked up brilliantly by Walter Lantz, who spoofed the fight as a boxing match in his cartoon *King Klunk*, only six months after *Kong*'s release.

However, many post-1933 generations only knew an expurgated *Kong*. In the uncut version (now restored from a British print), people writhe in close-up in Kong's jaws. He stomps a luckless native into the

mud, twisting his foot to finish the job. Kong was softened both by censors and by later films where Beauty tamed the bestial ape; *Mighty Joe Young* (1949), or the 2005 *Kong* remake. In the latter, Kong and Naomi Watts slide round on a frozen pond, for all the world like *Bambi** critters. As Armstrong said in the first film, Kong got sappy.

True, the new CGI Kong is laudably expressive, with the computer-captured presence of Andy 'Gollum' Serkis. But the 1933

Kong was no new ape; he was a chest-beating lummox, as dopey as he was vicious. He's childishly aggrieved when a human stabs his paw; he plays curiously with the head of the T-Rex he's broken; and even his death agonies are pathetically doltish as he sways, bullet-ridden, on the brink. *Contra* fan hagiographies, he has no soul. He's anthropomorphised only to the level of a crude cretin, a hairy Id glorying in carnal satisfactions. Kong stands alone, still bristling from his maker's touch, swatting planes from the sky.

Kung Fu Panda
US, 2008 – 91 minutes
John Stevenson, Mark Osborne
[CGI]

One of the cartooniest kinds of fantasy worlds rarely appeared in cartoon features before CGI. This is the 'funny animal' world, where humans don't exist (or they're in the minority) and the players are birds or beasts. They're a staple of short cartoons, TV and comics, such as Carl Barks's famous Disney strips starring Scrooge McDuck. However, even lightweight Disney animal features such as *The Jungle Book** and *The Aristocats* (1970) have people in the background, and a moment's thought suggests why.

A family audience in the cinema may be happy to watch *Funny Little Bunnies* (a 1934 'Silly Symphony') for seven minutes. The same audience may need persuading to stay with an all-animal cast in a feature without at least an *implicit* human context. The classic implicit-humans film is *Bambi**, with its Unseen Hunter. Even *The Lion King** lets us *presume* there are people living in the film's world, though we never see them. Paradoxically, animal worlds are fine in animations with an overtly adult perspective – *Fritz the Cat**, or the stop-motion *Fantastic Mr Fox** (in which the human villains are almost incidental).

In the noughties, though, there were several CGI films that were set in animal worlds, or other worlds without humans, such as Disney's *Chicken Little* (2005), Pixar's *Cars* (2006), Blue Sky's *Robots* (2005) and Sony's *Surf's Up* (2007, about surfing penguins). The successful studios could experiment; they also needed films to stand out from the glut of competition. *Kung Fu Panda*, for instance, opened three weeks before Pixar's *WALL·E**. One was a cute robot romance; the other was about, as the directors put it, teddy bears getting into kung-fu fights.

DreamWorks' sixteenth cinema feature toon (its tenth CGI), is a beast fable. The ungainly panda is scorned by the other animals: so far, so Ugly Duckling. He's presented with a 'magic' token, which he's told will let him beat the world. At the crucial point, though, he realises the item is a symbol, standing for what he hated about himself. Lesson learned, he turns his flaws into strengths and soars in a barnstorming finale.

It's *Dumbo** in a funny-animal China, but whereas Dumbo was only dressed up as a clown, *Kung Fu Panda* has a real one. Jack Black voices Po, the panda, as an excitable martial-arts fanboy ('Woah! The Sword of Heroes! Said to be so sharp that you can cut yourself just by looking *OW!*'). As with Winnie the Pooh's Tigger, he's the sole panda around. His dad is a noodle cook and also a duck, which is a zoological mystery the film leaves hanging. The other characters are mostly cute ducks, pigs and rabbits (the marching ducks are a gem).

Po is inexplicably chosen as a destined warrior over the resentful kung-fu masters, including a monkey (Jackie Chan), a viper (Lucy Liu) and a tigress (Angelina Jolie; both Jolie and Black get much better parts than in DreamWorks' irksome cartoon, *Shark Tale*, 2004). Dustin Hoffman voices a grumpy red-panda mentor, desperate to kick Po out. 'There is now a level zero,' he says sonorously after Po is pulverised by the training equipment. Only a hate-maddened warrior (Ian McShane) can force teacher and pupil to bond.

DIRECTOR John Stevenson, Mark Osborne
PRODUCER Melissa Cobb
STORY Jonathan Aibel, Glenn Berger, Ethan Reiff, Cyrus Voris
DESIGN Raymond Zibach, Nico Marlet
ANIMATION Don Wagner, Manuel Almela, Manuel Aparicio, Jeremy Bernstein, Arnaud Berthier

There are funnier DreamWorks cartoons, but this is one of the studio's most *likeable*, and certainly its loveliest. The meticulously expressive colour schemes were influenced by recent *wuxia* films such as *House of Flying Daggers* (2004). (In *Panda*, blue stands for fear and melancholy, saturated gold for heroism). It's also – and this is the surprise from *Shrek**'s studio – self-consciously elegant, both in the writing and the action. The battles are hugely impressive to watch, as much for their humour and invention as for their overblown staging, with a vertical fight up a hollow mountain, a tightrope clash over a chasm, a chopstick duel for a dumpling and a stylised 2D dream that gloriously spoofs anime.

And yet the film is deeply earnest, with a subplot about how the 'villain' is emphatically Hoffman's character's fault, and a sweet post-credits moment that would please Hayao Miyazaki. With its echoes of superheroes, the film inadvertently asks which is harder to take seriously: a knockabout world of cartoon animals, or live-action sagas of masked men in leotards. Most critics plumped for *WALL·E*'s robots over *Panda*, as did the Oscar voters, but there was one big holdout. At the 2009 Annie animation awards, *Kung Fu Panda* went head-to-head with Pixar, and trumped *WALL·E* in every major category.

Laputa: Castle in the Sky
Japan, 1986 – 123 minutes
Hayao Miyazaki
[Drawings]

Laputa: Castle in the Sky, directed by Hayao Miyazaki, begins in mid-air. A band of sky pirates swoop down from moon-silvered clouds to attack an airship. Their target is a scared young girl, Sheeta, who's the captive of a forbidding government agent. In the ensuing mayhem, Sheeta falls from the vessel and plunges headlong into clouds, but a magic stone she's wearing comes to fiery life and levitates her to safety.

She wakes in a mining village (the setting is a fanciful nineteenth century) where a local lad, Pazu, is fascinated by this angel from the sky. Both children are drawn into a treasure hunt for Laputa, the fabled flying island. The name and concept come from *Gulliver's Travels*, where it was one of the realms that Swift's hero visits after Lilliput, but Miyazaki refashions it from the same dream-stuff as his sea-going trains and cat-faced buses in other films. In fact, one of the joys of seeing *Laputa* for the first time is that for most of the adventure, there's almost no hint of what Laputa will be *like* when we get there, only for it to exceed our soaring expectations.

Released in 1986, *Laputa* was the first cartoon from the newly established Studio Ghibli, though Ghibli itself counts an earlier Miyazaki film, *Nausicaa of the Valley of the Wind* (1984), as its starting point. (*Nausicaa* had been produced by the publishing company Tokuma, which established Ghibli in the wake of the film's success.) *Laputa* was also Miyazaki's first stand-alone film. His début, *The Castle of Cagliostro* (1979) had been spun off from the popular 'Lupin the Third' franchise about an audacious thief, though Miyazaki reworked the roguish Lupin into a foolhardy romantic hero.

Nausicaa, Miyazaki's next film, was extracted from his work-in-progress comic about a wind-riding princess in a world of giant insects. Miyazaki was dissatisfied with the film, saying that that he didn't understand his own story yet. He was also surprised to see children in the audience, having meant it for older viewers. With *Laputa*, he set out to make a cartoon for kids, describing the film as 'truly classical in structure', and aiming it at elementary fourth-graders. But, like *Treasure Island*, one of *Laputa*'s influences, the story is far denser and richer than the average children's tale, influenced by themes and ideals that Miyazaki was still working out in his *Nausicaa* comic.

Typically for Miyazaki, *Laputa* is about innocence, its child heroes open to a marvellous cosmos which unfurls all the way through the film. At the beginning, Pazu's ground-level world is ostensibly one of hard, simple surfaces, stone, wood and metal. It can be transfigured, though, by a morning sunbeam or by lights deep beneath the earth. Early on, an underground cave is turned into a luminescent orrery as the children gaze around in wonder.

When we get back into the sky, it's a tempest of towering clouds and leviathan battleships, the vessels dependent on nuts, bolts and screeching machinery. Miyazaki treats the air as a place of spiritual immersion, as Jules Verne did the ocean in *20,000 Leagues under the Sea*. *Laputa*'s lyrical title sequence depicts

DIRECTOR/STORY Hayao Miyazaki
PRODUCER Isao Takahata
SCORE Joe Hisaishi
ANIMATION Yoshinori Kanada, Masako Shinohara, Masaaki Endo, Makiko Futaki, Michiyo Sakurai, Noriko Moritomo

fantastical flying machines as hatched engravings; whether Miyazaki knew it or not, he was following the lead of Karel Zeman's Czech film, *The Fabulous World of Jules Verne**. The island of Laputa is reconceived by Miyazaki as an outgrown war machine. Living tree roots have penetrated its cold crystal heart, so that the villain must tear his way through the foliage.

Pazu and Sheeta are simple characters, but Miyazaki gives them moments of pungent drama. In the opening sequence, a terrified Sheeta brings a glass bottle down on her grown-up captor's head. Later, when the villain captures the children, he snidely pays off Pazu with silver pieces that the penniless, broken boy is unable to throw away. At this point, the sky pirates must step in to save the story, led by a hulking, almost bestial matriarch called Ma Dola, who tears slabs of meat with her teeth and teaches Pazu masculinity.

Yet the pirates – who are essentially kids themselves – are won over by the children's earnestness, and become their loyal allies. (Miyazaki transforms Ma Dola the same way he does the witch Yubaba in *Spirited Away**; he gives her granny glasses.) Pazu and Sheeta are inspired in turn by a gentle race of chiming, swaying sky-robots, servants of the towering world-tree that roots Laputa in the air. The tree itself shields the children during the cataclysmic finale. Innocence prevails, even as Laputa is unglued and showers down into the ocean. 'The roots protected us!' says Pazu, awed.

'La puta' is a Spanish profanity, a point that may have been known to Swift when he wrote *Gulliver's Travels*. Consequently, the American (though not British) DVD release was renamed *Castle in the Sky*. Composer Joe Hisaishi reworked his score for the English version by Disney, which sadly can't match the original.

Lilo and Stitch
US, 2002 – 85 minutes
Chris Sanders, Dean DeBlois
[Drawings with CGI and brief live-action]

Lilo and Stitch opened in 2002, when Disney animation was at a precipice – indeed, when it had gone over the cliff for many artists. There had been crises at Disney before: the flops of the 40s, the studio strike, Walt's death and the decline that followed. Now, though, the executives deemed that hand-drawn cartoons weren't wanted in the computer age. In March, weeks before *Lilo* opened (and just after the release of the hugely successful *Ice Age**, a non-Disney computer film), more than 200 animators were laid off at Disney's Burbank studio. The carnage had begun.

Over at Disney's Florida studio, *Lilo* directors Chris Sanders and Dean DeBlois knew their history. *Snow White**'s success had fatally led Walt to top that film with ever-more lavish, expensive blockbusters: *Pinocchio**, *Bambi**, *Fantasia**, all money-losers. The same blockbuster mentality had predominated since *The Lion King**, while costs rose and revenues fell. (Disney's *The Hunchback of Notre Dame** opened two years after *The Lion King*, and earned less than half as much.) Wasn't it time Disney tried another model? The cheap, cartoony, unspectacular *Dumbo** had made money in the cash-strapped 40s, becoming an evergreen classic. Why not do it again?

Sanders pitched *Lilo and Stitch* as 'a love story of a girl and what she thinks is a dog'. The girl is Lilo ('Lee-lo'), a six-year-old cutely stumpy eccentric child savant, living amid the surf and greenery of Hawaii. Her 'dog' is Stitch, a delinquent blue alien with opaque black eyes who looks like, as the script notes, an evil koala. In everyone's favourite gag, he builds a model city from bric-a-brac, then stomps around it like a mini-Godzilla, cackling and howling in Sanders's voice. Hunted by the galactic authorities, he's adopted by Lilo, who takes it on herself to tame her new puppy. *Lilo* was the first Disney cartoon since *Dumbo* to have watercolour backgrounds, depicting a softly luminous Hawaii of transparent paints. Sanders's characters are chubby, stubby and bottom-heavy. Lilo in her swimsuit resembles a little round teddy; her adult sister Nani has thighs to impress the cartoonist Robert Crumb.

Beneath the ostensibly silly story is a drama about two damaged, angry infants. Lilo and Stitch are paralleled from the start, using teeth and drool against their foes, though Lilo shocks viewers more; she's a cartoon girl who punches a classmate and has screaming matches with Nani, who struggles to be her guardian. (The background to this situation is left implicit until late in the film.) As the critic Glenn Kenny noted, *Lilo* 'has to be the first Disney animation to contain the line, "The social worker's gonna be here any minute".' Both Lilo and Stitch lash out at a world they're terrified will reject them. One minute, Lilo is cheering Stitch on – 'Oh good, my dog's found the chainsaw!' she chirps during a comic battle with bumbling aliens. The next, she's blanking him with a little girl's hate: 'Get out of here, Stitch.'

Stitch is set up as a mischievous force of nature, *Gremlins* (1984) meets the Tasmanian Devil. It was always going to be difficult to sell his rehab, with an awkward subplot where he starts identifying with the

DIRECTOR/STORY Chris Sanders, Dean DeBlois
PRODUCER Clark Spencer
SCORE Alan Silvestri
DESIGN Paul Felix
ANIMATION Andreas Deja, Alex Kupershmidt, Stephane Sante Foi, Byron Howard, Bolhem Bouchiba

character of the Ugly Duckling. (It feels even more heavy-handed if you associate that tale with the Disney brand through the 1939 'Silly Symphony'.) It might have worked better had Lilo shaped him through her own idiosyncratic tales; we know she has the imagination.

Sanders and DeBlois considered going dark; an early version had Stitch killing Lilo's beloved sandwich-eating fish, then getting his nose rubbed in his own blithe cruelty. In the final film, the directors played up comic interludes, such as one where Lilo moulds Stitch into her model citizen, Elvis. It's witty on several levels, but the silliness makes it harder to appreciate the very grown-up scenes that follow. For Lilo's animator Andreas Deja, the key scene is when the girl tells

Stitch about her parents, fearing and hoping for a response. 'What happened to yours? I hear you cry at night … I know that's why you wreck things and push me …'.

Like *Dumbo*, *Lilo and Stitch* turned a tidy profit, too late. After the calamitous flop of its sci-fi *Treasure Planet* (2002), Disney continued to shut studio after studio, including the Florida outfit that made *Lilo and Stitch*. Disney's hand-drawn tradition ended up being mothballed until John Lasseter revived it in 2009 with the staid, expensive *The Princess and the Frog*, whose takings were dwarfed by Pixar's *Up**. With Sanders and DeBlois migrating to CGI (see p. 89), the prospects of another *Lilo and Stitch* look as uncertain as anything in old-school animation today.

The Lion King

US, 1994 – 88 minutes (slightly extended in a 'special edition' DVD version)
Roger Allers, Rob Minkoff
[Drawings with CGI]

DIRECTOR Roger Allers, Rob Minkoff
PRODUCER Don Hahn
STORY Irene Mecchi, Jonathan Roberts, Linda Woolverton
SCORE Hans Zimmer
DESIGN Hans Bacher, Jean Gilmore, Joe Grant
ANIMATION Mark Henn, Ruben Aquino, Andreas Deja, Tony Fucile, James Baxter, Tony Bancroft, Michael Surrey

'You are more than what you have become,' says the lion in the sky, rebuking his prodigal son. The vision is voiced by James Earl Jones, who immortalised 'I am your father' in celluloid, now playing another patriarchal monolith. The Lion King is dead: long live the Lion King.

The film may be Disney's tribute to David Lean, but its vast African landscapes don't diminish the players for long. The ghost king bestrides the rolling clouds. The lion villain sings while rising volcanically on a pinnacle of rock. The lions' castle is another rock, jutting massively over the plainlands. By the end, it seems lion kings even command the weather; they make the land grey or green, cause fiery storms or bring the sun out to baptise a newborn hero.

As of writing, *The Lion King* is the highest-grossing 'traditional' cartoon feature (though on deflated figures, its take is below those gathered over successive reissues by *Snow White**, *Fantasia** and *One Hundred and One Dalmatians**). Its critical standing is lower. Many reviewers found the film impossible to engage with except as phallocentric kitsch and dangerous ideology. The black-maned villain and social-deviant hyenas – racist. The African story of monarchy – colonialist. The creatures great and small who converge in biblical crowds to honour their prince – fascist. *The Lion King*'s songs, composed by Elton John to Tim Rice's lyrics, were an especially easy target for Disney-bashers. Who could have foreseen *Blackadder*'s Rowan Atkinson as a hapless blue hornbill, mouthing lines like, 'I've never seen a king of beasts with quite so little hair'?

But then British viewers could enjoy the highest-profile panto ever seen in a Hollywood film, courtesy not of Atkinson but Jeremy Irons's bad lion, Scar. He's a bitchy, slinky Widow Twankey: 'Ooh, I shall practise my curtsey!' he simpers. During his song 'Be Prepared', he squeals, 'Prepare for *sensational* news!' This stereotyping was added to *The Lion King*'s charge-sheet, though Scar's campy scene-stealing was drawn by a gay animator, Andreas Deja. The staging of 'Be Prepared' slides between Busby Berkeley and Leni Riefenstahl, with formation-goose-stepping hyenas that trump the whole of *Fantasia* for gratuitousness.

Of course, Scar's posturing is a baddy's drag act. He usurps his brother Mufasa (Jones) from spite and jealousy, not megalomania. Luring Mufasa's cub Simba into a canyon, he unleashes a wildebeest stampede, the grand setting matched to the computerised spectacle as they pour down the slopes in their thousands. Mufasa saves Simba, but not himself. 'Long live the king!' Scar gloats, staring into his doomed brother's eyes. An earlier version had him say, 'Goodnight sweet prince.' Mufasa's death lacks the poetry of *Bambi** (which was, from an animal viewpoint, a natural tragedy), but it's intense. It would be rash to assume it didn't affect its generation of kids just as much. Scar turns the knife on the distraught Simba, who thinks he's responsible: 'Run, run away, and never return.'

Simba, who's hardly domineering even when he gets his roar, recalls Disney characters like Mowgli or Pinocchio. Like them, he spends a lot of the film being passed between good, bad or happy-go-lucky fathers.

The happy-go-luckys are a pig–meerkat duo called Timon and Pumba, the new Baloo. Their manufacturing is obvious, but their stargazing scene is very funny. This being 90s Disney, though, Simba needs a formal hero's journey to take. Early on, he puts his paw on his father's footprint and sees how much greater it is. Later, a shaman baboon (another dad) drives the adult Simba through a dark and treacherous mythopoeic forest, while Hans Zimmer's score swells with chants and drums. The payoff is overworked with the ghost in the sky, but the night journey is enough. It conveys the force of the material, and carries the film's cheesy antics and missteps before it, much as the African chorus bears up the weak 'Circle of Life' song.

'People really seemed to relate to the story of a character that has lost his father yet his father was always there with him,' said Disney producer Don Hahn. Or perhaps *The Lion King*'s popularity is down to its cute cub, its father–son sentimentality (no one says a line like 'Nobody messes with *your dad*,' like a jovial James Earl Jones) and the charismatic interplay between the innocent Simba (supervised by Mark Henn) and Deja's sneaky Scar, running through to their last face-off. (Scar, wheedling: 'You wouldn't kill your old uncle?') *The Lion King* is both more intimate and open-ended than its debunkers allow, a tale of a daddy lion, his little boy and the landscape that parts and unites them. Even a prefabricated blockbuster can be more than it was.

There's a notorious debate among cartoon fans about whether *The Lion King* took ideas and images from a Japanese TV cartoon, *Kimba the White Lion* (1994) (see p. 208). The most balanced account is in Frederik L. Schodt's book, *Dreamland Japan*. However, it's worth noting that early Japanese animation lifted from Disney shamelessly; just watch the first *Astroboy* (1963) TV episode beside *Dumbo**.

The Little Norse Prince
Japan, 1968 – 82 minutes
Isao Takahata
[Drawings]

DIRECTOR Isao Takahata
PRODUCER Hiroshi Okawa
SCORE Michio Mamiya
ANIMATION Yasuji Mori, Yasuo Otsuka, Hayao Miyazaki

Animation history, like any other, has its ironies. Consider: *Snow White and the Seven Dwarfs**, Disney's first feature in 1937, had two songs about the joys of work. Three years later, Disney's own workers were joining an independent union, the Screen Cartoonists' Guild, which warred on the studio in the bitter strike of 1941. Walt denounced the strikers as Communist subversives and later told HUAC, the House Committee on Un-American Activities, that Communists 'ought to be smoked out [of the film industry], and shown up for what they are'.

A quarter of a century after the Disney strike, a group of leftist union troublemakers at Japan's Toei studio marched in demonstrations, cocked a snook at their employers, and plotted a cartoon feature about worker solidarity. Remarkably, the film was made, complete with agitprop images of the proletariat uniting against a common foe. The punchline? One of this rabble of activist animators – a Marxist, if not a partisan Communist – was Hayao Miyazaki, who would be one day dubbed a Japanese Disney.

In Japan, the film was called *Prince of the Sun Hols's Greatest Adventure*. It was part of a line of Toei cartoon features that began with *The Legend of the White Serpent* in 1958. That was Japan's first colour animated feature, released in America as *Panda and the Magic Serpent*. Toei's president, Hiroshi Okawa, spoke of making a 'Disney of the East', but Miyazaki and his friend Isao Takahata preferred the Mouse's rivals, such as the Fleischer studio's *Hoppity Goes to Town** and France's *La Bergère et le ramoneur* (1952) (see p. 172). *The Little Norse Prince* was visibly influenced by another film they liked, Lev Atamanov's Russian *The Snow Queen* (1957).

All these films lay under Disney's shadow. (Even *The Snow Queen* pinched its insect-sized narrator from Disney's *Pinocchio**.) Miyazaki described his generation's anxiety of influence.

> We wondered if we would ever catch up to the level of what was being done in France, America or Russia … .
> We began to develop an inferiority complex; we wondered if we even had the basic talent needed to proceed.

Toei's cartoons couldn't match Disney's character animation, so they innovated elsewhere. For example, 1963's *Little Prince and the Eight-Headed Dragon* has a splendid ten-minute battle between the writhing snake-necked monster and the darting gadfly Prince (on his pint-sized Pegasus), scored by *Godzilla* composer Akira Ifukube.

The Little Norse Prince, directed by Takahata, begins in a similar heroic mode. A young barbarian, called Hols, fights wolves in a savage stone landscape. It's dynamic, elementally aggressive and so far removed from Disney that it's a shock when Hols gets paired with a talking bear-cub. Such animal familiars were a Toei staple, though *Hols's* animators were more inspired by Sanpei Shirato's ninja strip, *The Legend of*

Kamui. The action is ruggedly, if sometimes raggedly narrated. Hols vies with giant birds, an icy-skinned tyrant and a huge fish. The latter monster was bruisingly animated by Yasuo Otsuka, who'd drawn much of the Eight-Headed Dragon. These dynamic set pieces compensate for the disappointing moments when *Prince* resorts to storyboards, a compromise when the production ran late.

Finding a hardy fishing town, Hols becomes its defender, bringing it prosperity and unity. The villagers harvest fish and dance through town, but the joyous celebration scenes are interrupted by a stranger. Hilda is an enigmatic girl harpist, whom Hols finds singing lullabies in a lakeside ghost town ('I'm a happy singing girl,' she introduces herself). In her way, Hilda is as vital to *Prince* as Grumpy was to Disney's *Snow White*, shifting the film to an alien and alienated perspective. 'We [the animators] didn't grasp what Takahata was trying to do,' Miyazaki said. 'He was really pushing back the limits of animation.'

Largely drawn by veteran animator Yasuji Mori, Hilda projects a complex and enigmatic presence from her simple-seeming design. Meanwhile Takahata projects her lonely psyche onto unpeopled, expressionist landscapes. Hilda is an Other, an insidious siren, but she's also a tortured villainess who slowly realises she's on the wrong side. Miyazaki would borrow this plot several times, while Hilda's take-over of Hols's story anticipates Takahata's shifting narrative strategies in *Only Yesterday** and *Pom Poko* (1994).

More broadly, Hilda foreshadows the troubled young protagonists of anime sagas such as *Neon Genesis Evangelion**, and the amoral *Death Note*. Both titles turned her into a boy, as did the more earnest treatment of her story in Goro Miyazaki's underrated Ghibli film, *Tales from Earthsea* (2006). The latter perhaps owes more to *Prince* than it does to *Earthsea*'s author, Ursula Le Guin.

Memories
Japan, 1995 – 113 minutes
Koji Morimoto, Tensai Okamura, Katsuhiro Otomo
[Drawings with CGI]

Memories is a Japanese triptych of short stories, all broadly SF, but more interesting in their differences than in what they share. Each is made by a different director – 'Magnetic Rose' by Koji Morimoto, 'Stink Bomb' by Tensai Okamura and 'Cannon Fodder' by *Akira** creator Katsuhiro Otomo, who was *Memories*' executive producer. As the big name, Otomo pervades the other two segments – 'Magnetic Rose' was based on his story, while 'Stink Bomb' uses his storyboards. Yet fifteen years after the film was made, his co-directors are major players in the animation industry, while Satoshi Kon, who scripted 'Magnetic Rose', became a celebrated auteur (see *Tokyo Godfathers**). As the critic Jonathan Clements notes, *Memories* may have been sold on Otomo's name, but it was also a highly successful apprentice piece.

Like *Fantasia**, the film is shaped musically, with even less of a bridging theme. (Only the first story concerns memories.) 'Magnetic Rose' is an operatic tragedy, weaving strands from *Alien* (1979), *Solaris* (2002), *The Shining* (1980) and *2001: A Space Odyssey* (1968) towards a cataclysmic catharsis of its own. A crew of blue-collar space salvagers is lured by a celestial siren, an opera diva haunting a spaceship shaped like a rose. The characters move through a vivid succession of increasingly Freudian spaces, from the weightlessness of their ship to the female depths of the rose; then into the palatial opera house that nestles within, projecting holograms of sunshine and flowers to hide the mucky swamps below. Yet this is no simple misogynist fable. One of the siren's male victims is a deluded and arrogant womaniser; another is emotionally blocked, denying a tragedy that's cruelly re-enacted for him as a stylised but heart-rending performance. The final bells-and-whistles cataclysm sees the diva resplendent in her crimson gown, singing Puccini amid a maelstrom of wind and metal.

'Stink Bomb' is a Godzilla-sized fart joke. A lab employee with the sniffles ingests the wrong pill – a bioweapon developed on the premises – and starts emitting killer gases as he cycles innocently towards Tokyo. Early on, there are lightly surreal elements, with sunflowers and cherry-blossom blooming in midwinter. A classic Hollywood animator would have taken them much further but Okamura – and crucially Otomo, who plussed the storyboards at every turn – glory in omnidirectional military carnage. The hero is chased by missiles from seemingly every tank and plane in Japan, hand-drawn in pornographic detail, while Jun Miyake's wailing jazz score riffs off the explosions. (The music anticipates Yoko Kanno's celebrated work for the TV action series *Cowboy Bebop*, 1998; Kanno herself provided the classical stylings for 'Magnetic Rose'.) Imitating many of his *Akira* set-ups, Otomo willingly Tex Averys his trademark action into farce.

If 'Stink Bomb' plays to fan expectations, Otomo's own 'Cannon Fodder' is a departure. It envisions a nineteenth-century city overbuilt to Metropolis proportions, festooned with hissing pipes and ducts and dominated by huge cannons aimed at a foe unseen. The images are effectively posterised; the industrial palette is mostly reds and greys, faces shaded and cartooned. Through the twenty-minute segment (the

DIRECTOR Koji Morimoto, Tensai Okamura, Katsuhiro Otomo
PRODUCER Shigeru Watanabe
STORY Katsuhiro Otomo, Satoshi Kon
SCORE Takkyu Ishino, Yoko Kanno, Jun Miyake, Hiroyuki Nagashima
ANIMATION Toshiyuki Inoue, Hirotsugu Kawasaki, Morifumi Naka, Shuichi Ohara

shortest), the image scrolls in a manner mimicking an extended camera take. The DVD 'Making of' shows the giant-sized cel backgrounds. One of the last vertical transitions looks like a deliberate homage to the elongated opera house in *Citizen Kane* (1941). Although computer-aided, the images celebrate *drawn* perspectives and spaces, like *The Thief and Cobbler** or *The Secret of Kells**.

'Cannon Fodder' has little plot or payoff, its pressure-cooker pace set by the regimented firing of the big gun. There's everyday humanity in the Gilliamesque world, and implicit sadness in the juxtaposition of an eager little boy and the haggard father he seems destined to become. But 'Cannon Fodder' and 'Stink Bomb' lack the catharsis of 'Magnetic Rose', and are thereby reduced to showpieces that impress with their skill and wit. If *Memories* had come to Western cinemas before *Akira*, it might have been better reviewed and won more prizes, but the teen tantrums of its messy, overspilling predecessor are just more memorable.

A Midsummer Night's Dream
Czechoslovakia, 1959 – 75 minutes
Jirí Trnka
[Stop-motion]
[Reportedly the original Czech release ran 80 minutes.]

A Midsummer Night's Dream was the last feature directed by the Czech stop-motion animator Jiří Trnka, working at his Puppet Film Studio in Prague. (See *The Emperor's Nightingale**.) By rights, his sublimely lovely rendering of Shakespeare's comedy should be easy to see today, but its Anglophone life has been limited. In 1959, Trnka presented *Dream* at the third London Film Festival, where it had an English voice-over. A more verbose dub was released in America two years later, featuring the voices of Old Vic actors led by Richard Burton. Because the British rights were sold to an American distributor, the dub didn't reach the UK until 1971, two years after Trnka's death. The film still has occasional screenings, but seems never to have gone to video in Britain or America.

The Old Vic version is far removed from Trnka's concept. The director had purposefully kept speech to a minimum; in fact, he'd hoped not to have speech at all. His film is a puppet ballet, his figures acting through their bodies and silhouettes, like dimensional equivalents of Lotte Reiniger's cut-outs (see p. 9). The Old Vic dub, with its long recitations from the text, weighs the exquisite mime down with voice-over.

On first viewing, it's hard not to feel Disney-induced bias; why are we waiting for Puck and the fairies? (Trnka, keeping to the play's chronology, introduces them at the quarter-hour mark.) Indeed, the magic cast is vivid. There's the brooding stag-like king Oberon, his close-ups startlingly sensual; the languidly feline queen Titania, her gown made of fluttering fairy-sprites; her cute acorn familiars which fall to the ground and sprout little legs; and the adorable donkey-headed Bottom, who licks Titania's caressing hands and munches her garlands. Puck is a russet-haired Peter Pan in leaves, who teases a mortal with the mirror routine from *Duck Soup* (1933) and sometimes becomes a bunny. In one of the new scenes, we see Puck collect the 'Love-in-Idleness' aphrodisiac, causing amour in snails, statues and a passing ram.

Small wonder foreigners found the film Disneyesque in its humour and dancing figures. Trnka, though, is egalitarian in the way he treats characters, never letting the jokes undercut the refinement (even the ram is elegant!), and uplifting even the potentially dull lovers, Lysander and Hermia. The pair introduce the film in a beautiful dance, the light-footed Lysander climbing to the window of his beloved in a nod to another play. In the CinemaScope version of the film (see below), the opening is played out on one broad stage, capitalising on the stop-frame medium. The motions are illusory, but the stage is real. There's a slight echo of Olivier's *Henry V* (1944) in the way Trnka begins with filmed theatre, then opens out the action.

Dream impresses with its splendid sets, its latex-moulded, five-fingered puppets and its intricate choreography, further manipulated by split-screen. And yet it never becomes an appropriation of the source like the Disneys of the 50s, *Alice in Wonderland* (1951) and *Peter Pan* (1953). Trnka's big change to the text could even be an anti-Disney gibe. Like the play, the film ends with Bottom and his fellow actors struggling through

DIRECTOR Jiří Trnka
PRODUCER Jiří Trnka, Jaroslav Možíš, Erna Kmínkovà
STORY Jiří Trnka, Jiří Brdečka
SCORE Vàclav Trojan
ANIMATION Stanislav Látal, Břetislav Pojar, Bohuslav Šràmek, Jan Adam, Jan Karpaš, Vladimír Jurajdovà, Marie Vlčková

a stage performance of the tragedy, 'Pyramus and Thisbe'. (Trnka has most fun when the 'lovers' must speak past a human wall.) The magic Puck, though, is watching. He turns Bottom into a great actor for a glacial tragic ending, with Bottom led by the ethereal Puck and a Méliès moon. It could be Trnka's rebuff to Disneyfied classics milked for laughs, and also anticipates *Shakespeare in Love* (1998), another comedy that ends with the triumphant performance of a tragedy.

Dream's delicate music was by Trnka's regular composer Václav Trojan (heavily muted in the 'Old Vic' dub), while six animators handled the central puppets. Stanislav Látal, for example, moves the imposing Theseus and his Amazon queen Hippolyta, who slips off a horse and chases a deer barefoot. (Latal's own features include a version of *Robinson Crusoe*, 1981.) Trnka disliked CinemaScope, a format which he called a 'mailbox slot', but he was leant on by the state-run trade body, Czechoslovak Filmexport. In the event, the director used parallel cameras to make a distinct cropped version of *Dream*, with different editing, compositions and camera angles.

Mind Game
Japan, 2004 – 103 minutes
Masaaki Yuasa
[Miscellaneous techniques]

If the astounding *Mind Game* didn't exist, then indie-minded animation fans would invent it, just to throw the cartoon establishment out of whack. *Mind Game* is spectacular, spontaneous, confusing, kooky and hilarious. It's an anti-realist bricolage whose hero is a struggling cartoon artist. In Japan, the staff at a *rival* cartoon studio, Madhouse, loved *Mind Game* so much they started a cheerleading squad to promote the film. It's been lauded by luminaries of progressive animation: Bill Plympton (p. 95), Satoshi Kon (p. 212). Yet as of writing, it's still obscure, a festival favourite awaiting a Western DVD release (though the Japanese DVD has English subtitles).

As a fable, *Mind Game* is a gonzo variant on *A Christmas Carol*, *It's a Wonderful Life* (1946) and even *Spirited Away**. Robin Nishi is a twenty-year-old wannabe comic artist, sharing his name with the creator of the source *Mind Game* comic. He's a loser, too much of a coward to make a move with the girl he's adored since grade school. A chance meeting leads him to an Osaka bar which his sweetheart runs with her sister. Gangsters show up too, looking for the girls' wastrel father. This part of the film is tough for viewers unused to nasty cartoon violence, but it's worth getting over the hump.

Nishi ends up with a gun pressed between his buttocks, grovelling on the floor. *Then* he tries to be a hero. Result: Nishi is probably the first film protagonist to have his brains blown out by a hot lead enema. Meeting God on oblivion's threshold, Nishi defiantly dashes back to the world of the living. From then on, as we spiral into demented fantasy, *Mind Game* is one long affirmation of life. Nishi drags the girls into madcap car chases and introspective sojourns; much of the story takes place in the belly of a whale. But even here, everything turns into new and unforeseen adventures, expressing *Mind Game*'s existential ethos: your life is the result of your own decisions.

Directed by Masaaki Yuasa, *Mind Game* was created by Tokyo's Studio 4°C, whose first major production was the slick anthology *Memories**. However, there's nothing in *Mind Game* to suggest it's from the same studio; rather, it feels indie to the core. The lopsided, freehand, cut-out character designs mutate cheerily and fluidly, sometimes transforming into animated photos of the voice-actors. Instead of distancing us, the shifting style makes the characters feel vital, multitudinous. The mutable aesthetic is taken to extremes when Nishi meets God, flashing from one cheesy toon shape to another like *A Scanner Darkly**'s scramble suit drawn by Rolf Harris.

The film starts and ends with dizzying montages, where we see dozens of glimpses of the players' pasts and maybe-futures, woven with modern Japanese history and an Astro Boy-like hero who manipulates time. The images switch so fast that most viewers would need to freeze a DVD to follow them, but the overall impression is of a world teeming with people, each and every one cartooned into quirkily striking individuals in daily life. It would be hard to create a live-action montage that carried the humanist message so vibrantly, or with such humour. As *Tokyo Godfathers** director Satoshi Kon said,

DIRECTOR/STORY Masaaki Yuasa
PRODUCER Eiko Tanaka
SCORE Seiichi Yamamoto, Yoko Kanno, Fayray
DESIGN Yuichirou Sueyoshi, Masahiko Kubo
ANIMATION (DIRECTOR) Koji Morimoto

'While they may be the recreation of everyday scenes, drawings are the essence of such scenes … . In animation, only what is intended to be communicated is there.'

Mind Game's high-speed chases and races feel like conscious celebrations of the medium. A crazy car chase seems to parody the quasi-animated *Matrix* films, as one yakuza finds himself super-sprinting at 100 miles an hour, only to smack into a concrete barrier. The climactic sequence, which takes six exhausting minutes, is perhaps the *only* set piece in a toon feature to match the mania of Tex Avery. The characters race up a raging crimson ocean in a frantic flurry of flailing limbs, dodging randomly placed planes, skyscrapers and ocean-liners, to a pounding drumbeat that was surely composed by Animal from *The Muppet Show* (1976).

Other set-piece crowd-pleasers involve the characters' experiments with sex and gender-bending, including a funny and lyrical love-making; the hero's body becomes a winged grub, the couple dissolve into bubbling paints and a smiley-faced train collapses into the sea. *Mind Game*'s ode to joy could be a riposte to the adolescent tantrums of the *Evangelion* franchise (p. 135), though there are also parallels with *Heavy Traffic* (1973), Ralph Bakshi's early film about a struggling comic artist, his fantasies in the raw, and the lives he could lead.

Monsters, Inc.
US, 2001 – 92 minutes
Pete Docter
[CGI]

It's a situation familiar to any parent. You're trying to persuade a boisterous child to go to sleep. Even when she's tucked in, there's a problem; she's scared of the closet with its ominous door. You sigh, you open the closet to show it's empty (the moppet squeaks and ducks behind the bedsheet). You even go in to prove there's no monster there. Then you pause. After all, you *are* eight feet tall, with huge horns, a boulder-sized head and a pelt of blue fur. 'Well, *now* there is …' you admit.

In Pixar's fourth feature, parents are represented as monsters (but *nice* monsters); monsters are terrified of children; and children make the world go round. It's hardly surprising that a cartoon would play to its traditional demographics of parents and offspring, but audiences sometimes forget that animators are parents too. The great Disney artist Bill Tytla drew Dumbo the baby elephant with his two-year-old son in mind (p. 57). 'I saw a chance to do a character without using any cheap theatrics,' Tytla said. 'There's nothing theatrical about a two-year-old kid. They're real and sincere – like when they damn near wet their pants from excitement when you come home at night.' Consider Tytla's peekaboo play between Dumbo and his mother, cartoonily cute and ecstatically lovely.

At Pixar, Pete Docter started developing *Monsters, Inc.* just as his son was born. Although the film had other permutations – one version had an adult man, not a child – it resolved into a parenting comedy that happens to involve monsters and magic doors. As in *The Nightmare before Christmas**, the 'monsters' are everyday folk who scare kids for a living. Their world is powered by screams, which the elite 'scarer' monsters race to extract before the kids turn blasé. The twist is the monsters are *more* scared of the children than the children of them (the monsters think kids are toxic, though why isn't clear). 'She got this close to me!' wails one T-Rex type. 'She wasn't scared of you?' asks his assistant. 'She was only *six*!'

For Sulley, the horned hairy voiced by John Goodman, things get worse when he finds a stowaway toddler on his back. Cue a bellowing blue colossus pursued by 'Boo', a pig-tailed little girl chuckling 'Kitty!' The child causes monster movie panic; we see a swish sushi bar 'decontaminated' with thrumming SFX from George Pal's *The War of the Worlds* (1953). Before long, though, Sulley is bonding with Boo in hide-and-seek. Unlike *Dumbo**, the weight is on the parent's enjoyment ('*Where did she go?*' Sulley asks theatrically, hunting Boo). It carries through to the last shot, where we hear Boo say 'Kitty!' and Sulley's face dissolve into a smile rivalling Boo's for adorableness. Docter animated the grin himself, though not Sulley's luxuriantly strokable hair, which had the virtual intelligence to move on its own. It contrasts oddly with the stop-motion of *King Kong**, where rippling hair was a sign of the animator's presence.

Monsters, Inc. was Pixar's first feature not directed by John Lasseter, the most famous maker of toon features since Walt. The film's huge success raised the Pixar brand higher than any director. As in *Toy Story**,

DIRECTOR Pete Docter
PRODUCER Darla K. Anderson
STORY Andrew Stanton, Jill Culton, Jeff Pidgeon, Ralph Eggleston, Daniel Gerson
SCORE Randy Newman
DESIGN Ricky Vega Nierva, Bob Pauley, Dan Lee, Harley Jessup
ANIMATION Glenn McQueen, Rich Quade, Doug Sweetland, Scott Clark

there's a crowd-pleasing buddy thread – Sulley forms a double act with his assistant Mike, a fast-talking beach-ball with legs and one eye, chirpily voiced by Billy Crystal. In one draft of the film, Mike was about to propose to his sweetheart Celia, the snake-haired receptionist voiced by Jennifer Tilly. The relationship was toned down because it suggested Mike and Sulley were already parting, whereas the film-makers wanted *Boo* between them. The buddies face off in an ice-cave, where Mike asks the deadly question. 'I'm your pal, I'm your best friend. *Don't I matter*?' It's a polished stock moment, yet Crystal has far more pathos as a great green pea than his usual flesh and blood self.

As with Docter's later *Up**, the emotion rises over the uneven action. Considering we're in a fantasy world, there's too much running and skulking in locker rooms and corridors, and even the film's visionary climax – a chase through a city-sized hangar of magic doors – is schematised into a rollercoaster. There's also an ill-fitting comedy scene where the distraught Sulley thinks Boo has been pulverised in a trash compactor. It homages a famous Chuck Jones cartoon (*Feed the Kitty*, 1952), cartoon expressions and all, but it makes nonsense of how we've been encouraged to see Sulley and Boo as a real parent and child. Then again, the scene would have fitted right into *Shrek**, which beat *Monsters, Inc.* to the first Animated Feature Oscar.

My Life as McDull
Hong Kong, 2001 – 75 minutes
Toe Yuen
[Miscellaneous techniques]

DIRECTOR Toe Yuen
STORY Brian Tse, Alice Mak
MUSIC Steve Ho
DESIGN Alice Mak

McDull is a kindergarten-age little boy, living in the urban jungle of Kowloon in Hong Kong. He's drawn as a piglet; other everypigs in cartoons include Miyazaki's middle-aged Porco Rosso (p. 162) and the witty *Peppa Pig* (2004), a British kids' TV cartoon about a little girl. But what's remarkable about *McDull*, and what makes it so affecting even on repeat views, is the way it changes from the second kind of cartoon into the first. The film begins as an idiosyncratic children's charmer, and ends as a grown-up elegy.

McDull grew out of *McMug*, a magazine comic strip written by Brian Tse and designed by Alice Mak. (The pair co-wrote the film, which Tse executive-produced.) The original strip was about *another* little-boy piglet, the eponymous McMug and his Hong Kong friends, who include cats, cows and ducks, all two-legged. The gang acquired its own magazine (*Yellow Bus*) and a line of designer merchandise, before being animated in a 1998 *McMug* TV show. But when the film was greenlit, Tse decided that McMug was inadequate for the lead.

According to Gigi Hu Tze Yue, writing in *Asian Cinema*:

> Tse explained that in the process of conceptualising the film, McMug and his nuclear family of a father, a mother and two elder siblings became too boring for him to improvise and to catch creative ideas. In comparison, McMug's cousin, McDull, and his high-spirited mom, Mok Tai, and the one-parent family set-up offered more avenues for creativity.

Indeed, *McDull*'s heart is the relationship between the boy and his mother. (The dad is hardly mentioned, though his story is told in the second McDull film, *McDull, prince de la bun*, 2004). Mok Tai is a white-collar superwoman, working in 'insurance, real estate and trading'. We see her battle through Kowloon's streets and shopping malls in the style of a left-to-right videogame. There are also clips of her cookery programme, where she makes 'Chicken Bun Paper Bunning a Bun'. These food jokes may be mostly aimed at Hong Kong locals, but the demented word-circles are funny enough in themselves. The whole end credits are taken up with Mok Tai's efforts to order *anything* in a café.

The story and style are both collages. The characters' animation is charmingly simple, as are their picture-book pastels; the same look defines McDull's home and school. Beyond them, there are dizzying CGI cityscapes, Photoshop montages and live-action; one key episode is in minimalist pencil animation. Hong Kong's highrises had previously been presented in animation in Japan's *Ghost in the Shell* (1995) (see p. 78), which made the city into an exotically alienated tone poem. *McDull*, though, makes us part of this thriving, dirty concrete hive. In one interlude, we pass over the grimy CGI rooftops, accompanied by a dazed-sounding rendition of 'All Things Bright and Beautiful', as construction cranes turn like spinning wheels.

Mok Tai tells McDull frightening bedtime stories, whether the boy wants them or not. ('One day a boy slept a lot, next day he died.') But she's loving enough to fake a holiday for McDull in the Maldives (convincing him that a tram is an aeroplane) or to write a painstaking letter to the international Olympic committee, asking that her son be entered in the local sport of bun-throwing. 'Let the world know the talent of your children,' she declares. 'Parents will do anything for that.'

And yet the film *doesn't* have the happy ending we expect. Instead the final section switches to a grown-up perspective to examine the death of parents and childhood. Graceful and a little shocking, the transition may owe something to one of Tse's influences, Raymond Briggs, the pessimist British cartoon artist who drew *The Snowman* (1982) and *When the Wind Blows**. Briggs's Snowman melts, while McDull has the sober revelation that, 'A no is a no; Stupid leads to failure, to disappointment; Disappointment is not funny.' We end with McDull as a live-action grown-up, all the fantasy gone, just getting on with his life as best he can. Ironically, *McDull*'s huge success in the real world brought the piglet back, with three McDull sequels to date.

My Neighbour Totoro
Japan, 1988 – 90 minutes
Hayao Miyazaki
[Drawings]

DIRECTOR/STORY Hayao Miyazaki
PRODUCER Toru Hara
SCORE Joe Hisaishi
ANIMATION Tsukasa Tannai, Shinji Otsuka, Masako Shinohara, Masaaki Endo, Toshio Kawaguchi

My Neighbour Totoro, in which two young girls discover magic creatures in the Japanese countryside, was swifly nominated by Akira Kurosawa as one of the 100 greatest ever films. Everyone else played catch-up. Hayao Miyazaki's fourth animated feature did lukewarm business in Japan, and was first distributed in America by a subsidiary of the schlock studio Troma. It got only one thumb up from TV critics Siskel and Ebert; Ebert called *Totoro* 'a discovery' while Siskel was 'bored right off the top'.

Totoro is turgid if one expects a film primarily about the furry, funny, bear-like creatures of the title. The Totoro are on screen for less than a quarter of the film, the rest establishing the context that makes them wonderful. Japan's lost landscape of wood and water, slugs and snails, wind and rain, is rendered through the craft of art director Kazuo Oga. *Totoro* is an animist poem, a series of haiku: rain plopping on an umbrella, a leaf floating down a stream, a snail sliding up a grass blade. There are echoes of *Bambi*: the transparent flow from scene to scene, the child's-eye view of the sublime, and the straightforward honesty about death. *Totoro*, though, is an immeasurably more personal film.

Miyazaki first meant to have one child protagonist, but the sisters' mutual relationship makes each more real than other Miyazaki characters, a lesson that *Totoro* fans Chris Sanders and Dean DeBlois would take for Disney's *Lilo and Stitch**. The girls' reactions to the countryside recall Tolkien's walking tree in *The Lord of the Rings*, who laughed if the sun came out from behind a cloud or if he came upon a stream. Early on, the girls race round their 'new' country home, a venerable wooden house that's welcoming yet mysterious, carrying the weight of time like the haunted town in Miyazaki's later *Spirited Away**. Miyazaki said wryly that *Totoro*'s crew all wanted to live in the house, but without lowering their modern standards of living. Foreigners may see it as a quintessentially Japanese home, but its gabled front is Western; compare the pseudo-Western architecture of *Spirited Away*'s bathhouse.

The girls' follow-the-leader playtimes, where the toddler Mei obsessively copies her big sister Satsuki, are counterpointed by their grown-up fears. The girls' mother is sick in hospital. When she seems in danger, the children's beautiful country playground suddenly looks vastly indifferent. The girls' situation matches Miyazaki's childhood; his mother had had spinal TB. *Totoro*'s threatened tragedy, the girls' terror and hysterics, become the film's artistic measure. You can compare the unforeseen ending of Yasujiro Ozu's *Tokyo Story* (1953), or the wholly anticipated end of *Grave of the Fireflies**, with which *Totoro* was double-billed in Japan.

In Miyazaki's words, 'Satsuki and Mei are saved just by Totoro's existence, by his being.' The first Totoro to appear is a small creature who's chased by Mei in an invigorating toon set piece. The Totoro does broad double-takes, while Mei skids and crashes with a kid's hard-edged enthusiasm, Mickey Moused by composer Joe Hisaishi's exclamations and mini-melodies. 'Children aren't conscious of wanting to run, they're only

aware of wanting to get somewhere quickly,' Miyazaki said. 'I made *Totoro* hoping that children would run around the fields, or become excited while peeking in the crawl spaces under their houses.'

The Totoro's appearances grow into wondrous encounters, most famously an appearance by the giant King Totoro at a woodland bus-stop. The masterclass build-up – the lamp that turns on in the dark, the stately frog that crawls along the ground – recalls the crop-duster overture in *North by Northwest* (1959), or the Central Park scene in *Cat People* (1942), replacing the suspense with a softly sung dread. Later, when the girls and three Totoro join forces to raise a tree from the soil, Miyazaki turns a game for laughing children into a numinous ode to the earth. Intended or not, the sprouting tree's similitude to a mushroom cloud suggests a forcible reversal of symbols, an icon of death reclaimed for life.

Miyazaki's greatest film wasn't a success in cinemas, but its intimate story, so achingly centred around the home spaces of childhood, is tolerably suited to the small screen. *Totoro* is partly grounded in a line of TV series with which Miyazaki and his colleague Isao Takahata were heavily involved in the 1970s. Called *World Masterpiece Theater*, these were annual adaptations of foreign children's books, each serialised over a year. Leisurely by nature, they focused in great detail on home and community life, be it in the Alps (*Heidi*, 1974), Genoa (*From the Apennines to the Andes*, 1976) or Prince Edward Island (*Anne of Green Gables*, 1979). Miyazaki, though, was aggrieved that Japanese animation avoided its own country. 'Why don't we make fun, wonderful films actually set in Japan?' he asked.

On the other hand, much of *Totoro*'s comic business comes from *Panda! Go Panda!* (1972), a pair of cinema featurettes for grade-schoolers, written by Miyazaki and directed by Takahata in 1972–3. Miyazaki let the same whimsy predominate in his thirteen-minute *Totoro* sequel, called *Mei and the Baby Cat-bus* (2002), a straight cartoon that enjoyably extends the film's magic menagerie. As of writing, the sequel has played in the Ghibli Museum in Tokyo, where it rotates with other short Miyazaki films.

Neon Genesis Evangelion: The End of Evangelion
Japan, 1997 – 90 minutes
Hideaki Anno, Tsurumaki Kazuya
[Drawings with CGI and live-action]

DIRECTOR Hideaki Anno, Tsurumaki Kazuya
STORY Hideaki Anno
PRODUCER Mitsuhisa Ishikawa
SCORE Shiro Sagisu
DESIGN Yoshiyuki Sadamato, Ikuto Yamashita
ANIMATION Yoshimasa Yamazaki, Mika Nakabayashi, Hiroyo Izumi, Hiromi Igarashi, Satsuki Wada

Think of a popular fantasy franchise; *Star Wars* (1977 on), for instance. Now imagine a version of *Return of the Jedi* (1983) which begins with the hero Luke Skywalker committing an act of gross indecency over the comatose, half-naked body of Princess Leia. Later, he finds his true self by throttling her. Meanwhile, the *Star Wars* universe is being ripped apart by Rebel authorities murdering their own. Screaming people are gunned down mercilessly, brains spattered on walls. Elsewhere, feral giants engage in spine-snapping, flesh-eating carnage. Finally the diminutive Jedi Yoda manifests as a giant world-devouring god.

Switch the *Star Wars* characters for those in the Japanese sci-fi TV saga *Neon Genesis Evangelion*, and all the above happened in the big-screen 'last' chapter, *The End of Evangelion*. It was produced by the Gainax studio, whose past productions included the cinema *Wings of Honneamise* (1987), an alternate-world vision of the space race. The TV *Evangelion* was serialised in twenty-six parts in 1995, followed by the *End* feature two years later.

The series began from a familiar Japanese plot template; the adolescent boy who drives a giant robot (or in *Eva*'s case, cyborg), using the huge and frightening body to fight monsters and save Earth. In *Evangelion*, the world is being rebuilt after a terrible cataclysm when it's attacked by a succession of titans called Angels. An enigmatic scientist recruits his fourteen-year-old son, Shinji, to pilot a saurian-looking colossus, the Eva or Evangelion. So far, so familiar.

Evangelion, though, set out to do for the robot show what the comic *Watchmen* did for superheroes. Its boy 'hero', Shinji, is a hive of hang-ups, complexes and relationship phobias. In the first TV episode, when he's charged with being a defender of the Earth, he doesn't jump for joy; rather, he shrieks that he *can't* and that it's not *fair*. In other episodes, and for much of the *End* film, he slips into catatonic self-loathing, but then most of the *Evangelion* cast is damaged or dysfunctional, including the other two Eva pilots. Both are girls; Asuka, a firebrand megalomaniac with repressed horrors in her psyche, and Rei, a blank doll-figure whose true nature is shocking. Another female, the soldier Misato, takes Shinji into her home when his dad won't, but her private screw-ups are paraded before us.

The TV show mixed dark heroics, low-brow slapstick, in-jokes, psycho-drama and fan-baiting literary and theological allusions. But was it all bluff? After weeks of sometimes shambolic, sometimes inspired telefantasy, the twenty-fourth part resolved little. The last two TV episodes (25 and 26) were conceptual performance pieces on cartoon equivalents of bare stages: slideshow images, flipbook doodles and gnomic therapy-speak. Some fans saw the TV ending as an inspired avant-garde deconstruction, or as a raspberry from series creator Hideaki Anno to his fans, or both together. It's easy to read both the TV and film endings as Anno's psycho-portrait of the fantasy-media fan, fixated on cartoons and robot kits, and alienated from adulthood and reality.

The film *The End of Evangelion* follows from the twenty-fourth TV episode, and is split into replacement parts 25 and 26 (each with its own end-credits). Compared to the series, the film recalls a certain kind of fan-fiction which proclaims its nature through sex and violence forbidden in the source, like an X-rated *Star Wars*. Paedophilia and incest figure in barely sublimated forms, though the most shocking scene (the first) has a hysterical Shinji masturbating over the body of one of the main female characters, before the film is amped up to feverish *Sturm und Drang*. Few of the characters (or audience) know what's happening, but suddenly everyone is fighting and dying horribly.

Snapping off her hairband, Misato becomes an ultracool assassin, smiling 'Nothing personal!' as she blasts an enemy soldier in the head. Asuka curls into a foetal ball in darkness, compulsively repeating 'I don't want to die!' – a fine example of Gainax's limited (or rather, non-existent) animation which suddenly explodes into berserk motion. In her giant Eva steed, Asuka wields battleships, punches air-to-ground missiles and fights *Alien*-style monsters with luscious rosebud lips.

Part 26 offers an Armageddon of *Evangelion* characters bursting ecstatically into pools of primordial soup, interspersed with spaced-out album-cover imagery, religio-sexual symbols, subliminal death threats (that had actually been sent to the director) and imagined killer dialogues between the lead characters (reworked from the TV ending). Some of the eye-bleeding montages were created by filming the backs of the animation cels. An almost comically avant-garde interlude shows a little boy's tantrum in a playground modelled, Magritte-like, on the female anatomy. The abject epilogue mirrors the first scene, asking if we've gone anywhere at all.

As of writing, Anno is remaking *Evangelion* as four cinema features, starting with *Evangelion 1.0: You Are (Not) Alone* in 2008. Typically for Anno, he leaves open the possibility that this new version could be a restart-the-world sequel, unravelling *Evangelion*'s ends yet again.

Nezha Conquers the Dragon King
China, 1979 – 58 minutes
Yan Dingxian, Wang Shuchen, Xu Jingda ('A Da')
[Drawings]

The hero's journey starts early in *Nezha Conquers the Dragon King*. A mere infant, Nezha fights demonic dragons which eat children and scourge the land with floods and thunder. Rather than bloodshed, the battles play out through flying dances and gyring acrobatics. *Nezha* was shown at Cannes in 1980, back when Asian animation was an exotic novelty for most Westerners. How many of the festivalgoers knew that Chinese animation, just like Nezha, had fought for its existence?

China's first animators were four siblings, the Wan brothers, who made cartoon shorts from the 1920s. Two of the four, Wan Laiming and Wan Guchan, went on to *Princess with the Iron Fan* (1941), the first hand-drawn feature made outside America. Remarkably, it emerged during an invasion. *Princess* was at least partly made in Shanghai, which Japan occupied from 1937. The brothers were based in the city's French Concession district, where they had what historian Giannalberto Bendazzi called 'shaky diplomatic protection'.

Largely rotoscoped in black and white, *Princess* featured a legendary Chinese hero, the Monkey King, later known in Britain through Japan's live-action TV version, *Monkey!* (1978). Like Bugs Bunny or Daffy Duck, Monkey conquered enemies with irreverent trickery. The defiant subtext was hailed by a Japanese fan, Osamu Tezuka (p. 207), who saw *Princess* as a teenager. It also inspired Japan's first feature cartoon, the openly jingoistic *Momotaro's Divine Sea Warriors* (1945).

Wan Laiming returned to the Monkey King twenty years on, in a very different Shanghai. A lavish two-part colour feature, *Havoc in Heaven* (1961/4) was made at the Shanghai Animation Film Studio established by Mao's regime in 1957. Here, cel animation developed with other crafts; animation based on puppets, brush strokes, folded paper and paper-cuts. But by *Havoc*'s completion, the People's Republic was turning against animators. *Havoc* was screened at the Locarno festival, then shelved by the Chinese authorities. The American animator Dave Ehrlich speculates that, 'Perhaps the leaders now saw Monkey as rebelling against their own kind of authority.'

Even before the Cultural Revolution, Chinese animation was being denounced as reactionary intellectualism. Artists were expelled and 'sent to peasant villages to learn humility and revolutionary consciousness from the uneducated peasants' (Ehrlich). One of *Nezha*'s future directors, Yan Dingxian, was separated from his family and banished to the countryside. Another, Xu Jingda ('A Da') fed pigs, dug septic canals and drew forbidden cartoons of the Gang of Four, the Cultural Revolution's leaders. *Nezha* celebrated the end of that era, the Gang of Four's fall and the animators' return from exile. (In *Nezha*'s climax, it seems hardly accidental that the reborn hero battles *four* dragon monsters.)

Watched today, *Nezha* looks like a precursor to the French films of Michel Ocelot (p. 37), with their radiant colours and delicately balanced compositions. (And also their casual nudity – Nezha sometimes wears an apron-like garment, like the giant baby's in Miyazaki's *Spirited Away**, which leaves him mostly in the

DIRECTOR Yan Dingxian, Wang Shuchen, Xu Jingda ('A Da')
PRODUCER Liu Guimei
STORY Wang Wang
SCORE Jin Fuzai (Chinese version) Ivor Slaney (English version)
ANIMATION Lin Wenxiao, Chang Gwangxi, Zy Ranglin

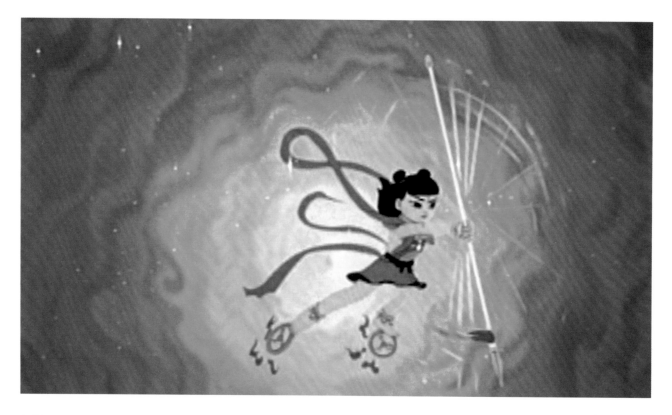

buff). The aesthetic is set by the fabulous overture, in which the dragons emerge from a funnelling ocean, writhe through the heavens and rain hail and brimstone on the land. The landscapes, tsunamis and storm clouds are ripples on ripples on ripples, delighting the eye.

While contemporary Japanese cartoons were minimising motion in fight scenes for budget reasons, resulting in the rigid poses homaged in *The Matrix* (1999), *Nezha* stylises its battles into flowing dances which Westerners could recognise from the Beijing (or Peking) Opera. Any rotoscoping is absorbed into the flow of sometimes extraordinary movements. During the last undersea battle, Nezha is swallowed by a whale, only to puncture it from inside with his spear. He rides two golden rings like celestial rollerskates, and wields a whirling gymnast's sash, crimson as if for the bloodshed *Nezha* mostly eschews.

The film was reportedly shown dubbed by the BBC, and English-subtitled DVDs can be found online. Judging by web comments, many Western viewers were enchanted by *Nezha* as children, perhaps partly because it *breaks* our rules for family films. One child is devoured (off screen) by monsters; another commits heroic suicide – with a sword! – shocking viewers who don't know the source myth. The latter tragedy ends with a deer bounding forlornly along a shoreline, before we switch to a cartoony underwater concert. This transition is one of *Nezha*'s few overt debts to Disney, and specifically to Walt's handling of tragedy in *Bambi**.

Night on the Galactic Railroad
Japan, 1985 – 108 minutes
Gisaburo Sugii
[Drawings (with brief CGI)]

DIRECTOR Gisaburo Sugii
PRODUCER Hiroshi Masamura
STORY Minoru Betsuyaku
SCORE Haruomi Hosono
DESIGN Takao Kodama
ANIMATION Marisuke Eguchi, Koichi Mashimo, Yasunari Maeda

Racing from the void, golden against the blackness, a square of light fills the universe. 'It's a field of corn!', exclaims one of Night on the Galactic Railroad's child adventurers, who happens to be a human-sized cat. Their steam train pulls in at a deserted, sun-drenched platform. Overheard, suspended from nothing, is a clock from which a gleaming pendulum swings, crisply clacking like a heartbeat. Music throbs softly through the cornfield from an invisible orchestra. A human girl leans forward. 'That sounds like the New World Symphony …'.

To Westerners, it sounds like a pastiche of a Hayao Miyazaki animated fantasy. Actually, it's a cartoon version of a far older source, a Japanese novella by the author and poet Kenji Miyazawa (1896–1933), published posthumously. The story tells of a boy, with the un-Japanese name of Giovanni, who finds himself atop a starlit hill on the night of the 'Milky Way' festival. Down from the heavens comes the wonder train, and Giovanni boards, finding his friend and classmate Campanella already a passenger. Their cosmic journey interleaves Miyazawa's devout Buddhism with allusions to contemporary physics, astronomy, palaeontology and – perhaps most surprising for Westerners – Christianity. The boys witness shining celestial crosses ringing with 'Hallelujah' choruses, visit a Pliocene coastline to pick million-year-old walnuts, see a puckish birdcatcher snatch herons from heaven, and must finally part on the threshold of a black hole.

The animated film is an uncompromisingly stately, poetic and haunting meditation on Miyazawa's text, a study staple in Japan. Reviewers often claim that it's not a children's film, but Miyazaki cartoons such as My Neighbour Totoro* and Spirited Away* – both influenced by Miyazawa's writing – form bridges to their mystic, melancholy predecessor. Railroad's drawing, by the studio Group Tac, is far simpler than Studio Ghibli's, but the beautiful colour co-ordinations and picture-book look are gracefully self-effacing. What matters is the experience of a child, Giovanni, who barely comprehends the story he's in. Throughout the film, he moves or is moved through a series of evocative illustrations. On the dark hill where he boards the train, the trees are globular, feminine and mysterious. Later the film's designs become frightening, with deadly dark water and the bottomless sky-tunnel.

Like the book version of Grave of the Fireflies*, Railroad was written as a requiem for a lost sister, adding resonance to the cartoon's female imagery. However, the director, Gisaburo Sugii, played down the story's history, saying that he wanted to universalise Miyazawa's vision. Thus Giovanni and Campanella are drawn as solemn-looking cats (which nicely reflects their uncertain nationality in the story). More than the animation, Giovanni's character is conveyed by the lucid designs and layouts, and by the melodic transcendence of one of the best scores to ever grace a cartoon.

Giovanni is receptive, sensitive, a chronic outsider. His consciousness is established in the film's leisurely first third, before he even boards the train. The shadowy, clanking printworks where he runs errands is, for

him, a mystical piece of isolated spacetime. Later, taunted by other boys, Giovanni flees the festivities that turn his cobbled town into a citadel of light. The true magic lies in the shadows. Aboard the echoing train, he can only see the wonders from behind a carriage window, and sense an understanding he can't share between Campanella and the other travellers.

Despite the cornfield and other ecstasies, Giovanni's journey is one to a mysterious deeper darkness that's never really broken by the strange lights – glowing stars, luminous flowers, the light bulbs in the train – that limn his journey. For Miyazawa, the dream-odyssey is an inherently moral inquiry, and his thoughts will shock some viewers. At one point, the train turns into a sinking ship (modelled on the *Titanic*)

for a fable about acts, omissions and drowning children. But the film is a call to reconcile love, sacrifice and moral engagement; and certainly *not* a film about suicide, as some books have suggested.

The director's eclectic résumé includes animated versions of the eleventh-century novel *Tale of Genji* and the arcade game *Street Fighter II*. The composer was Haruomi Hosono, a sometime bandmate of Ryuichi Sakamoto, and the script was adapted by the prolific playwright Minoru Betsuyaku, whose works include *Godot Has Come*, a comic sequel to Samuel Beckett's *Waiting for Godot*. Miyazaki fans may recognise Giovanni's Japanese voice, actress Mayumi Tanaka, who went on to voice the boy-hero in *Laputa: Castle in the Sky**.

The Nightmare before Christmas

US, 1993 – 73 minutes

Henry Selick

[Stop-motion with drawn and computer elements]
[A 3D version was released in 2006.]

The Nightmare before Christmas's most potent stop-frame image unites three disparate graphics into eldritch beauty. A rolling hill tapers, with absurd elegance, into a spiral of earth. A round yellow moon hangs behind it. Standing on the first against the second, a spindly stick figure – Jack Skellington, the skeleton king – moves with intricate, elongated grace as the spiral slope unfurls to form a tentacular bridge to the ground. It's no stranger than what happens in many early, wild cartoons, but Jack's refined poise is more Fred Astaire than Felix the Cat.

Jack sings of the ennui of mastering a craft – for him, the craft of scaring the pants off people – only to be doomed to repeat the performance *ad nauseam*. *Nightmare* is the first Hollywood cartoon feature to foreground an *artist*, whose Felliniesque frustrations drive the story; and the first since Walt Disney's death to highlight a flesh-and-blood artist over the animation. Tim Burton, whose name precedes the full title, designed the spiral hill, though he hadn't visualised it unrolling. That was Henry Selick, the film's actual director, who realised, 'It just seemed a moment … begging to happen.'

Halloweentown, *Nightmare*'s grey but gay setting, is stocked with vampires, werewolves, witches and ghouls. They're nearly all childish and lovable, only scary on 31 October. (One of them looks like the 'Creature from the Black Lagoon', of whom Marilyn Monroe said, 'I think he just craved a little affection, y'know?') Bored with the festival routine, Jack wanders off and falls into Christmastown, the domain of elves and Santa, who look toy-like and mechanical beside the Halloweeners' spontaneity. When Jack sets his empty eyes on the snowy landscape, his bewildered, newborn expression cracks into a grin of greedy delight. 'I want it, O I want it!', he crows. He's sung by Burton's collaborator Danny Elfman, whose ten restless songs smother or transfigure the film, depending on your taste. (Jack's speaking voice is provided by Chris Sarandon.)

Jack usurps Santa's job, with chaotic results. Kids open presents to find shrunken heads or monstrous parodies of Mickey Mouse and Donald Duck. But *Nightmare* spends less time on its crowd-pleasing climax than on Jack's vainglorious struggles to comprehend Christmas, to have it for himself. 'These dolls and toys confuse me so, Confound it all, I love it though!' Like Burton's live-action *Ed Wood* (1994), *Nightmare* celebrates its hero's glorious disasters, which supersede a pat final moral about Jack realising his place (like a patronising Disney short, 1934's *The Flying Mouse*).

Disney had done *animation macabre* in 1929's *The Skeleton Dance*, which *Nightmare* homages as much as Fleischer's Betty Boop film, *Minnie the Moocher* (1932). The latter turned jazz singer Cab Calloway into a dancing ghost walrus, while *Nightmare* serves up Oogie Boogie, a heavyweight sack-monster and brilliantly charismatic bully. In the 1990s, a hulking, dice-throwing boogieman with a black singer's voice (Ken

DIRECTOR Henry Selick
PRODUCER Tim Burton, Denise Di Novi
STORY Caroline Thompson, Michael McDowell
SCORE Danny Elfman
DESIGN B. J. Fredrickson, Gregg Olsson, David Cutler, Barry Jackson
ANIMATION Eric Leighton, Trey Thomas, Timothy Hittle, Michael Belzer, Anthony Scott, Owen Klatte, Paul Berry

Page's) brought charges of racism, but if only Oogie's henchmen – three tiresome brats – were half as fun. The same goes for Jack's arbitrary love interest, Sally, a stitched-together girl-doll who should have been a knockout, with terrifying subversive potential in her casually shed, shapely limbs. Instead, she mopes and pines interminably for Jack, who needs no help dominating the film.

Burton shot his live-action features *Batman Returns* (1992) and *Ed Wood* while *Nightmare* was being made by Selick, his longtime friend. The story, characters and design templates came from Burton, who paid occasional visits to Selick's studio in San Francisco. 'It's as though [Burton] laid the egg, but I sat on it and hatched it, so it came out looking a bit like both of us,' Selick told *Sight and Sound*. 'It was my job in a way to make [*Nightmare*] look like a Tim Burton film.' Indeed it does, full of curving camera moves, deep-etched lines, curlicued details and crooked, looming edifices. Beside them, Jack's extravagantly articulated leaps and poses look almost normal.

Ironically, Burton developed this style to *resist* an overbearing brand. He and Selick had worked at the fading Disney studio in the early 80s, where Burton made the short film *Vincent (*1982), a stop-motion dirge about a morbid little boy. It matched *Nightmare* so closely that *Vincent* supported the feature in British cinemas, as if to muddy the question of who was *Nightmare*'s true author: Burton, Selick or indeed Elfman. A month before *Nightmare*'s release, Disney started marketing it under the 'full' name of *Tim Burton's The Nightmare before Christmas*. 'I just wish (Burton) had been a little more generous,' Selick told *Empire* in 2009. 'And I hope it was Disney marketing who made the ultimate decision … . But if nothing else, I can always make a living winning bar bets on who directed *The Nightmare before Christmas*.'

Ninja Scroll
Japan, 1993 – 90 minutes
Yoshiaki Kawajiri
[Drawings]

The backdrop is the isolated, feudal Japan of the seventeenth century. The players are monsters and superfighters. *Ninja Scroll* is an icon of Japanese animation, not in Japan but abroad. It influenced the Wachowski brothers when they made *The Matrix* (1999) (you can see it in the way the warrior heroes bound up cliffs and from branch to branch). It was a linchpin of the Japanese animation video market after *Akira**, and a cash-cow for Western distributors.

Some fans now see *Ninja Scroll* – a shockingly violent film – as a relic from the days when Japanese animation was marketed to foreigners *on* shock value. But the film holds up now, and *not* because of its sex and gore. The plot is a B-movie's. Jubei is a wandering swordsman, based on a semi-mythical personage, and lightly voiced by the actor Koichi Yamadera, whose later roles include the lead in the TV animation series, *Cowboy Bebop* (1998). Following tradition, Jubei stumbles by chance into an uneven conflict. On the one side are monstrous brigands who are *actually* monsters, controlled by puppeteers in the shadows. On the other is an ill-starred woman ninja, Kagero, whose comrades were bloodily obliterated at the beginning of the film. The monsters are led by a man Jubei beheaded, with the scarred neck to show it.

Animated by Tokyo's Madhouse studio, *Ninja Scroll* focuses less on details than atmospherics: lightning, fog and fireflies, backgrounds that depart into monochrome blue and red, a characters' emotions being unashamedly (and unobtrusively) expressed in white light and golden flowers. The magic is casual: one character turns into a tree branch, while the villains control and command each other through endless threads that run from their mouths across the country.

As in *Akira*, many of the most outrageous and offensive images are in the first few minutes, as if to clear out anyone who didn't know what they were getting into. It's not so bad to see Kagero's ninja allies getting sliced in half, like a cartoony *Final Destination* (2000). But then a stone-skinned hulk rips a man's arms from his sockets, drinks the blood and violates Kagero, whom Jubei saves by planting an arrow in the beast's eye. (The attack on Kagero was censored in 1990s UK videos, but restored in the 2004 anniversary DVD.)

The film then 'settles' into a merely violent action-adventure that's tersely told, ruggedly staged and – astonishingly – touching, even tender in the story between Jubei and Kagero. That's not to say *Ninja Scroll* isn't sexist and exploitative. Director Yoshiaki Kawajiri had form in this area, having made the horror animation *Wicked City* (1987), containing pornographic sexual violence. It came out in the same year as *Legend of the Overfiend*, the most notorious sex animation of all.

Yet the women in Kawajiri's films frequently bite back, such as *Wicked City*'s spider-woman with her snapping *vagina dentata*. By *Ninja Scroll*, the sexual violence is brief, and there's more emphasis on the gross, complacent men who mete it out. After surviving her ordeal with the stone-monster, Kagero finds her clan-lord abusing a female chattel; the point is obvious but well made. Kagero is a poison-taster, whose beautiful,

DIRECTOR/STORY Yoshiaki Kawajiri
PRODUCER Shigeaki Komatsu, Haruo Sai, Masaki Sawanobori
SCORE Kaoru Wada
DESIGN/ANIMATION Yutaka Minowa

toxic body is death to all men but one. The sly monk orchestrating the story calls her, 'A perfect woman for this hellish world.' Though when Kawajiri was invited to expound on *Ninja Scroll*'s social stance on women, he had the grace to decline. This is pulp fantasy, after all.

Jubei's and Kagero's other opponents are reliably colourful; the best are a snake-tattooed, skin-shedding lady, a man who conceals a bee swarm on his back, and a Zatoichi-style blind swordsman. The latter's duel with Jubei in a bamboo forest stands out less for its stylised animation than for the complementary rhythms of its staging, sound and editing. The last fight is a true epic, set in the hold of a burning ship. The absurd brutality is joyful, the bonecrunching of the supermen topped off by a tide of molten gold that carries us sated away.

One Hundred and One Dalmatians
US, 1961 – 79 minutes
Wolfgang Reitherman, Hamilton Luske, Clyde Geronimi
[Drawings]

One of the most delightful notions in Disney's *One Hundred and One Dalmatians* is that domesticated dogs see humans as *their* pets, to protect and make happy. It's a joke for both parents and children, though perhaps kids relate to it more. As in many children's stories, normal power frameworks are inverted, and the (literal) underdogs are in charge. Later, though, we're shown this is a lie. A Dalmatian couple, Pongo and Perdita, have their beloved puppies stolen, and are frantic for news. While walking 'their' humans, Pongo barks his plea, but is pulled away by the man who's now plainly his master.

At this point, the film becomes a different kind of fantasy, in which a parallel animal society works heroically to save the pups. It's a precursor to *Toy Story**'s parallel world of playthings, and like *Toy Story* this isn't a simple children's film. Rather it's a comedy-thriller, mixing *The Great Escape*'s derring-do (1965) with Hitchcock's playful suspense. In one marvellous scene, a brave cat tries to marshal the kidnapped pups into fleeing their prison, while their captors watch a TV game-show where toffs quiz criminals ('Did you … *do someone in?*'). Earlier the dogs saw an adventure show, containing all the thrills (a maniacal villain, fast-flowing rivers) they must later face for real.

Visually, *One Hundred and One Dalmatians* moved Disney into graphics-led modernism, when most of the studios who'd championed the style as a reaction *against* Disney – most famously, UPA – were on the way out. As often happens in animation, the aesthetic came from cost-cutting technology. Mickey Mouse's first animator, Ub Iwerks, developed a variant of the Xerox process ('Xerography') that transferred animation drawings to cels without the need for tracing. The characters were defined by black outlines which Walt disliked. However, the film's designer/art director Ken Anderson envisioned a cartoon *built* out of those lines.

The style snowballed. In the final film, lines are the measure not just of the characters but the backgrounds as well. Painter Walter Peregoy's loose, mood-creating colour blotches and the Xeroxed lines look like what they are – separate elements of a picture, kept apart for deeper stylistic harmony. The spotted opening titles have the visual puns, spiky unpredictability and self-referencing of an ad campaign. (Peregoy's colours wash over the screen when his credit comes up.) Pongo – whose cut-out style hind leg in the first scene is brazen for Disney – even inspects a chic art magazine, *Lilliput*.

The outlines redefine motions, especially the characters' struggles for traction. When the pups slide on a frozen river, the outlines convey the *contact* of an ice surface even more than *Bambi*'s famous skating. The characters are infused with modern voices. Pongo narrates the opening like a cooped-up bachelor, following the suburban comedy of Disney shorts such as *Donald's Diary* (1954). His 'pet' human Roger, an impish bluesy songwriter, supplies an almost naturalistic diegetic soundtrack.

Parents, not orphans, are valorised, and Pongo and Perdita are grown-ups who know their enemy. Wholly animated by Marc Davis, the dog-skinning devil Cruella De Vil is a customised, bisexual fiend, with

DIRECTOR Wolfgang Reitherman, Hamilton Luske, Clyde Geronimi
STORY Bill Peet
SCORE George Bruns
DESIGN Ken Anderson
ANIMATION Milt Kahl, Frank Thomas, Marc Davis, John Lounsbery, Eric Larson

her black-and-white hair, sallow skin, goblin cheeks, phallic car and cigarette-holder, and swathing fur coat. She was partly inspired by the overbearing actress-personality Tallulah Bankhead, whom Orson Welles called 'the most sensational case of the ageing process being unkind'. In a cartoon so broad, the metaphorical devils are no different from real ones. Cruella hurls a bottle into a fire where it explodes in orange smoke.

The film's slightly odd structure – Pongo and Perdita almost vanish in the middle act – matters less than the moment-to-moment thrills. The puppies' trudge through snow swells into an epic, and their final perilous escape in a furniture van finds suspense in artful animation cycles, as the identical dogs creep past the villains. The film delighted animators, critics and audiences. It did not please Walt. Ken Anderson recalled, '(Walt) said, We're never going to do another one of those *goddamned* things like Ken did … . He didn't talk to me for about a year.'

Only Yesterday
Japan, 1991 – 114 minutes
Isao Takahata
[Drawings]

DIRECTOR/STORY Isao Takahata
PRODUCER Yasuyoshi Tokuma,
Yoshio Sasaki, Ritsuo Isobe
SCORE Katsu Hoshi
DESIGN Yoshifumi Kondo, Yoshiyuki
Momose
ANIMATION Yoshifumi Kondo,
Katsuya Kondo, Yoshiharu Sato,
Shinji Otsuka, Masako Shinohara

Released in 1991, *Only Yesterday* was the fifth theatrical feature from Japan's Studio Ghibli. Hayao Miyazaki picked the property, a strip about a perky ten-year-old girl in 1960s Tokyo. It was a series of childhood vignettes rather than a narrative, so Miyazaki gave it to his senior colleague Isao Takahata, director of *The Little Norse Prince** and *Grave of the Fireflies**. 'I knew instinctively that he was the only person who could turn it into a film,' Miyazaki said, joking that Takahata's approach was 'typically complicated'.

In the film, the child scenes remain vignettes. We see the girl, Taeko, in family squabbles and schoolyard embarrassments, some linked to intimations of puberty. (The giggling schoolboys overhear that girls have periods, which they think are worse than nits). These scenes are funny and charming, especially a class meeting about school rules, where the swots clash with the clowns. However, there are also abrasive moments that it's hard to imagine in a Miyazaki film. For example, Taeko's father strikes his little girl angrily in the face, then can't hide his guilt.

On top of all this, Takahata invented a framing story, half-romance, half-documentary. In this second narrative, a twenty-seven-year-old Taeko remembers her childhood as she travels to the country for a working holiday, picking flowers for rouge and dye. Taeko was born and bred in Tokyo, but her soul belongs to the country. There are passages of reverie, successive snapshots of pastoral tranquillity. Rather than Miyazaki, they recall Mamoru Oshii's rhetorical visuals in *Patlabor 2* (1993) and *Ghost in the Shell* (1995).

Taeko's girlhood predominates in *Only Yesterday*'s first half; then the adult scenes take over, though we often return to ten-year-old Taeko. Viewers may find the farm scenes interminably preachy, yet they seem purposefully provocative as Takahata buttonholes us with his pastoral hard sell. The director busts animated form, showing Taeko and a cute male farmer, Toshio, on a long car drive through a misty dawn while Toshio explains his calling ('We bring out the plant's life force'). Many *live-action* films, let alone animated ones, would avoid the scene as undramatic. Even the extended stoner conversations in Richard Linklater's *A Scanner Darkly** give us images of famous actors to look at. Takahata, though, plonks the scene in for us to like or lump.

The realism of *Only Yesterday*'s grown-up scenes is broken by heavily stylised elements. Three farm workers are introduced, each smiling in layered rural backgrounds like diorama figures while pan-pipes play. These artificial devices lend irony to Toshio's later speech, where he explains that the 'wild' Japanese woods and streams are crafted by humans, while we see *drawings* of those same woods and streams. 'I don't think audiences watch live-action features carefully,' Takahata said. 'However, they'd be forced to for an animated feature, because animation catches things we do and reflects reality more solidly than it actually is.'

The child scenes, though, are less solid. There are delicate watercolours, simplified characters with cartooned expressions, and white spaces that have an especially interesting effect when a boy baseball star appears in sports whites. The contrasting styles suggest two different films entwining, as personal identity (Taeko's memories) is set against national identity (Japan's farm heritage).

The young Taeko shyly meets a boy at sunset and the backgrounds glow pinkly, till the scene tips into first-love fantasy and she runs up into the sky. Soon after, there's a ravishing hyperrealist scene where the adult Taeko sees the sun rise over dewy fields. It's part of Takahata's overtly pro-country propaganda, yet he later shows an equally realistic, adult encounter, no less delicate or touching than the children's. Again it's set in the car, where Taeko talks out a troubling memory that Toshio finds he can enter.

Thinking back, the adult Taeko abruptly generalises about her sex. 'We girls were livelier and more spirited than guys; it was like we'd finally found our wings. But looking back now, maybe we were just flexing them pointlessly.' At the end, Taeko is encouraged to marry Toshio and stay in the country, forsaking her urban career. Yet whatever Takahata's prescriptive intentions, his film inclines us to trust less the teller or tale than Taeko herself. The reverse of the quailing Seito in Takahata's *Grave of the Fireflies*, she's driven to excel in arduous experiences: farming, acting, bathing in a hot-spring *onsen*, even eating an exotic pineapple. Sensitive, articulate and forthright, Taeko brings this contradictory film together.

Persepolis
France, 2007 – 95 minutes
Marjane Satrapi, Vincent Paronnaud
[Drawings]

At the start of *Persepolis*, the film's Iranian characters are shown partying like it's 1979. Through the story, which covers a dozen years of fall-out from the Shah's overthrow, there are many scenes of dancing, at parties and in other contexts. Some are joyful, some rebellious, some struggling against despair, all experienced by Marjane Satrapi, the author of the graphic novel-memoir on which the film is based. It's a highly coloured story, told almost entirely in black and white.

When revolution hits Tehran, Marjane's father – a firm but warm patriarch, his gentleness encapsulated in his droopy moustache – picks up his daughter and whirls her around to celebrate the moment. Only a few scenes on, Marjane is dancing in darker places. Her heroic uncle twirls her to try and make her forget she's visiting his death cell. An older Marjane riffs on an imaginary guitar to the screeches of Iron Maiden. We saw how she bought the illegal music from a street of trench-coated vendors hawking Abba, Pink Floyd and 'Jikael Mackson'.

When Marjane is sent to Vienna for safety, she headbangs with metalheads in a basement dive, but it's not the same. What was rebellion in her country is dissolution for an exile, hanging with dropouts who preach nonchalance and nihilism. Returning to Iran, she's picked up by a new soundtrack, singing 'Eye of the Tiger' and making herself over in a high-energy combo of education, depilation and aerobics. The last party in the film is broken up by Iran's Guardians of the Revolution. Revellers flee over rooftops; one straggler tries jumping a chasm, clutching at the crescent moon in the sky, but we never see him land.

Marjane is ungrounded; the film revolves around scenes of her at an airport, stranded between states and identities. (These melancholic scenes are the only ones in colour, a stylistic joke.) Her heritage is remarkable: her uncle strove for an independent republic, her great-grandfather was the Shah of Persia. As a jumping bean child – not dissimilar from Taeko in the previous entry, *Only Yesterday** – Marjane knows she's the nation's saviour, as she chats with a white-bearded God in her bedroom. When she's a rootless teen exile, she pretends she's French to a youth ogling her low-cut top, and is haunted not by God but her gran for denying her roots.

Persepolis suggests an analogy, which Satrapi herself might well reject, between the conflicted girl and her conflicted nation. The personal narrative is drawn in Satrapi's faux-naif comic style, modified for clean movement, with characters often caught in ominously encroaching black frames. When Marjane is faced with an unspeakable horror of war, her background plunges into darkness while her face mimics Munch's Scream. Iran's history is told through agitprop silhouettes (black blood pooling under a murdered boy), satiric caricatures (a puppet show retelling of the rise of Reza Shah) and fairytale (the richly drawn adventures of Marjane's uncle).

Marjane has all our sympathies by the time she moves to Vienna, letting us see the West through a migrant's eyes. Her uncertainties and wrong decisions suggest a real-world version of Kiki, the trainee witch

DIRECTOR/STORY Marjane Satrapi, Vincent Paronnaud
PRODUCER Marc-Antoine Robert, Xavier Rigault
SCORE Olivier Bernet
ANIMATION Christian Desmares, Olivier Bizet, Damien Barrau, Franck Bonnay, Jean-Yves Castillon

in Hayao Miyazaki's *Kiki's Delivery Service**. Yet the reality-based *Persepolis* raises a possible contradiction in cartoon form.

Satrapi said bluntly that,

> With real actors ... (*Persepolis*) would have been an ethnic movie about the problems of people ruled by God in a distant country. Whereas drawings bring a universality ... . Dictatorships can happen to anybody, whether you live in Chile, China or Iran.

But would her grandmother have placed universality over ethnicity? The film plays up Marjane's reactions to Western music and well-stocked supermarkets – this Iranian girl, she likes the things we do! – even as the anarchists tell her Father Christmas works for Coca-Cola.

Perhaps Satrapi should have followed another graphic novel-turned-film, 2003's *American Splendor*. She could have cameoed in *Persepolis* as her live-action, ethnic self.

Having first made us fall for the little girl Marjane, the film accelerates and fragments as she grows up. Perhaps it's a ploy to avoid neatly packaging her life, or perhaps just the consequence of compressing a 350-page comic into ninety-five minutes. Marjane's love life is reduced to annoyingly flip jokes, like a *Rashomon* gag reducing an ex to a buck-toothed snot. The high-speed approach works better in depicting Marjane's pneumatic physical development (a gloriously funny cartoon interlude) and her pill-popping plunge into depression. The course of her life is as chaotic as a blown blossom; all she can do is honour the good times and dance through the bad.

Pinchcliffe Grand Prix
Norway, 1975 – 88 minutes
Ivo Caprino
[Stop-motion]

The mere existence of *Pinchcliffe Grand Prix* should gladden the jaded cinephile. Made in Norway, it's a stop-motion yarn about a middle-aged bachelor bohemian. An inventor, he lives in a house on a craggy Norse hilltop with a maudlin shaggy hedgehog and a sly blackbird. They're both human-sized and anthropomorphised (the bird, for instance, has a snappy muffler and jacket and zooms round on a motorbike). The three build a giant racing car, bankrolled by a millionaire sheikh who uses dollar bills as flywhisks. Released in the shadow of the OPEC oil crisis, *Pinchcliffe*'s Middle Eastern caricatures would launch a thousand protests today. There's even a 'sexy' avian belly dancer with a jewelled navel.

Like France's *Le Roman de Renard**, *Pinchcliffe* was a family affair. Ivo Caprino (1920–2001) made puppet shorts from the 1940s. His first feature, *Ugler i mosen* (*Owls in the Marsh*, 1959), mixed live-action and stop-motion; it featured the child actress and future singing star Grethe Kausland. By the time of *Pinchcliffe*, Caprino's son Remo had joined his father's studio, serving as co-writer, producer and second-unit director. Caprino's daughter Ivonne assisted, while *Pinchcliffe*'s characters came from the author Kjell Aukrust.

Pinchcliffe was planned as a TV show for NRK, the Norwegian Broadcasting Corporation, but the station turned it down. Remo then suggested making the material into a feature. According to the publicity, *Pinchcliffe* sold five and a half million tickets in Norway, a country of *four* and a half million people. For British viewers, *Pinchcliffe* brings two mini-institutions to mind. The inventor hero and the provincial whimsy anticipate Wallace and Gromit (p. 219), though the roles are reversed. Caprino's inventor, Theodore Rimspoke, is quiet and level-headed, leaving the humour to his animal friends.

Pinchcliffe's look and feel, meanwhile, evoke the string-puppet series by Gerry Anderson (*Thunderbirds*, 1965–6). Despite the fluid stop-motion, the puppets have limited faces and unbendy frames, while the roads and race tracks suggest ornate train sets. Even the sheikh's smart gorilla (a bouncer, chauffeur, chess player and drummer rolled into one), seems no stranger than Parker, Lady Penelope's cockney driver in *Thunderbirds*.

Pinchcliffe also delights in artisan engineering, foreshadowing *Porco Rosso** by Hayao Miyazaki. The building of *Pinchcliffe*'s racing car is detailed at leisure, down to its technical specs, so it comes as little surprise to learn that the studio built a *real* version of the car to promote the film. (It was twenty-two feet long from crank to exhaust.) Like *Porco*, *Pinchcliffe* climaxes in a racing duel with a caddish baddie who not only steals Rimspoke's patent but insults him as an eccentric rustic. The fifteen-minute race masterfully assembles low-tech effects, from back-projection to simple toys, heavily relying on editing, sound and small-scale camerawork, including remarkably dynamic moving shots.

For viewers not drawn to the visual style, *Pinchcliffe*'s main appeal is its gently quirky incidental humour: the avuncular voice-over narration, a TV anchorwoman who looks like Barbara Cartland, and a hilariously shapeless band performance composed by Danish musician Bent Fabric, who scored the film. Otherwise the

DIRECTOR/ANIMATION Ivo Caprino
PRODUCER Remo Caprino
STORY Kjell Aukrust, Remo Caprino, Kjell Syversen, Ivo Caprino
SCORE Bent Fabric

music and story has the cosiness of Wallace and Gromit, as *Pinchcliffe* starts and ends at home. As the narrator concludes, the characters will 'be back at their daily chores tomorrow, with petty quarrels, inventions and the manufacture of flagpoles for the Swiss navy'.

A region-free DVD (PAL) of *Pinchcliffe* is available from the Ivo Caprino studio website, featuring English-dubbed and subtitled versions of the film.

Pinocchio
US, 1940 – 88 minutes
Ben Sharpsteen, Hamilton Luske
[Drawings]

Disney's *Pinocchio* is the first cartoon feature to allegorise animation's miracle, the creation of life. By *Pinocchio*'s release in 1940, cinema audiences had seen many fantastic births, but usually of monsters: Paul Wegener's clay Golem, Fritz Lang's robot Maria, the lumbering Boris Karloff. Early cartoons, meanwhile, reduced their life-giving magics to jaunty conjuring, inspired by the lightning artists of vaudeville. The connection is explicit in J. Stuart Blackton's *Humorous Phases of Funny Faces* (1906), perhaps the first cartoon ever. The first chalk drawing is by a visible hand, but then the magician drops out and the faces move by themselves.

In contrast, Disney couches Pinocchio's birth in wondrous fairytale metaphor, but with a showman's wink to the audience. A winged Blue Fairy in a glittering dress touches her wand to a boy marionette and declares, 'Little puppet made of pine; Wake, the gift of life is thine!' Pinocchio wakes amid sunbursts, stretches and blinks his blue painted eyes, and we cut to the gnome-like spectator Jiminy Cricket, voiced by vaudeville star Cliff Edwards. Jiminy looks at us, lets out an impressed 'Phew!' and chirps, 'What they can't do these days!' You can almost see Walt beaming with pride.

Pinocchio was the second cartoon feature released by Disney, three years after *Snow White**. It was a flop; war in Europe blighted foreign sales, while some critics argue the film was too dark for American viewers. Yet many reference books cite *Pinocchio* as the greatest cartoon feature ever, even if its images and characters haven't sunk into the popular memory as deeply as *Bambi**, *Dumbo** and *Snow White*.

The technology unites handicrafts with high-tech. *Pinocchio*'s pictures were interpreted in 3D through the multiplane, a giant camera holding glass sheets on which cels, backgrounds and overlays were painted separately. When Pinocchio's alpine village wakes, we swoop and turn overhead like a bird, looking down at the flocking crowds, though it's typical of the pell-mell narrative that we never see this bustle again.

The film's greatness is haphazard, its magic almost shapeless. It has *five* villains (including a monster whale), untidily sprawling set pieces, broad panto knockabout (exaggerated double-takes abound) and moments of high terror. There's the horror-film shadow of a doomed delinquent, turning from boy into donkey, and the shock-and-awe climax, where Pinocchio and the toymaker Gepetto are chased by a whale like a roaring locomotive. If *Pinocchio* has a self-metaphor, it's Gepetto's fantastic toyshop array of clocks shaped like animals, birds, dancers and delinquents, all brassily chiming the hour – though Gepetto must still check what time it actually *is*.

The carvings and clockwork of Gepetto's home advertise the animators' handicraft. The toyshop scenes drip enclosed and intimate charm, modulated by Gepetto's cranky cat (animated by Eric Larson). Cliff Edwards as Jiminy was the first celebrity voice in Disney's features, a precursor to Phil Harris in *The Jungle Book** and Robin Williams in *Aladdin**. Edwards, though, can mix fanny gags with snowy purity, and his

DIRECTOR Ben Sharpsteen, Hamilton Luske
STORY Ted Sears, Otto Englander, Webb Smith, William Cottrell
SCORE Leigh Harline, Need Washington, Paul J. Smith
DESIGN Joe Grant, Al Hurter, John P. Miller
ANIMATION Frank Thomas, Ollie Johnston, Milt Kahl, Bill Tytla, Ward Kimball, Wolfgang Reitherman, Eric Larson, Art Babbitt

tenor singing of 'Fate steps in and sees you *through* …' conjures a lost world of Hollywood gentility.

Disney's Pinocchio is an adorable child, far from the devil doll created by Italian author Carlo Lorenzini, writing as Carlo Collodi. The original character swung between cruelty, indolence and prima-donna sentimentality, more 'Looney Tunes' than Disney. Walt didn't corrupt the source; Pinocchio was already an innocent in a popular 1938 US stage version directed by Yasha Frank. Disney's and Collodi's Pinocchios are often contrasted by pundits looking to denounce one or the other, but they can co-exist. (Spielberg references Disney's Pinocchio in *Close Encounters of the Third Kind*, 1977 and Collodi's in *Artificial Intelligence, AI*, 2001.)

Collodi's puppet is the hero of a rickety junior *Bildungsroman*, a round of painful falls and lessons. Disney's Pinocchio just needs to become a real boy to escape wicked exploiters, like the foxy J. Worthington Foulfellow with his red fur and quizzical, questing malignity, voiced by a bluff Walter Catlett. Far worse is the coachman who takes urchins to Pleasure Island, a cockney fiend who leers, 'They never come back … AS BOYS!' and turns into a penny-dreadful cross between a gargoyle and Batman's Joker (invented that year). The whinnying puppet master Stromboli, animated by Bill Tytla, is a campily monstrous Santa Claus whose rolling flesh and scarlet mouth foreshadow the rampaging whale at the end.

None of these evil-doers are punished or destroyed, but just melt away like lemon drops, ready to entrap the next careless child. Even at the happy ending, we're not allowed to linger at the celebrations, but follow Jiminy out into the cold night – though a night suffused with light, where each twinkling star equates to a small but sturdy conscience. Disney pours New World optimism over unkillable European nightmares; *Pinocchio* opened just as Europe was falling under tyranny.

The Polar Express
US, 2004 – 99 minutes
Robert Zemeckis
[CGI, also released in a 3D IMAX version]

The Polar Express depicts an enchanted journey into magic and fantasy, framed by snow-filled skies, a vast frozen wilderness and Santa's kingdom at the end of it. The transport is a giant old-school locomotive, all blasting steam and heavy metal, crossing a thrillingly rugged landscape of mountains, valleys and an iced-over sea. Of course it becomes a rollercoaster, the precipitous scenery turning into a cine-carny backdrop for a runaway train.

The slight fable, from a picture-book by Charles Van Allsburg, concerns a boy who's become a Doubting Thomas about Father Christmas. Invited onto the Polar Express on Christmas Eve, the boy meets other children and some strange grown-ups – a gruff conductor, a frightening hobo – who strongly resemble each other. When the boy meets Santa, he has the same look, but in a kingly, messianic (though rather stiff) way. All these adults seem to be versions of the boy's father, who's glimpsed at the start with a Santa hat in his pocket. It echoes director Zemeckis's earlier *Contact* (1997), another faith tale, where Jodie Foster met an alien with her father's face.

The Polar Express's characters are mostly one-note figures. They sometimes break into song, a first in a big CGI film, though the songs themselves are weak. The film was plainly aimed at younger viewers than *Shrek** or *The Incredibles**, but the whirligig spectacle has Zemeckis's flair. At the start, the Polar Express train roars to a steam-swathed halt outside the boy's snow-bound house. Later, a lost ticket flutters through a mile-high landscape of eagles and wolves. The hero boy trudges through a rushing vortex of snow, and he and his friends inch across a slippery rail over a bottomless pit. The ruddy illuminations and children's night-gowns are homely defences against the dark and snow.

The Polar Express was marketed as a miracle, capturing actors' living presences and infusing them into a new medium *between* animation and live-action. Naysayers called it a clunky gloss on an old technique, rotoscoping, which dated back to 1916 when Dave Fleischer donned a clown suit and was filmed by his brother Max, then traced to create a cartoon clown. Eighty-eight years on, Tom Hanks and other *Polar Express* actors wore 'motion-capture' suits, resembling Lycra wetsuits. These were covered by reflective markers, which showed up on a computer as dots building the characters.

Hanks provided the movements of the central boy and his father-figures (the conductor, Santa *et al.*). But the boy was *modelled* on a real child, who looked like Hanks as a youngster, and had his face scanned by computer before Hanks 'animated' his likeness. This was tantamount to possession; an actor appropriating someone else's appearance and walking round in his skin.

For critics, though, it was as absurd as Lewis Carroll's map that's as big as what it shows. All animators knew that humans were the hardest species to simulate believably, because we know the true article so well. *The Polar Express* opened to jeers that the characters were animatronic zombies, ludicrously affectless and inhuman. Their shiny doll-eyes were a special *bête noire*.

DIRECTOR Robert Zemeckis
PRODUCER Steve Starkey, Robert Zemeckis, Gary Goetzman, William Teitler
STORY Robert Zemeckis, William Broyles Jr, Malia Scotch Marmo
SCORE Alan Silvestri
DESIGN Rick Carter, Doug Chiang
ANIMATION Keith Kellogg, John Clark Matthews, Kenn McDonald, Jeff Schu, Chad Stewart

The Polar Express popularised the phrase, 'Uncanny Valley' (coined by Japanese roboticist Masahiro Mori), referring to simulated humans who look *just* wrong enough to prompt revulsion. The idea of a luminal film between cartoon and live-action, importing actors' performances into new-minted, cohesive virtual territory was compelling. It would lead on to *A Scanner Darkly** and eventually to *Avatar**. But *Polar Express* was *far* from cohesive. In a few shots, you could be seeing real humans; more often they were jerky and robotic; and mostly they were somewhere in between.

*The Incredibles'** director Brad Bird pointed out how a previous motion-captured character, Gollum (Andy Serkis) in *The Lord of the Rings* (2001 on) film trilogy was tweaked and massaged by animators. In part, they key-framed his crucial facial expressions, injecting the believability Zemeckis lost. Moreover, *Polar*'s blockbuster spectacle resembled a train set beside more modest cartoons. The puffing locomotive can't compete with Casey Jr in Disney's *Dumbo**. The epic landscape has less magic than the hand-drawn Brighton Pavilion seen from the air in Britain's *The Snowman* (1982).

Yet *The Polar Express*'s imaginative shortcomings and bad animation matter less in king-sized 3D. As of writing, *The Polar Express: An IMAX 3D Experience* has been reissued every Christmas since its release. Scaled up to IMAX, the characters' fakeness is far less notable, and the hero boy's adventures are wholly immediate as he rides mountains like rollercoasters and delves into Santa's cavernous realm. The payoff is touching – a leap of faith in the ringing of a tiny bell – and the celebrations and return home are shown at enough leisure to convey a journey travelled.

Ponyo
Japan, 2008 – 101 minutes
Hayao Miyazaki
[Drawings]

DIRECTOR/STORY Hayao Miyazaki

PRODUCER Toshio Suzuki

SCORE Joe Hisaishi

ANIMATION Atsuko Tanaka, Shinji Otsuka, Katsuya Konda, Megumi Kagawa, Hiromasa Yonebayashi

Hayao Miyazaki aims his tenth animated feature at young children, with a cute magic character as its star – Ponyo, a perky red goldfish who turns into a little girl. Fans wondered if Miyazaki was remaking *My Neighbour Totoro**, his previous children's classic about a cute fantasy creature. But *Ponyo*, while delightful, doesn't really feel like *Totoro*, nor like Miyazaki's other films, though it has some things in common with his later ones. There's an array of strange creatures and characters, an unpredictable plot, and offbeat ideas spun into cartoon spectacle.

A boy, Sosuke, lives in a clifftop house with his excitingly reckless mother, Lisa, who treats Sosuke as a grown-up in every important decision. The five-year-old's characterisation switches between a near-toddler and a mini-adult, distending the careful portrayals of kids in Miyazaki's *Totoro* and Disney's *Lilo and Stitch**. In *Ponyo*, realism is rarely a priority.

Sosuke's father is away at sea, and Lisa's exasperation with this is comically exaggerated when the family communicates through ship-lamps and Morse. Miyazaki has confessed to being a largely absent husband and dad, and that's represented here. Both husbands in *Ponyo* revere and are terrified by their wives, their femininity linked to the crashing sea.

Playing by the water, Sosuke finds the Ponyo fish stuck in a jam jar. He rescues and cares for her, carrying her around in a bucket and forming a bond, which spills over into love when she speaks to him. Later, Ponyo gains spectacular powers and turns the sea into a tsunami of giant foaming fish-shaped spirits, on which she bounds confidently on her new-grown legs. The bravura animation, showing the magic waves crashing explosively against a coastal road, conveys mighty nature even more forcefully than Miyazaki's epic *Princess Mononoke**.

The flood engulfs Sosuke's town, but no one is hurt or hysterical. Instead, the event is treated like a child's first snowfall, turning familiar scenery into magic. As a children's story, *Ponyo* draws on 'The Little Mermaid' (and 'Cinderella' in the way Ponyo's transformation has a time-limit) but it also recalls how L. Frank Baum described his book, *The Wizard of Oz*: 'A modernised fairy tale in which the wonderment and joy are retained and the heartaches and nightmares are left out.' True, there's brief distress when Sosuke fears he might have lost his mother, but Ponyo is there to bolster him up.

As animation, *Ponyo* rolls back the frightening shadows of *Coraline**, *Toy Story** and even *Snow White**. To use a contentious distinction, it might be better called a cartoon than an animation, though grown-ups can enjoy it as a lovely, witty fantasy. Like many Miyazaki films, it stresses how children *negotiate* their surroundings. In a beautifully observed and paced early scene, Sosuke paddles cautiously out to rescue Ponyo, who flaps around with her head in the jam jar.

Miyazaki also makes play with magic undersea membranes that Ponyo must breach, sluicing water

deliciously back and forth. The sequence is humorously contrasted with Ponyo's experience of dry land, where she dashes uncontrollably round in Sosuke's house and bangs into a door. Later, she and Sosuke sail a magically grown toy boat across the flooded town, peering at prehistoric fish swimming placidly down roads and over houses.

Structurally, Ponyo recalls The Little Norse Prince*, on which Miyazaki worked under Isao Takahata. The first half focuses on Sosuke's fascination with the magic alien. The second shows Ponyo learning what humans are and how to be one. Her exciting first dinner in Sosuke's home is shown at length, as is her inspection of a glowering baby. Her heritage is borrowed cheekily yet majestically from Norse myth. Her given name is Brunhilde, her mother is a serene red-haired giantess and the score spoofs 'The Ride of the Valkyries' during Ponyo's plucky wave-top dash.

Ponyo, though, finally breaks free of parents and magic to live her chosen life, reprising themes in Miyazaki's Howl's Moving Castle (2004). As in Howl and Spirited Away*, the final reckoning is thrown away insouciantly. Sosuke's last 'challenge' is just to confirm what he's proved, that he loves Ponyo whoever she is. The build-up to the climax is the climax.

The hand-drawing involves flattened perspectives, soft-textured pastel backdrops and humped-up seas as massive and dynamic as Laputa*'s clouds. Straight lines are out; the wavy, childish opening titles recall those for the vintage Japanese puppet show Hyokkori Hyotanjima, which was sampled in Studio Ghibli's Only Yesterday*. At times it seems that every frame of Ponyo wriggles with mundane and magical fishy creatures, foaming waves and crawling critters.

Porco Rosso
Japan, 1992 – 93 minutes
Hayao Miyazaki
[Drawings]

DIRECTOR/STORY Hayao Miyazaki
PRODUCER Toshio Suzuki
SCORE Joe Hisaishi
ANIMATION Megumi Kagawa,
Toshio Kawaguchi, Shinji Otsuka,
Yoshifumi Kondo, Yoshinori Kanada,
Yoshiyuki Momose, Katsuya Kondo

Japanese director Hayao Miyazaki uses flight so often in his animation that it's become his trademark. For example, when Pixar announced that the studio's 2009 feature *Up** would involve a flying house, journalists quickly linked the film to Miyazaki's oeuvre, having presumably not seen Winsor McCay's 1921 short actually called *The Flying House*. *Porco Rosso*, though, nods respectfully to vintage Hollywood animation. The setting is 1930s Europe, and there's a sweet scene in a Milanese cinema where kids gawp at a mouse aviator fighting a bad-guy pig. (Disney's first Mickey Mouse cartoon was a flying caper, 1928's *Plane Crazy*.)

'This is a lousy film,' grumbles Porco Rosso, a fighter pilot with a pig-face himself. 'This is a good film,' demurs his companion as the mouse gets the girl. It's a cute moment, perhaps asking us what cartoons are *for*. Miyazaki wanted to make a silly, irresponsible picture, 'that (would be) frowned on by the PTA'. He drew a fifteen-page comic in which the high-flying Porco competes with a cocksure American and clownish air-pirates, to the cheers of ordinary people. The final punch-up between the main rivals, played for laughs, recalls John Wayne fighting Victor McLaglen in *The Quiet Man* (1952).

All this is in the film, but the comic omitted some important things. It didn't have Gina, who in the film is the graceful and beautiful chanteuse who remembers Porco from when he had a human face, and fondly calls him 'baka' (perhaps best translated in this context as 'fool'). A *Porco Rosso* film poster showed Porco, Gina and a sunset sky, positioning the film as a romantic drama distinct from Miyazaki's kids' fantasies. Disney had already used this strategy, promoting *The Little Mermaid* (1989) and *Beauty and the Beast** with romantic silhouettes.

The film also gives Porco a melancholy history, making him a larger-than-life hero who's tired, middle aged and socially alienated (the reason for his magic-realist appearance as a pig). Pixar's later *The Incredibles** has a similar premise but at least gives Mr Incredible a family. Porco is a loner on a sheltered island beach, though, unknown to him, the thrice-widowed Gina waits in a jewel-like walled garden, the ocean between them. Planes loop and dive, swooping over flowing cartoon landscapes, but the underlying situation is static – the opposite of Miyazaki's children's films, which are forever *going* somewhere.

Miyazaki said the film's sombre elements were inspired by the conflicts in Eastern Europe – Porco's island is supposedly off Croatia – much as his later *Howl's Moving Castle* (2004) would be influenced by Iraq. However, the director's comments also suggest that *Porco*'s deeper themes were forced on him when the film became a feature, having been planned as a thirty- or forty-five-minute featurette.

His producer Toshio Suzuki was involved in the extended, faintly postmodern story. At the start, Porco lies on the beach with his face under a film magazine. Soon after, he leans on a bar at Gina's hotel and blows cigarette smoke, looking so much like a film star that we laugh in recognition. Gina looks no less a starlet, especially when holding her broad-brimmed sunhat in an exquisitely framed moment of remembrance. The American 'villain' Curtis *wants* to be a movie star, though Gina warns him, 'Life here is more complicated than where you're from … . You go to Hollywood, kid.'

Like all Miyazaki films, *Porco Rosso* features a wide-eyed young girl (the seventeen-year-old engineer Fio), but even she feels like a self-conscious pastiche of the Miyazaki type, outrageously competent and cute. Befitting a grown-up film, Fio flirts playfully with Porco, while demanding he live up to the stories she heard as a child, so he can be changed by her kiss. Gina arrives at the end like the world's loveliest schoolmarm (or mother) to bring the brawling males to order. For all the testosterone, Miyazaki portrays masculinity as nobly idealist and hopelessly childish, except when redeemed by a woman – a theme developed in *Howl's Moving Castle*.

Howl, incidentally, is usually seen as Miyazaki's first film of a British book (by Diana Wynne Jones). *Porco Rosso*, though, borrows a scene from Roald Dahl – namely a story Porco tells Fio, about when he flew through a cloud of light and saw hundreds of ghost-planes in a pure blue sky, carrying dead airmen's souls. The beatific image isn't from Dahl's children's fiction, but his 1940s story, 'They Shall Not Grow Old', inspired by Dahl's experiences as a fighter pilot, which Miyazaki surely envied. The scene lets romantic, Hollywood-style fantasy soften the war looming round *Porco*'s edges. However, the ending gently conveys that the film's Adriatic dream is passing, dispersed like the rude revellers by darker human follies.

The Prince of Egypt
US, 1998 – 98 minutes
Simon Wells, Brenda Chapman, Steve Hickner
[Drawings/CGI]

Animation is a medium of strange movements, and of strange transitions in image and tone, far more elastic than in live-action. In DreamWorks' Bible epic, *The Prince of Egypt*, the title character Moses falls into a troubled sleep. We close in on his twitching eyelid, which hardens into stone, as Moses finds he's turned into a figure in a wall-carving. Later, as Egypt burns and Moses and the Pharaoh Rameses sing out their joint angst, the characters' faces are bisected and merged. Such effects are inherently pictorial, more self-consciously filmic than cartoon squashing and stretching, but forceful because these characters are drawings turning into other drawings.

In Hollywood cartoons, slapstick routinely gives way to song, to spectacle, to terror, to tragedy, to slapstick again. The critic Gary Westfahl suggested the ancient Greeks would have found *The Prince of Egypt* like their theatre, with the eclecticism and variety praised by Aristotle. In animation, scenes supersede each other, melting time and emotion. Even Bambi's mother's death gave way to a silly spring symphony. *The Prince of Egypt* endeavours to do the same with Old Testament cruelties, banishing them with a song number or a cartoon camel.

DreamWorks' co-founder Jeffrey Katzenberg claimed, 'The tradition up to now has been to do things cartoony, and we don't want to be pretentious, but we set out to do fine art … I'm not saying cartoony isn't fine art, just very, very different styles.' In the event, *The Prince of Egypt* – retelling the Exodus story of Moses freeing the Hebrews – has the most self-important Hollywood cartoon opening since *Fantasia*. Following black title cards and a scriptural disclaimer, its opening images feel immediately like a misstep. Huge, affectless crowds of slaves toil to a booming chorus ('Deliver Us', by Stephen Schwartz), when the inhuman scale of the *mise en scène* demands live performers. Suddenly, we're against the limits of cartoon flexibility.

Part of *Prince's* problem is its monumentalism, its giant edifices and endless wilderness sapping spontaneity from the players. (Rameses and his father are framed beside gigantic statues of themselves.) At the same time, the film *wants* to be a passionate drama. When Moses meets but doesn't recognise his Hebrew siblings, voiced by Sandra Bullock and Jeff Goldblum, the acting is laughably melodramatic. Throughout, the script is talky and portentous, the humour forced, most tediously with the Vegas-style wizard flunkies voiced by Steve Martin and Martin Sheen.

But live-action epics have similar issues, and *The Prince of Egypt* remains impressive. Most viewers remember the third-act spectacles (the apocalyptic plagues, the Red Sea's parting, a majestic Exodus), but it's the propulsive middle act that raises the temperature. Moses's desert exile is portrayed through stately, near-static dissolves, balanced a few scenes later by a contrived but lively song, 'Through Heaven's Eyes', played with humans rather than the dancing scorpions of an early draft. The Burning Bush and Angel of Death have a numinous power matching Miyazaki's recent *Princess Mononoke** (see the next entry). The Burning Bush

DIRECTOR Simon Wells, Brenda Chapman, Steve Hickner
PRODUCER Penney Finkelman Cox, Sandra Rabins
STORY Philip LaZebnik, Nicholas Meyer
SCORE Hans Zimmer
DESIGN Carter Goodrich, Carlos Grangel, Nicolas Marlet, Darek Gogol
ANIMATION Kristof Serrand, William Salazar, David Brewster, Serguei Kouchnerov

scene is uplifted by the sensitive animation of Moses drowning in light, drawn by British animator James Baxter. The Angel of Death that slaughters the first-born is a divine killer wind, realised through stark chiaroscuro drawings of blasted buildings.

Yet it's followed by *Prince*'s queasiest moment, as the freed Hebrews break into a song of joy while the audience is still digesting God's genocide. What worked in the intimate, rhythmic *Bambi** can't sugarcoat a harsh Bible epic whose dramatic arc is bleak. Moses and Rameses are spiritual brothers who start as chariot-racing buddies but end up parted by a pitiless sea, the defeated Rameses screaming 'Moses!' into the wind. As of writing, no other recent Hollywood cartoon has dared as much.

Princess Mononoke
Japan, 1997 – 133 minutes
Hayao Miyazaki
[Drawings with CGI]

In Hayao Miyazaki's *Princess Mononoke*, the hero is a warrior youth in a mythical, medieval 'Japan' not yet a nation; rather it's a fantasy bordering on Middle Earth and the Wild West. Clear-eyed Ashitaka's village is attacked by a monster, a massive bellowing boar that initially resembles a spider, made up of foul black worms leaping and writhing through the wilderness. Mostly hand-animated, the creature looks as unique as it sounds. Ashitaka slays the boar, but is cursed with a deadly scar. So starts his journey, as he rides out over a sweeping green landscape to learn what brought the monster home.

Ashitaka is young and earnest, but muted; he adds little colour to the world he travels. In Miyazaki's previous *Porco Rosso**, a romantic teen girl wished a grumpy old fighter pilot would live up to the stories she'd heard of him. In *Mononoke*, on the other hand, the innocent Ashitaka seems like a story-book figure even within the film's fantasy. The worldlier support characters view him with amusement and fascination (he even picks up girl groupies). It's indicated that Ashitaka is from an ancient tribe, already lost to Japanese history.

The film's forests are haunted by tree-spirits in the shape of capering white homunculi. Gods take the shapes of great wolves, boars and deer. A translucent giant strides through woods like an ethereal Godzilla while the spirits rattle their pebble heads. Amid the wonder, there's mythic violence; Ashitaka's curse lets him remove a bandit's arms with an *arrow*. The violence is fleeting (the film was rated PG in Britain without cuts) but this isn't *Spirited Away** or *My Neighbour Totoro**.

The wolves have raised a girl, Mowgli-style; she is San, or the Princess Mononoke. ('Mononoke' means ghost or spirit.) Ashitaka sees her by a river; her giant wolf mother has been shot, and San buries her face in its neck to suck out the poisoned blood. It contrasts with Disney's *Beauty and the Beast**, where Belle bathed the Beast's wounds to *stop* him licking them like an animal. San's feral femininity is 'naturally' sexual; *Mononoke*'s Japanese poster depicted her bloody glare. The gentle Ashitaka finds her heartbreaking, the yearning music telling his tale.

Yet San is limited too. She has the most power when she wears a clay face-mask, charging down a steep rooftop to attack the humans she hates. She and Ashitaka share only a few scenes that constitute a love story. They aren't unmoving, but they're distanced by the mythic tone, even when Ashitaka guilelessly calls San beautiful while she holds a knife to his throat. Like many Disneys, the leads are upstaged by everything else: earthy humans, angry monsters and the forest's mossy secret heart suggesting a cathedral and a womb.

Miyazaki traverses *Mononoke* in bold cuts, from a deer god padding silently on water to a samurai battle, or from charging monsters to a close-up of rain on stones. The film is about the conflict between humans and the elemental forces of nature, which Miyazaki had presented before in his 1984 film, *Nausicaa of the Valley of the Wind*. *Nausicaa* had a science-fiction setting, an alien Earth of huge fungi and insects,

DIRECTOR/STORY Hayao Miyazaki
PRODUCER Toshio Suzuki
SCORE Joe Hisaishi
ANIMATION Masashi Ando, Kitaro Kosaka, Yoshifumi Kondo, Shinji Otsuka, Masako Shinohara, Noriko Moritomo, Megumi Kagawa

but in both films, the idealist hero sympathises with the natural forces, while an older warrior seeks to destroy them.

That sounds like the plot of James Cameron's *Avatar**, but Miyazaki's 'older warriors' are tough women with strong morals. *Mononoke*'s Lady Eboshi is the decorous revolutionary head of a frontier foundry town. By the time San attacks, we know Eboshi saves prostitutes and tends to lepers, so we don't know who to root for. The neutral telling is reminiscent of Miyazaki's rival director, Mamoru Oshii, especially in the long passages where Ashitaka hears both the gods and humans present their causes.

One difference between *Mononoke* and *Nausicaa* is that the earlier film had a charismatic title heroine, voiced with gusto by Sumi Shimamoto. *Mononoke* splits Nausicaa into San and Ashitaka; San gets her love of nature, Ashitaka her fairness. But Nausicaa's charisma stays with Shimamoto, who returns in the Japanese voice-role of Toki, a feisty townswoman. She steals several moments, but her presence highlights what Miyazaki gave up for his reflective myth-making. Several of the other *Mononoke* actors are famed outside animation; the most striking is the cross-dressing 'actress' Akihiro Miwa, who voices San's wolf mother with a chilling laugh.

Many Miyazaki fans prefer *Nausicaa* to *Mononoke*, though neither film is wholly satisfactory. Miyazaki's vision can outstrip his resources; some of *Mononoke*'s later scenes, for example, have backgrounds that are jarring mixes of static, hand-animated and computer-mapped drawings. Miyazaki's definitive epic remains his 1,000-page comic version of *Nausicaa*, written from 1982 to 1994 and translated in seven volumes. It was here that some of *Mononoke*'s images – the foul curse-worms, the girl who selflessly sucks the blood of another – first originated.

The Rescuers

US, 1977 – 74 minutes
John Lounsbery, Wolfgang Reitherman, Art Stevens
[Drawings]

The Rescuers starts with pastel drawings by Disney animator Mel Shaw, showing a bottle drifting helpless through a stormy sea. It's a tempting metaphor for the Disney studio, ten years without Walt. In the summer of 1977, audiences saw and heard an Imperial battlecruiser howl overhead, a fantasy for pubescents who knew Disney as the tatty home of *The Love Bug* (1968) and *One of Our Dinosaurs Is Missing* (1975). *Variety* proclaimed *Star Wars* (1977) equal to the genius of Walt Disney. But when light-sabers and Darth Vader went up against cartoon mice and hag-ladies, surely it was *Disney* that was long ago and far away.

Actually, *The Rescuers* was popular and well reviewed, though it earned most of its money outside America (outdrawing *Star Wars* in France). No doubt some kids enjoyed both films. However, it's hard to imagine a playground Luke or Leia choosing to be Bernard, *The Rescuers*' timid mouse janitor (voiced by Bob Newhart), or the chic Miss Bianca (huskily voiced by Eva Gabor). Lucas had stolen the 'child in every adult' that Walt once cultivated.

Significantly, both Lucas and Spielberg drew on Walt's Old Testament giants: *Pinocchio**'s whale, *Fantasia**'s devil, *Sleeping Beauty*'s dragon (1959). For its part, *The Rescuers* climaxes with a lumpish scarlet harridan water-skiing through a swamp on the backs of her pet alligators and banging into a tin chimney. It was crassness unthinkable even in the slapstick-heavy *The Jungle Book** a decade earlier.

Thankfully the title mice have more charm. Bianca and Bernard are out to save Penny, a human girl trapped in a bayou swamp by the trashy Madame Medusa, who's plainly Cruella De Vil's brow-plucking slob sister. The animal cast is filled out by swamp critters, a stumblebum albatross and a bushy-tashed old cat, the last a self-portrait of animator Ollie Johnston.

Co-director John Lounsbery died of a heart attack during production, reminding the studio that the old guard was fading. Lounsbery, like Johnston, had been one of the 'Nine Old Men', Walt's favoured artists who shaped Disney from the 1940s. Another of the Nine, Milt Kahl, bowed out with Medusa; in his day, he'd drawn Jiminy Cricket and Shere Khan. Meanwhile, fellow veteran Eric Larson was supervising Disney's new artists, some of whom debuted on *The Rescuers*. They included Glen Keane (see p. 43), whose first Disney animation was of Bernard sweeping a floor. Don Bluth (see p. 183) drew the mice in a rainy zoo; his Bernard has the stagily studied cuteness that'd characterise Bluth's own films.

Most of *The Rescuers*' characters feel brassy or facile beside their predecessors, at least judged individually. Yet the film is well aimed at its audience of nostalgic parents and next-gen tots. Like *The Jungle Book*, its mawkishness is surprisingly melancholic. Penny's swamp prison is far less bad than Medusa's ruthless put-downs: 'What makes you think *any*one would want a homely little girl like you?' *One Hundred and One Dalmatians** had sophisticated suspense; *The Rescuers* goes for lurid but well-staged threats. Penny and the mice almost drown more than once; even a comic set piece with the mice trapped in an organ by

DIRECTOR John Lounsbery, Wolfgang Reitherman, Art Stevens
PRODUCER Wolfgang Reitherman
STORY Larry Clemmons, Ken Anderson, Vance Gerry, Frank Thomas
SCORE Artie Butler
ANIMATION Ollie Johnston, Milt Kahl, Frank Thomas, Don Bluth, John Pomeroy, Cliff Norberg

the gators is menacing. The mice are good 'parents', devoted to Penny, yet they're on her vulnerable level. If the film has a hidden message, it's that Penny must come up with their escape plan herself.

The Rescuers is mostly lifted by the easy chemistry between Newhart's and Gabor's Bernard and Bianca. 'Just went through a red light,' Bernard frets as the mice swoop through Manhattan on bird-back. 'Oh! I do that all the time, dahlink,' trills Bianca. The cartoon odd couple teaches children that adventures are both scary (Bernard) *and* enjoyable (Bianca). They would return in a thirteen-years-later sequel, *The Rescuers Down Under* (1990), which had showier effects but no sturdy story. *The Rescuers*' swamp setting came back in 2010's *The Princess and the Frog*.

Rock & Rule
Canada, 1983 – 77 minutes
Clive Smith
[Drawings with computer and live-action elements]

Watched now, *Rock & Rule* looks like part of the ragged cycle of ragged cartoon bids to attract older viewers to animation in the 1970s and 80s. However, the Canadian studio Nelvana had originally meant to make a children's film, building on Nelvana's half-hour TV specials. These included *The Devil and Daniel Mouse* (1978), an offbeat tale about a mouse singer who sells her soul to Beelzebub. The writer of this book saw it as a child, and was unnerved by the monstrous, many-formed demon that chases down the heroine. According to *Daniel Mouse*'s director, Clive Smith, its successor *Rock & Rule* began as a 'Grimm's fairy tale kind of story, and as it progressed it just got darker and darker'.

In *Rock & Rule*'s gloomy post-nuke America, humans are extinct. People are descended from dogs and rats, with sometimes rodent features, though they're minimised on the principals. Fading rock star Mok, energetically voiced by Don Francks (speaking) and Lou Reed (singing), wants to rule the planet by summoning a netherworld demon. He needs a diva singer's voice, but the feisty starlet he kidnaps isn't compliant and proves more capable than her male bandmates who rush to 'Nuke York' to save her.

The heroine is sung by Debbie Harry; her cocky love interest is sung by Robin Zander of Cheap Trick, with supporting numbers from Iggy Pop and Beloyd Taylor of Earth, Wind and Fire. All these names were dated by the time *Rock & Rule* opened, though the soundtrack holds up well enough, culminating in a high-powered Harry–Zander duet.

The film's impressive and embarrassing in equal parts, wonkily edited and narrated, and remorselessly juvenile. It actually seems better if you catch it midway through, as many viewers did on its TV airings after a minimal cinema outing. Beneath its clouds and synthesisers, though, it's refreshingly light-handed. The arch-fiend Mok introduces himself with an affable, 'Anyone want a beer?' and throws out laser-lights declaiming, 'My name is Mok, Thanks a lot!' Mok's egotism makes him a credible threat when he half-throttles the heroine and his frame-filling performance, drawn by Robin Budd, is perkily energetic.

The comic-book postures and gesticulations befit a far more likeable film than the nasty *Heavy Metal* (1981), or later slick and dull space adventures such as *Titan A.E.* (2000) and *Treasure Planet* (2002). *Rock & Rule*'s profanity and violence is tame now, but perhaps the film would have fared better in the 90s, following the success of *Akira**. The most memorable scene is the climax, where a slavering demon erupts from Hell and must be sung to death. Its tumescent texture was provided by cow brains on a rostrum, and the finale foreshadows *Akira* and Disney's *The Little Mermaid* (1989), where the fiend is a giant octopus.

Their common ancestor, though, is a glutinous, liquid behemoth called The Greedy in Richard Williams's 1977 *Raggedy Ann & Andy: A Musical Adventure* (see p. 205). Animator Tom Sito assisted on The

DIRECTOR Clive Smith
PRODUCER Patrick Loubert, Michael Hirsch
STORY Patrick Loubert, Peter Sauder, John Halfpenny
SCORE Patricia Cullen
DESIGN Frank Nissen, Louis Krawanga, Clive Smith
ANIMATION Anne-Marie Bardwell, Chuck Gammage, Dave Brewster, Frank Nissen, Robin Budd, Tom Sito

Greedy (primarily animated by Emery Hawkins), before co-creating *Rock & Rule*'s demon, and moving to *Mermaid* and other Disneys. Further down *Rock & Rule*'s credits, animator Roger Allers would one day co-direct Disney's *The Lion King**.

Rock & Rule is available on a two-disc DVD in America and Britain, including *The Devil and Daniel Mouse* TV special. The US – but not UK – DVD bundles in a slightly different cut of the film, screened on television by the Canadian Broadcasting Corporation.

Le Roi et l'oiseau/The King and the Bird
France, 1980 – 81 minutes
Paul Grimault
[Drawings]
[A 63-minute version of the film, disowned by Grimault, was released in 1953.]

Quoted in Michael Barrier's book, *Hollywood Cartoons*, the Disney animator Dave Hilberman said that Walt in his early days had firm ideas about cartoon scenery. 'He (Walt) emphasised it so many times. If you didn't know the backgrounds were there, they were good backgrounds.'

By Disney's feature films, though, scenery was taking on greater importance. *Snow White**'s grotesque, Rackham-esque trees showed the hand of Swedish illustrator Gustaf Tenggren, who also influenced the sliding planes and sloping architecture of *Pinocchio**'s Alpine village. Characters supposedly came first at Disney, but what of *The Old Mill* (1937) – probably Tenggren's first project – which made the edifice into a sensescent eco-sphere, roused to animist life by a storm? Two decades later, *Sleeping Beauty* (1959) wove backdrops and people into a single moving tapestry.

The French animator Paul Grimault went a step further. His film, today known as *Le Roi et l'oiseau*, let its characters be dwarfed by their background, for what a background it is. The story takes place in a castle the size of a city and the height of a mountain. The action alternates between courtly antics in stately rooms and runarounds on rooftops, Venetian canals that become waterfalls and mile-long stairways recalling the celestial escalator in *A Matter of Life and Death* (1946). The wicked king ascends to Olympian heights in his elevator, but it's a humble sweep and shepherdess – who enter the film by stepping from their paintings – who do the physical and spiritual climbing. In the sweetest interlude, they emerge from a chimney and sit on its top admiring the stars, an image from the Hans Christian Andersen story ('The Shepherdess and the Sweep') on which the film is loosely based.

The children are greeted by a bluff, portly bird – a mockingbird according to translations, like a burlesque Jiminy Cricket that capers and gesticulates and even presents the film in the first scene. Rather than conveying inner life, the characters' motions and emotions are elegantly studied, matched to the refinements of the score by Polish composer Wojciech Kilar. They belie a mad world where lions waltz, bowler-hatted policemen have wings and the king hides a big robot in the basement. (Not that he's the real king; in an odd story wrinkle, a wily royal portrait follows the shepherdess and sweep into the real world and dispatches his neurotically cross-eyed model.)

Grimault began the film in the late 1940s, collaborating with Jacques Prévert, the writer of *Les Enfants du paradis* (1945). On Grimault's account, he was removed from the project in 1950 by his producer, André Sarrut, who released a version of the film in 1953. Called *La Bergère et le ramoneur*, this version was indifferently dubbed into English with Peter Ustinov as the bird. Released under several names, it can be found on US DVD as *The Curious Adventures of Mr Wonderbird*.

Later, Grimault reclaimed the rights and negative, resuming work in 1977. His revision, *Le Roi et*

DIRECTOR/PRODUCER Paul Grimault
STORY Paul Grimault, Jacques Prévert
SCORE Wojciech Kilar
ANIMATION Marcel Colbrant, Alain Costa, Guy Faisien, Philippe Leclerc

l'oiseau, runs a quarter of an hour longer, but a comparison of the two versions doesn't support Grimault's claim to have stripped out a third of the old film. One big difference is the changed ending – *Wonderbird* has a conventional happy-ever-after, while *Le Roi et l'oiseau* ends on an angry symbolic note, with the giant robot crushing an empty cage. As well as fortifying some other scenes, Grimault inserts an arch, leisurely interlude in the first act, played out in dumb show, in which the king is silently offended by his new portrait. Like the new ending, it helps remove Grimault's film from Disney convention.

Le Roi et l'oiseau is available on a two-disc French DVD, which also includes *La Table tournante* (1988), a compilation of Grimault's shorts. There are no English subtitles, but the film can be easily followed without them. Outside France, *La Bergère et le ramoneur* was a profound influence on Japan's Isao Takahata and Hayao Miyazaki. Miyazaki homaged Grimault in his début, *The Castle of Cagliostro* (1979), though the Frenchman's legacy is equally visible in *Laputa**. Both directors destroy their hubristic worlds, but only after using them to lift us to the stars.

Le Roman de Renard/The Tale of the Fox
France, 1937 – 65 minutes
Ladislas and Irene Starewitch
[Stop-motion]

France's first feature animation, *Le Roman de Renard* was made nearly single-handedly by the stop-motion pioneer Ladislas Starewitch (born Wladyslaw Starewicz) and his daughter Irene, working at Starewitch's studio-home in Fontenay-sous-Bois. *Renard* premièred in April 1937, eight months before Disney's *Snow White**, though Starewitch had actually finished it back in 1930. Despite its long-delayed release, it may be the first feature to have an all stop-motion cast. (A 1935 Russian feature, *The New Gulliver*, blended live-action with stop-motion – see p. 103.)

Born in Moscow to Polish-Lithuanian parents, Starewitch started using stop-motion to simulate nature, not fantasy. He wanted to film stag beetles fighting, but they didn't perform under camera, so he animated their carcasses instead. In 1911, he made *The Cameraman's Revenge*, a startlingly modern comedy in which a vengeful grasshopper films a beetle *in flagrante delicto* with a dragonfly. Twenty years on, *Renard* has modernity overlap with nostalgia. A raspberry-blowing monkey hand-cranks a movie camera; then we leaf through a Disney-style story-book.

Unlike Disney fare, though, *Renard* is completely amoral. The story was based on a medieval fable that Disney considered but dropped; elements of it appeared in the studio's furry-animal *Robin Hood* (1973) after Walt's death. Notoriously, the same fable was reworked as an anti-Semitic Dutch cartoon, 1943's *About Reynard the Fox*.

In Starewitch's version, Renard (called Reynard in the DVD subtitles) is a vulpine aristocrat anti-hero who endlessly exploits and bamboozles the beasts of the animal kingdom. Starewitch's furry, oversized puppets (his 'Queen Lioness' stood fifty centimetres tall) will startle viewers weaned on the stop-motion of Henry Selick and Nick Park. *Renard*'s mammals bristle, drool and lick their lips. There are no saccharine doe-eyes, but tongues and teeth. The lion king sits on his throne in medieval regalia, as confrontational in close-up as King Kong. Renard's expressions recall Willis O'Brien's sneering Brontosaurus.

The most Gallic image is the needle-toothed cat serenading the moon-eyed lioness. The most disconcerting is a chick chirping 'Mama' beside the bones of one of Renard's victims. Other highlights include a rowdy drunken rabbit choirboy and a demented animal after-life of flying bunny heads and peeing beer-barrels. The narrative, however, is makeshift and repetitive, as Renard just fools the dumb animals over and over. Even when they besiege his castle (involving 273,000 puppet movements), it's just so they can be endlessly clonked on the head or knocked off the battlements.

Whereas Walt Disney was a beneficiary of sound, which he exploited in his seminal short *Steamboat Willie* (1928), sound stymied Starewitch. When he finished *Le Roman de Renard* in 1930, his producer Louis Nalpas meant to release it with a soundtrack on synchronised phonograph records, but the system became obsolete. Starewitch took back the film, and waited seven years until a German dub was created by UFA. The French

DIRECTOR/ANIMATION Ladislas Starewitch, Irene Starewitch
PRODUCER Louis Nalpas, Roger Richebé (French sound version)
STORY Jean Nohain, Antoinette Nordmann (French sound version), Ladislas Starewitch, Irene Starewitch
MUSIC Vincent Scotto

version was released by Roger Richebé, with music by prolific composer Vincent Scotto. It played to Occupation audiences, just as another trickster hero, the Monkey King, was playing to audiences in Japan-conquered China (see p. 137). Truly tricksters appear in times of need.

The Richebé version of *Le Roman de Renard* is available on French DVD, with English subtitles. But an arguably more iconic

Starewitch film is his short *The Mascot* (1933), whose revelry of demons, bones and bric-a-brac anticipates *Fantasia**, *The Nightmare before Christmas** and Jan Svankmajer. *The Mascot* is included on a US DVD, *The Cameraman's Revenge & Other Fantastic Tales*, which collects several Starewitch films, though not *Le Roman de Renard*.

A Scanner Darkly
US, 2006 – 96 minutes
Richard Linklater
[Rotoscoped animation]

The best-known Philip K. Dick adaptation is Ridley Scott's *Blade Runner* (1982), based on Dick's novel *Do Androids Dream of Electric Sheep?*. Its funniest scene is its opening, where an impatient interviewer psychoanalyses an apparent half-wit to check if he's human. (Spoiler: he's not.) The interviewer puts forth a hypothetical scenario, involving torturing a tortoise in a desert. 'A tortoise? What's that?' 'Do you know what a turtle is? Same thing.' 'Never seen a turtle.'

Richard Linklater's animation of Dick's novel, *A Scanner Darkly*, plays up this digressive humour, while bringing out the same concerns about our unreliable empathy towards turtles and people. Its first scene exemplifies our kindness to animals. A man, Freck (Robert Cochrane), finds segmented green bugs emerging from his scalp, running through his hair and over his arms as he dances a twitchy, whimpering fandango. But he's equally worried for his dog; he takes a bath with the puzzled animal, scrubbing it frantically. As Dick wrote in his book, 'It hurt to feel the dog suffer; he never stopped trying to help him.'

Freck is addicted to the drug Substance D, which stands for 'the desertion of your friends from you, you from your friends'. Two more addicts, Barris (Robert Downey Jr), and Luckman (Woody Harrelson) live in a bachelor crash-pad with its owner Arctor (Keanu Reeves). Their maundering, absurdum-on-absurdum dialogues take up much of the film. In one scene, Luckman collapses in their dirty shared kitchen. Barris watches; then he picks up a phone and fidgets girlishly while circumlocuting to the operator. ('I don't want to say that it's *not* cardiac arrest …'.) Barris, clearly, doesn't care about the world as he should. We've seen him rat on Arctor to a pair of disguised narc officers; but, in a Dickian turnabout, one of these officers *is* Arctor.

Mostly, though, we spy on Arctor's off-kilter consciousness, lost in the surveillance and double-crossing of the drug scene, in carnally frustrated love with a dealer (Winona Ryder) and brain-addled and bifurcated by Substance D. Arctor shields his police identity with a scramble suit, a sci-fi garment that makes him into a human kaleidoscope. Bits of faces – men, women, children, a glimpse of Dick himself – flicker through mix-and-match Identikits, while Arctor shrinks beneath. But he's not the only person with a scramble suit, and in an almost mellow scene of psycho-hazing – again, just two people talking, this time in an office – the suit declares what it always was: an unending acid trip.

'The whole process is hidden beneath the surface of our reality,' muses one of the few characters in the film who's *not* on drugs. Extending the conceit, the whole film is a rotoscoped mask for live-action, like *American Pop**, *The Polar Express** or the prince and princess in *Snow White**. Linklater called his version, 'interpolated rotoscoping'. In modern character animation, a computer can fill in frames between the main action poses, using software such as Flash or Toon Boom. Linklater used Rotoshop, a proprietary software developed by Bob Sabiston, to create transitory frames between tracings by *Scanner*'s artists. Prior to

DIRECTOR/STORY Richard Linklater
PRODUCER Anne-Walker McBay, Tommy Pallotta, Erwin Stoff, Palmer West, Jonah Smith
SCORE Graham Reynolds
DESIGN Bruce Curtis
ANIMATION Bob Sabiston, Jason Archer, Paul Beck, Sterling Allen, Evan Cagle, Nick Derington, Christopher Jennings, Lance Myers

Scanner, the technique was tried in Linklater's *Waking Life* (2001), a non-narrative film where people expound their philosophical creeds.

Linklater himself cameoed in *Waking Life*, presenting Dick's Gnostic notions on the world's unreality. But *Waking Life*'s world *was* clearly unreal. Eyes drifted off faces, backgrounds flapped loosely, abstraction dialled up and down. There were cartoon jokes and violent punchlines. In contrast, Linklater made *Scanner* to strict style guidelines, pushing for a liminally consistent world. *Scanner*'s texture is somewhere between a gloopily liquid oil painting and an expensive graphic novel, so even Arctor's scramble suit looks relatively mundane. The overt black outlines echo Disney's Xeroxed *One Hundred and One Dalmatians**. *Scanner*'s plot concerns the murky human soul, but a prop such as Arctor's car is geometrically rigid, unyielding. Linklater only lets his world slide occasionally in mellow counterpoint to the action.

'I think this animation process f***s with your brain in a really great way,' Linklater claimed, arguing that *Scanner*'s semi-reality was trippy enough. In his view, a woozier, *Waking-Life* approach would have pulled viewers out of the plot (already hard to follow) and out of the stoner camaraderie between the subdued Reeves and the live-wire Downey and Harrelson – though for my money, the star is Cochrane's twitchy, gauche Freck. These male friendships are at *Scanner*'s heart, even if they're only half-real like everything else. The treacherous Barris stays cool when his 'friend' Luckman collapses before him. Conversely, Arctor clings on to his consciousness of friends even when the poor guy's mostly gone, kneeling on the earth in a corrupt field of dreams.

The Secret Adventures of Tom Thumb
UK, 1993 – 61 minutes
Dave Borthwick

[Stop-motion and pixillated live-action. A short 'pilot' version was screened by the BBC Christmas 1988.]

Stop-motion is magic made nightmare. Screen sorcerers from Georges Méliès to Jan Svankmajer taught us that inanimate things dream of a twitchy, juddering dimension where time is twenty-four fleeting presents to a second. It can wear the goofy, crooked leer of King Kong; it can be brainless and headless, like the dancing chickens in the 'Sledgehammer' animated music video. In Christmas 1993, it had the baleful, yellow-beaked stare of a gangster penguin in Nick Park's *The Wrong Trousers* (1993) (see p. 219).

Park's wry but cosy film was screened in Britain on Boxing Day, two days after *The Secret Adventures of Tom Thumb* offered a shadow-world of buzzing insects, wriggly things, dark alleys and dirty houses. The worst monsters, though, were the *people*. They were plainly real actors; they were also not-quite-human Hogarthian proles who'd sipped a stop-frame elixir and moved in the slithy, time-lapsed way of drunk model dinosaurs. Long before Uncanny Valley, stop-motion animators travestied flesh-and-blood humans on purpose.

'When you read a kid a fairytale, it scares the shit out of them when they go to sleep, and the adults think they're doing a good turn,' said Dave Borthwick, *Tom Thumb*'s director.

> I wanted to turn the tables a bit, make a film that would affect adults that deeply … . Once you can put it in the past or future, you can say, 'Well, it's not here now so it doesn't bother us.' I tried to create a world you couldn't quite put your finger on, whether it was in the past, future or some really demented present.

Cartoons are often about underdogs. *Tom Thumb* is about abjects. Tom is a Pinocchio abortion, a puppet mutant sprog, the cute sibling of the *Eraserhead* baby (1976). He's raised by lumpen but loving giant parents, then taken by Men in Black and put in a Frankenstein torture-chamber. He escapes to an outside world of models like him, at which point the film feels almost like conventional stop-motion. However, Tom must return to giant-land, accompanied by a warrior called, with due irony, Jack. There's almost no dialogue, people grunting and mumbling in the manner of *One Million Years BC* (1966), or (Borthwick claimed) Bristol pub dialect.

Like *The Wrong Trousers*, *Tom Thumb* came from Bristol's burgeoning animation community, some of whom appeared as giants. Following the lead of 'Sledgehammer' (another Bristol production), *Tom Thumb* treats humans *like* stop-motion models, a process called pixilation. An actor splits an expression or action into twelve or twenty-four poses, holding still as each frame is shot. Borthwick found an action of five seconds could take three or four hours to complete.

DIRECTOR/STORY/DESIGN Dave Borthwick
PRODUCER Richard Hutchison
SCORE Startled Insects
ANIMATION Dave Borthwick, Frank Passingham, Lee Wilton, Cathy Price

Thesp actors found it difficult to grasp the idea of working in increments, so we ended up working with colleagues who understood the technique. We were lucky a lot of these people were quite weird-looking anyway, which we wanted for the film.

Despite his strangeness, Tom's father (Nick Upton) is a sympathetic presence with his string vest and beefy arms. Thanks to the pixilation, he can touch and hold Tom in the same stop-frame reality. All creatures are equalised; the omnipresent flies, squelched and mashed through the film, are beatified in the closing shot, while religious icons are mocked through a model of Santa on the cross (taken from a mythical Tokyo display). Like much Japanese animation, the blue-and-white cloudscapes give way to a transcendent coda, making it fitting that the film was distributed by Britain's Manga Entertainment.

The drawback is that solipsist, stylised mundanity often ends up feeling samey, especially in animation. Reviewers repeatedly linked *Tom Thumb* to the live-action *Eraserhead* and *Delicatessen* (1991), for which one could substitute any number of angsty festival animations. Technique aside, *Tom Thumb* is saved by its humour, grot and tenderness. In Borthwick's words, 'I see us as just scratching the surface of what a weird life really is.'

The Secret of Kells
Ireland/France/Belgium, 2009 – 75 minutes
Tomm Moore
[Drawings with CGI]

DIRECTOR Tomm Moore
PRODUCER Ivan Rouvreure
STORY Tomm Moore, Fabrice Ziolkowski
MUSIC Bruno Coulais
DESIGN Tomm Moore, Barry Reynolds, Jean Baptiste Vendamme
ANIMATION Fabian Erlinghauser, Nora Twomey, Alberto Cassano, Alessandra Sorentino

In the 2000s, cartoons sprouted virtual dimensions, and in 3D to boot. Irish director Tomm Moore wanted to move the other way, towards artistically animated *flatness*, but he didn't know how the *Shrek** generation would take it. A grown-up, Moore loved the 'boldness and designy-ness' of independent animators. 'But as a kid it seemed just weird,' he confessed, 'and I probably would have rejected much of it (for) something like the Don Bluth stuff.'

Bluth, a pretender to Disney's legacy (see the next entry), had set up a studio in Dublin in the late 1980s. It had one big hit, *The Land before Time* (1988). Bluth also helped start an animation course at Ballyfermot Senior College, where Moore graduated in the 90s after Bluth's studio had already closed down. Moore co-founded Cartoon Saloon, based in his hometown of Kilkenny, and began developing a feature. Les Armateurs, the French producers of *Belleville Rendez-Vous**, invested in the project. 'The sales boost that *Belleville* got from its [2003] Oscar nomination helped finance *Kells*,' Moore said. Meanwhile, the animator Michel Ocelot (*Azur & Asmar**) encouraged Moore to swim against the tide.

'The French producer really wanted me to push the designs further,' said Moore.

> I resisted at first, but then I met Ocelot on a trip to Paris and he said the same thing, that (the) designs were too Disney and traditional, that I should use the chance to do something different. That night I started sketching something really flat … I was aware the budget would be quite limited, so it made a kind of sense to push the design, as traditional designs animated on a budget can look really bad.

The production spread to studios in France, Belgium, Hungary and Brazil.

In *The Secret of Kells*, the drawn style *is* the subject. The setting is an Irish monastery weathering the Dark Ages, where monks struggle to preserve civilisation through illuminated manuscripts, the greatest of which is *The Book of Kells*. (The real book, Ireland's national treasure, is on display in Dublin.) Brendan, an orphan boy, is torn between two father figures. The heavy-handed, looming Abbot, voiced by Brendan Gleeson, wants the lad to succeed him. The jovial Aidan knows the boy is the artist to inscribe the Book's ornamental heart. With Aidan's encouragement, Brendan overcomes his fears and slips into the wild wood to meet Aisling, a quicksilver little-girl Puck, though her liking for Brendan seems partly maternal. (Aidan's character was inspired by Moore's kid sister, while Brendan himself was named for Moore's son.)

Medieval art had been the impetus for Disney's *Sleeping Beauty* (1959), but the film's fabulously stylised backgrounds (created by the painter Eyvind Earle) couldn't lift a plain Disney fairytale. Another mountain of cartoon design was Richard Williams's unfinished *The Thief and the Cobbler**, based on Persian art, whose story barely registered beside its mad-architect ornamentalism. Confined to a far- lower budget, Moore sought to mix lavish backgrounds with elegantly limited animation *à la* Genndy Tartakovsky, the creator of TV's *Dexter's Laboratory* (1996) and *Samurai Jack* (2001).

Kells is built from swirls and semi-circles, jigsaw-shape collages and a funhouse of perspectives disguised as flat backgrounds. Initially, it's a playful, endearing world, presented in an archetypal toon set-up: Brendan and his monk mentors chase a worried goose, and the multiformed mob pile up in a heap like Tetris shapes. Later, Aisling and Brendan climb a huge tree, only the tricksy perspectives make it as much a climb *into* the tree, finishing up in the fold of a curlicued manuscript letter. The film's second half is darker. A monster serpent is trapped in a circle and eats itself; Viking raiders are inhuman parallelograms, turning the world red. The interlacing designs encompass story and characters; even when the principals age, they do so by traversing a medieval stained-glass triptych.

The most unexpected design in the film is its downbeat arc. Brendan is helpless to stop a slaughter and flees Kells to become a wandering teacher of the living Book, whose pictures move like an intricate organism. For me, *Kells* felt awkwardly like part one of a longer story, perhaps a trilogy; though objectively it's no odder-shaped than some of the auteur Japanese films by Miyazaki and Oshii, which slot into larger oeuvres much as *Kells'* abstract shapes build into objects, people and more. As of writing, Moore is preparing his next feature, *Song of the Sea*: doubtless his designs will become clearer with time.

The Secret of NIMH

US, 1982 – 83 minutes
Don Bluth
[Drawings]

In the opening moments of Don Bluth's *The Secret of NIMH*, we're presented with a gnarled hand writing with a quill on parchment. Yet this antique craft is overlaid – some would say smothered – by razzle-dazzle. Rather than ink, the unseen writer uses what looks like glittering fairy-dust which flares on the page, then burns in the letters the hand has traced. What you think of *NIMH* may depend on whether you see this as vulgar kitsch or a lovely gilding.

Either way, it's a Spielbergian touch; and Spielberg liked *NIMH* so much that he executive-produced two of Bluth's later films, *An American Tail* (1986) and *The Land before Time* (1988). Both Spielberg and Bluth share a deep nostalgia for Disney animation circa 1940s *Pinocchio**, which Spielberg referenced in *Close Encounters of the Third Kind* (1977). Bluth himself had been a Disney animator, working there on and off since 1955 (his first work was on *Sleeping Beauty*, 1959). But according to John Taylor's book, *Storming the Magic Kingdom*:

> In 1979, Bluth walked out of Disney, complaining that the studio was skimping on the production values that made the classics so remarkable. Lakes no longer reflected their surroundings, raindrops no longer glistened when they hit the ground, curls of smoke no longer floated from fires … . Bluth also declared that Disney's stories had degenerated into saccharine mush, devoid of the dark undercurrent of fear, loss and death that linked the classics to traditional fairytales.

Many other Disney artists quit with Bluth, causing Walt's son-in-law, Ron Miller, to call him a son of a bitch. More temperately, Disney production chief Tom Wilhite said that, '(Bluth) seems to be obsessed with recreating the Disney of the Forties.' By implication, Bluth was competing not only with the *real* Disney classics (*NIMH* opened in Britain against a digitally re-recorded *Fantasia**), but also with the cyber-spectacles of Disney's *Tron* (1982).

Bluth fought back by pumping up his drawings. He used multiplane cameras and multiple passes to layer up his dense imagery, and backlit animation to create sparkling dewdrops and a shining magic amulet. Bluth claimed that the more stylised, graphic kinds of animation could never create life. 'An audience can't identify with a drawing,' he said, surprising anyone who remembered, for instance, the dogs in Disney's *One Hundred and One Dalmatians** (see also the previous entry on *The Secret of Kells**).

NIMH's setting is a farmer's field, where rodents wear clothes but a monster house-cat does not, as in Disney's *Cinderella**. The heroine is a fieldmouse, Mrs Brisby (understandably changed from 'Frisby' in the source book, *Mrs Frisby and the Rats of NIMH* by Robert C. O'Brien). To save her sick son, the widowed Brisby ventures into thorny, cobwebbed dragon's lairs, an owl's tree, a kingdom of rats. In an especially intense

DIRECTOR Don Bluth
PRODUCER Don Bluth, John Pomeroy, Gary Goldman
STORY Don Bluth, John Pomeroy, Will Finn, Gary Goldman
SCORE Jerry Goldsmith
ANIMATION John Pomeroy, Gary Goldman, Don Bluth, Lorna Pomeroy, Skip Jones

scene, she's attacked by a giant rat sentinel that wields a glowing sword. The second half of the film brings in SF and fantasy. The rats, it turns out, were mutated into higher beings by human experiments, with a lurid rodent transformation that purposefully recalls the queen-to-witch scene in Snow White*.

Judged against Bluth's own ambitions, NIMH fails. Neither Mrs Brisby nor her clownish crow sidekick voiced by Dom DeLuise (an interminable presence in later Bluth films), are compelling enough to compete with Disney's stars. Nor can they save a broken-backed story, which collapses into a sword-fight between half-baked secondary characters, only to bring Brisby back for a makeshift deus ex machina. Yet NIMH is more interesting than many sounder films. Making a widowed mother the protagonist is a bold move, with the anthropomorphism highlighting Brisby's struggles with her timorous mouse nature. The situation is powerful, though the character is not.

NIMH's visual ornateness is part of its overripe texture, together with Jerry Goldsmith's swelling score and Brisby's stagey but rather charming acting, which oscillates between grown-up and childish and recalls Hollywood acting before 1940. Her mouse children are indulgently saccharine (another pitfall in Bluth's later cartoons), but the film has thoughtful nuances for the real child viewers to pick up. For example, a dowager shrew is first introduced as a figure of fun, then matter-of-factly shown as braver than Brisby herself. It's the non-formula thinking, more than the sumptuous pictures, which make NIMH a precursor to better brand-breaking films: The Nightmare before Christmas*, The Iron Giant* and Toy Story*, all made by disgruntled Disney artists.

Shrek

US, 2001 – 89 minutes
Andrew Adamson, Vicky Jenson
[CGI]

A Disneyesque forest unspools on screen. A repellently cute squirrel prances over grass, collecting nuts. He's stopped by a disreputable red rodent, whose ungainly design and nasal tones have the aesthetic impact of Monty Python's foot. 'Hey, what kind of cartoon is this going to be anyway?' demands the newcomer. 'Well …', whines the nut-collector, cuddling his bushy tail in a masturbatory gesture, 'my name is Sammy Squirrel, and this story is about me and my cute furry friends …'. 'Oh, brother, not that!', exclaims the delinquent, leading Sammy behind a tree. Bang, bash, thump.

The scene is from a Tex Avery cartoon, *Screwball Squirrel* (1944), made half a century before *Shrek*. DreamWorks' film was praised for skewering the cutesy Disney formula, as *South Park: Bigger Longer and Uncut** had done two years earlier, as TV cartoons (*The Simpsons*, 1989–, *Animaniacs*, 1993–5) had done before that and as Avery had done before them all. What *was* new about *Shrek* – the fifth big CGI-animated feature, after two *Toy Story**s, *Antz** and *A Bug's Life* (1998) – was that the cartoon players were no longer rodents, toys or insects. Instead, they were near or actual humans, presented in what the DreamWorks studio's publicity called 'stylised realism'.

The title green ogre (Mike Myers with a brogue) enjoys a life of earthy hedonism. His swamp is invaded by a pestilence of fairytale characters ('Dead broad off the table!', Shrek snaps at seven dwarves bearing Snow White's casket). A tent-pole action sequence stars a bellowing hormonal dragon that falls, King Kong-style, for Shrek's sidekick Donkey (Eddie Murphy). A feisty princess, Fiona (Cameron Diaz), joins the fun and the loose later scenes become a star-crossed, shape-changing romance, echoing the live-action *Ladyhawke* (1985) and, more overtly, Disney's *Beauty and the Beast**.

All this is accompanied by family-friendly farting, belching and slick pop numbers. The CGI comprises lushly lambent scenery and quasi-human extras that hardly qualify for Uncanny Valley (see p. 157). *Shrek's* look was gulped down by the mainstream, while a vocal minority followed French animator Michel Ocelot (p. 37) who reportedly almost shrieked: 'Not that! I cannot watch it! I suffer because of the ugliness.' Backlashers complained of *Shrek's* numbing realism, lumpish designs and abjection of organic caricature.

The poison dwarf villain, Lord Farquaad (John Lithgow), brought further baggage. Anyone who read film magazines 'knew' that Farquaad (a name to swear by) was really a mockery of Michael Eisner, Disney's CEO, who'd usurped Walt's son-in-law in 1984. Eisner's team included Jeffrey Katzenberg, who oversaw Disney's revitalised animation until he fell out with Eisner a decade later. Katzenberg co-founded DreamWorks with Steven Spielberg and David Geffen, and promoted *Shrek* at Cannes (where it was the first cartoon feature to compete since 1953's *Peter Pan*). All of this made *Shrek* into Katzenberg's revenge on Eisner, whether Katzenberg meant it or not.

Yet *Shrek's* still funny minus the fart and Disney jokes. There's sound cartoon humour; at one point,

DIRECTOR Andrew Adamson, Vicky Jenson
PRODUCER Aron Warner, John H. Williams, Jeffrey Katzenberg
STORY Ted Elliott, Terry Rossio, Joe Stillman, Roger S. H. Schulman
SCORE Harry Gregson-Williams, John Powell
DESIGN Tom Hester, Raman Hui, James Hegedus
ANIMATION Tim Cheung, Paul Chung, Denis Couchon, Donnachada Daly, James Satoru Straus, Raman Hui

Shrek's characters skid down a slope, Fiona gracefully, Donkey like a four-legged snowball and the ogre like a slimy rock. More memorably, Fiona sings to a bluebird *à la* Snow White, and inadvertently blows it up. The joke is imperfect – the princess's power comes from nowhere, like her martial arts skills later on – but the best laugh's in the capper, when Fiona guiltily takes the bird's eggs and serves them up to her friends.

There are nastier jokes – many viewers don't spot what happens to the 'Mummy' of the Three Bears, reduced to a rug. But most of *Shrek*'s would-be subversive gestures are torturous or half-cooked, without the inspired fudging of *Antz*. The ethnic cleansing of the fairytale characters has undertones too dark for a summer comedy. (Ray Bradbury had poetically portrayed such a genocide in his story, 'The Exiles'.) *Shrek* starts with the bold declaration that fairytales are 'a load of …', but by the end Fiona has been transfigured into a buxom green-skinned cherub in a half-hearted stand against body fascism.

The film-makers talked of 'dialling' Fiona's realism up and down to achieve the desired stylisation, and it's striking how Shrek and his sweetheart can suddenly look startlingly real, as in a quiet supper scene where the blunt movements give way to nuance. As realism vies with CGI artifice, the scene is elevated like the CGI ballroom at the peak of *Beauty and the Beast*. The characters often look unstable in themselves, yet they inhabit their world compellingly. When Shrek and Donkey climb a sunflower-covered slope, it's to a new vantage point in vibrant virtual landscapes.

The ogre–donkey buddy story is more engaging than the heterosexual romance, thanks to the reliably hilarious exchanges between Myers and Murphy. *Shrek* queers itself as Donkey, imploring, rests his hooves on Shrek's chest: 'That's what friends do, they *forgive* each other!' The sequel, *Shrek 2* (2004) became the top-grossing animated film until *Toy Story 3* (2010), with a popular new character (Puss in Boots, voiced by Antonio Banderas) distracting from the largely rerun plot. *Shrek the Third* (2007), though lucrative, drained the franchise of spontaneity; *Shrek Forever After* (2010), ostensibly the last chapter, was an intermittent return to form.

Sita Sings the Blues
US, 2008 – 81 minutes
Nina Paley
[Flash animation with After Effects]

DIRECTOR/PRODUCER/STORY/
DESIGN/ANIMATION Nina Paley

Sita Sings the Blues is wondrously preposterous and whole-heartedly retro. It's full of curvy shapes and bouncing rhythms, all converging in a Betty Boop Hindu goddess. Any film that subjects vintage torch songs and cartoon styles to DIY karaoke needs no further reason to exist, but *Sita* is also an exegesis on broken love stories, personal and universal. *Sita* itself couldn't be any *more* personal. Its eighty-one minutes were entirely animated, edited, designed and written (barring the improvised vox pops) by its creator, American animator Nina Paley.

In *Sita*, blues songs 'tell' the story of the selfless wife of the heroic Rama in India's epic poem, the *Ramayana* (animated as an Indo-Japanese film in 1992). Paley's approach is illustrated by how she handles a titanic battle where Rama and his simian army carve up the demon forces of a ten-headed king. In Paley's version, hordes of critters move in simple videogame cycles that make even the pooling blood look cute. It could be *South Park* (1997), but for Paley's inability to produce a displeasing, halting or vulgar composition, while Sita trills, 'Who's that knocking at my door?' in the archived voice of jazz singer Annette Hanshaw. Imagine Peter Jackson possessed by the Fleischers *circa* 1930.

But *Sita*'s uniqueness lies in its synergy of devices used by umpteen other animators. Its collage-style sequences recall the humour of Britain's Bob Godfrey or Aardman's vox-pop stop-motions. A trio of unscripted Indians, represented by shadow puppets, debate the details of Rama's and Sita's story, filling in the screen with contesting images and annotations. The switches in style, from Fleischeresque caricatures to expressionless paintings, improve on the cheesy comic mutations ('superdeformities') in Japanese cartoons. An expressionist rotoscoped dance takes *Sita* into transcendental territory, like the 'Lucy in the Sky with Diamonds' scene in *Yellow Submarine**.

Submarine, though, was psychedelically ecstatic, while *Sita*'s fiery dance expresses the heartbreak and trauma of a woman dumped. Yet it has its own masochistic exaltation. Paley extends Sita's story to herself in autobiographical interludes, which she draws in loose lines and colours recalling Godfrey's *Roobarb* (1974). It's a sketchier reality than the *Ramayana*, but Nina and Sita are similarly dropped by their men through no fault of their own (Nina via an email from her animator husband). The director presents her heartbreak as tragicomedy, deflecting any self-importance, before universalising her experience into dance.

But it's the *Ramayana* sections that dominate the film. The jointed flat Flash figures, in which Sita's spherical breasts are as pictorially fundamental as Mickey Mouse's ears, recall the paper cut-outs in Lotte Reiniger's *The Adventures of Prince Achmed**, the first cartoon feature authored by a woman. But *Sita* is as representative of the strong women's voices in animation today. It won Best Animated Feature at Annecy in 2008, a year after Britain's Suzy Templeton had taken the short-film honours for her stop-motion *Peter and the Wolf*, while Marjane Satrapi's *Persepolis** had shared the Jury Prize at Cannes.

Not that Paley shows herself strongly. In a drawn-from-reality scene, the cartoon Nina (voiced by Paley) hysterically begs her ex to take her back. We cut to the three *Ramayana* commentators – two men and a woman – debating Sita's loyalty to Rama. The men say that Sita should move on, while the woman speaker invokes unconditional love. 'This is the part of the female perspective I disagree with,' one man complains. Paley the director chooses sympathy over closure, signing off with a wink from Sita, whose story Nina is reading at the end.

After winning a plethora of awards and plaudits, *Sita* fell foul of the rights to sync Hanshaw's songs to a moving picture ('sync rights'). Because of them, the film was denied a theatrical release. Paley points out these rights are held not by the singer's estate (Hanshaw died in 1985), but by corporations hoarding her music. For Paley, *Sita* depends on Hanshaw's songs dovetailing with the *Ramayana* with no causal or cultural link, so it would be pointless to use new songs.

Sita cost $200,000 (Paley's money plus donations and grants), yet the director released it free online, hoping her audience would support her. 'Annette Hanshaw's recordings got locked up so that no-one could hear them,' Paley says. 'I didn't want that to happen to my film.' A *Sita* DVD is now available.

The Sky Crawlers
Japan, 2008 – 122 minutes
Mamoru Oshii
[Drawings and CGI]

One of Japanese animation's most familiar visual tropes is the brilliant blue sky, dotted with white clouds. In Mamoru Oshii's *The Sky Crawlers*, it's a heavenly vault suggesting Elysium or Valhalla, where ageless warriors have brief and bloody duels in fighter planes, the battles recurring into timelessness. The celestial impression is heightened by the harp music of composer Kenji Kawai, Oshii's regular collaborator.

Fans of Oshii and Japanese animation won't necessarily like *The Sky Crawlers*, a leisurely low-key SF drama closer to *Moon* (2009) or *Gattaca* (1997) than to Oshii's worldwide hit, *Ghost in the Shell* (1995) (see p. 78). The air battles are beautiful but brief, and largely impersonal. If *The Sky Crawlers* isn't conventionally anti-war – Oshii glumly suggests that conflict is an immovable part of the human psyche – then it's emphatically anti-action. In *Ghost in the Shell*, a nude cyborg doll with a human soul dived from a skyscraper and was broken by a tank. These dispassionate images became pop-culture emblems, symbols of what Japanese animation 'was'. It's unlikely that *The Sky Crawlers*' CGI plane battles will become such icons, or that Oshii meant them that way.

The narrative is a mystery, a parable and a convoluted love story. Yuichi, a young fighter pilot, arrives at a small airbase. It's seemingly Europe a few decades ago, with an American-style diner nearby (the scenery was based on Ireland and Poland). Yuichi's memories are vague, as is his awareness of who and why he's fighting, though he's curious about his female CO, Suito (voiced by *Babel*'s Rinko Kikuchi), and the pilot he's replaced. Off the base, he's approached by a tattooed woman, more courtesan than prostitute. In bed, she comments on his innocent face; he blandly says he's just a kid. Later he asks a condescending older officer whether someone who might die tomorrow need grow up. Gradually we learn that Yuichi, and most of the other characters, aren't human but 'Kildren', artificial people in perpetual adolescence, fighting humans' wars.

The Sky Crawlers is divisive; it asks audiences to accept a serious drama within the tropes of SF, the anime medium and Oshii's neutral, walking-pace storytelling. (The first *Ghost in the Shell* was already slow and lyrical; *The Sky Crawlers* has less action and runs forty minutes longer.) Except in the last scenes, Oshii evokes emotion and pathos less through the principals' bland faces or their more expressive voices than through the small details; a disconsolate-looking man who sits outside the diner (joined later by another character), or a mordant visual joke when Yuichi and another pilot sit on playground rides meant for 'real' kids, bouncing blankly up and down. In the sky battles, Oshii shows us what *he* wants to show, not what we want to see. In the biggest battle set piece, he sets up lovely patterns of planes in formation, but soon cuts to screens of words and symbols when the fighting starts.

Such ploys are foreshadowed in Oshii's former films, going back to his early fantasy comedy, *Urusei Yatsura 2: Beautiful Dreamer* (1984), about characters in an infinite dream. This situation is increasingly

DIRECTOR Mamoru Oshii
PRODUCER Tomohiko Ishii
STORY Chihiro Ito
SCORE Kenji Kawai
DESIGN Tetsuya Nishio
ANIMATION Toshihiko Nishibuko, Akira Honma, Asako Nishida, Atsuko Nakajima, Atsushi Takeuchi

echoed in *The Sky Crawlers*' limbo present, which also takes strands from Oshii's *Patlabor 2* (1993) about what the director sees as the chimeric notion of world peace. Yuichi's ambiguous state recalls the cyborg heroine's in *Ghost in the Shell*, who feared that 'the real me died a long time ago'. *The Sky Crawlers*' post-credits epilogue, which viewers are liable to miss, offers not closure but renewal.

As usual with Oshii, there's an adorable basset hound (based on the director's beloved dog); characters musing on the strangeness of an existence they can't change; and slips into extended static monologues. Oshii keeps these back for the last act, where they're mostly delivered by female characters, though Yuichi reflects on what he's learned in a final voice-over. Overall, *The Sky Crawlers* is less about Yuichi than the women moved, in different

ways, by what he unknowingly represents. In a moment of melodrama rare for the director, Yuichi and Suito embrace *while* grappling over a gun, which Suito is desperate to use. Suito is mostly a doll-figure on which Oshii projects a scrutable humanity, like the cyborg in *Ghost in the Shell*, but her few human expressions animate her to pungent effect.

The film blends simple characters and handsome semilit interiors with near-photoreal CGI for the sky scenes. It won't please everyone; older Japanese animated films such as *Wings of Honneamise* (1987) and *Porco Rosso** created their superlative flight scenes by hand. However, I found *The Sky Crawlers*' hybrid style easy to accept, and far less jarring than Don Bluth's space film *Titan A.E.* (2000), or 2008's clumsily 'revised' version of *Ghost in the Shell*.

Snow White and the Seven Dwarfs
US, 1937 – 69 minutes
David Hand (supervising director)
[Drawings]

Disney's *Snow White* starts with a castle on the hill, foreshadowing *Citizen Kane*'s Xanadu (1941). In the latter film, we pass through a window to find a dying man dropping a snow-globe to smash on the floor. But Walt, too, had to show his fantasy world's fragility. In *Snow White*'s opening minutes, he presents his sweet princess in a typical cartoon situation, comforting a baby bird. Behind her, a huntsman approaches, face set and eyes fixed. His arm comes up, holding a knife.

And then, of course (*of course* in hindsight, though it's far less obvious when you're watching the film), the huntsman relents, drops his knife and lets Snow White flee. 'Everyone in this world was once a child,' Walt told Cecil B. DeMille in a radio talk.

> We grow up, our personalities change, but in every one of us something remains of our childhood … where all of us are simple and naive, without prejudice or bias. In planning a picture, we don't think of grown-ups and we don't think of children, but just of that fine, clean, unspoiled spot deep down in every one of us.

Snow White, or Rosebud.

'What funny names for children!', laughs the princess when she enters the dwarfs' cottage and sees their miniature beds. Then blobby noses pop up one by one over the bedsteads: 'Why, you're little men!' But she could have been right the first time. The bald-pated dwarfs resemble bearded babes (most nakedly the mute clown Dopey) or *Peter Pan*'s 'Lost Boys', needing to be told to scrub for dinner or go to bed. Their dialogue is rarely over children's heads; even when they mine for riches, they 'don't know what we dig 'em for'.

Snow White is also infantilised, but Grim Natwick, one of her animators and Betty Boop's designer, wanted a more womanly character who sometimes breaks through in the drawing. The historian John Canemaker flags a scene where she prepares a gooseberry pie. Significantly, she's making it for the misogynist Grumpy, with whom she has the most ambiguous relationship; mother, daughter or …? Unlike rival cartoons, which thrived on transsexuality (Bugs Bunny) or even bestiality (Tex Avery's anti-Disney *Red Hot Riding Hood*, 1943), *Snow White* sublimates such notions, using Prince Charming for that purpose.

Disney also blurs child–adult distinctions, taking startling swings into horror. Few film moments are more deliciously chilling than the evil Queen, her lovely, haughty face reflected in a bubbling glass, breathing, '*Now … begin thy magic spell*', then drinking deep and turning into a monstrous hag. Walt's four-year-old daughter, Diane, bawled at the scene. Nine years earlier, Walt had been relieved to hear audiences chuckling at *Steamboat Willie* (1928), his first sound short. Now he'd made a cartoon which – to paraphrase Edward van Sloan in *Frankenstein* (1931), one of *Snow White*'s likely influences – thrilled people, shocked them, even *horrified* them.

DIRECTOR David Hand
STORY Ted Sears, Richard Creedon, Otto Englander, Dick Rickard, Earl Hurd
SCORE Frank Churchill, Leigh Harline, Paul Smith
DESIGN Albert Hurter, Joe Grant
ANIMATION Hamilton Luske, Fred Moore, Bill Tytla, Norman Ferguson, Frank Thomas, Les Clark

It also made them sob, during the star-studded Hollywood première at the Cathay Circle Theatre. Snow White's teary elegy, as the dwarves mourn her in their darkened cottage, was animated by Frank Thomas. Later he would be known as one of Disney's 'Nine Old Men'; then he was in his twenties. His scene is famously subdued and brief, before the coming of spring and resurrection. But the rest of the film is a grand-standing performance; the posturing Queen, the singing princess, the wildly dancing (and yodelling!) dwarfs. Audience surrogates are constantly on screen, applauding, cowering, sneering (Grumpy grouches 'Mush!' during Snow White's love song) or plain enraptured. Even the Queen glowers from a window, and Snow White cringes from bodiless watching eyes in her forest nightmare.

Snow White's legend is festooned by tales of Walt's performances of the evolving story, acting each role from dwarf to Prince. He himself described showing the unfinished film to a sceptical banker, filling in the missing drawings with his sweat and oratory. Exaggerated or not, these tales suggest, as Neal Gabler argues, a man straining to embody himself in a film he couldn't actually draw. After Walt's death, revisionists argued he was the depthless Prince beside his animators' toiling dwarfs. Considering Snow White's torturous production, though, the critic Michael Barrier claimed it was 'not a story of how (Walt) Disney's men realised his conception … but of how Disney himself recovered from (his) potentially fatal mistakes and wound up making a much better film'.

For today's audiences, the great mistake may be the heroine's relentlessly winsome cuteness in the first twenty minutes, when she and the animals must carry the action before the dwarfs appear. But for animators and critics, the debate – as heated now as it was in 1937 – swirls round Snow White's pollution of cartoon with live-action. The film is a fairytale, but with realistic textures and illusory third dimensions. When characters proved hard to animate, Disney filmed actors as stilted motion references, the live-action footage guiding the artists. It's plainest with the affectlessly traced Prince Charming, who takes Snow White to his cloud-castle at the end. It's as if they're transcending lowly cartoon business, like Dopey chasing a soap bar, or Grumpy's halting, thready smile as he stomps away from Snow White's kiss.

Son of White Mare
Hungary, 1981 – 85 minutes
Marcell Jankovics, Elek Lisziak
[Drawings]

In one of its issues, [the animation journal] *Animafilm*'s editor asked three Hungarian animators what they thought was the special characteristic of the Hungarian school of animation. To his surprise, the interviewees replied that, to the best of their knowledge, no such school existed; nor was there any endeavour that they knew of to found such a school. They said that the individual artists and groups of film-makers, the small studios, producers and artists that worked in Pannonia Film Studio formed a new type of staff; they were seeking to differ from, not resemble, one another.

DIRECTOR Marcell Jankovics, Elek Lisziak
PRODUCER Emoke Marsovszky
STORY Marcell Jankovics, László György
SCORE István Vajda
DESIGN László Hegedus
ANIMATION Marcell Jankovics, Edit Baksa, Edit Szalay, János Uzsák

So reported *Hungarofilm Bulletin* in 1980. It was a time when, unnoticed by most of the world, Hungarian animation was going into overdrive, led by the state-funded Pannonia studio. Formed in 1951, Pannonia was invigorated by the sixties boom in TV animation, but it never abandoned cinema. Older viewers may remember *Hugo the Hippo* (1973), a nightmarish piece of *Yellow Submarine** psychedelia co-produced with America and designed by British illustrator Graham Percy. The writer of this book remembers *Hugo*'s heroes being assailed by an army of killer vegetables.

By 1980, Pannonia had released a contemporary adult cartoon musical (1979's *Foam Bath*, by György Kovásznai), and was embarking on the science-fiction *Time Masters* with France's René Laloux (see p. 69). It was also making *Heroic Times* (1983), a glass-painted medieval saga by József Gémes. From 1980 to 1989, Pannonia released around *twenty* animated cinema features, a rate probably unmatched by any other studio in the world.

Son of White Mare, though, was particularly auspicious. It was directed by the polymath artist Marcell Jankovics, an author and illustrator who'd joined Pannonia in 1961, a year after leaving secondary school. He made countless TV animations, a clutch of acclaimed independent shorts (including the brutally visceral *Sisyphus*, 1975) and a celebrated cartoon feature, *Johnny Corncob* (1973).

Its successor, *Son of White Mare*, is shocking, not because of its violence or subject, but because of its visual presentation. As Amid Amidi, the author of *Cartoon Modern*, said, it seemed impossible that a feature could be so visually *intense* throughout its length. Peter Chung, the creator of the series *Æon Flux* (2005), described *Mare* as a model of pure animation design. The film's unforgiving day-glo palette makes *Yellow Submarine* look muted. The hero's face burns gold against inky blues and throbbing rainbows; the characters' features and clothes are simple blobs of colour. Everything on screen is subsidiary to patterned near-symmetries, which morph liquidly and are stuffed with *single-entendre* fertility symbols. Nor is the soundtrack any softer, consisting of arid electronic ambiences by Istvan Vajda. Only the curvy motions of the flat graphics are conventionally pleasing, though Jankovics opposed toon caricature.

The story is an archetypal hero's journey. The titular white mare nurtures its human child in the hollow of a shining world-tree, thrown up by her birth-agony. She even lets herself be drained dry so her Herculean son ('Treeshaker') can fulfil his world-healing quest. This takes the form of a journey to the underworld, playing out in threes: three monsters, three princesses and so forth. *Mare* is one of the least-populated fantasies on screen; there are no extraneous crowds to distract from the magnificent monsters. The critic Michael Barrier wrote of Tex Avery's cartoon *King-Size Canary* (1947) that its comedy was 'as cold and impersonal as an asteroid hurtling through space'. The same is true of Jankovics's heroic archetypes. (The director has written extensively on mythology; one of his studies, *Book of the Sun*, is available in English.)

Mare's closest analogues are the stylised fairytales of Michel Ocelot (p. 37), the gentle French director of *Kirikou and the Sorceress* (1998) and *Azur and Asmar**. But *Mare* has no time for restful beauty.

'Without poetry, I feel the genre of cartoons is dead,' claimed Jankovics, but *Mare* is as rude as it's ornate. Robert Zemeckis's animated *Beowulf* (2007) would give us a puerile *Austin Powers* (1997) routine to spare us the hero's manhood, but Treeshaker's sword-phallus is as upfront as the Cerne Abbas giant. The many-headed monsters include a tank-creature festooned with gun-ports. Only at the end can a woman tame the hero-beast, with a last peacock collage that wouldn't look out of place in *Yellow Submarine*.

Jankovics's fourth feature, the long-awaited *The Tragedy of Man*, may be released by the time this book is published. Even before the fall of Communism, privatised outfits had altered Hungary's cartoon landscape, such as Varga Studios, which animated *The Simpsons*' (1989–) 'Do the Bartman' video. One of the most successful Hungarian cartoons of recent years is *The District* (2005) by Aron Gauder, a scabrous, rap-flavoured portrait of Budapest that sold over 100,000 tickets.

South Park: Bigger Longer and Uncut
US, 1999 – 78 minutes
Trey Parker
[CGI]

In *The Simpsons Movie* (2007), Homer shouts, 'I can't believe we're paying for something we get on TV for free! If you ask me, everybody in this cinema is a giant sucker! Especially *you*!' If so, it wasn't the first time. Eight years before, another TV spin-off, *South Park: Bigger Longer and Uncut*, had mocked its paying audience. Its horrid little blobby boys – Cartman, Stan, Kyle and the perpetually doomed Kenny – are barred from a film with naughty language. 'Ah, screw it, it probably isn't that good anyway,' rasps Cartman (voiced by director Trey Parker). 'The animation's all crappy.'

American TV toons have been blown up on the big screen since the 1960s, when Hanna-Barbera released *Hey There, It's Yogi Bear!* (1964) and *The Man Called Flintstone* (1966). Forty years later, though, it was the *grown-ups* going to the big-screen spin-offs. The *South Park* film was R-rated in America; *The Simpsons Movie* was PG-13. The drawings were still crude, but now they stood for huge commercial brands; or for the fervent fans, they were ironic reflections of the postmodern *Zeitgeist*. *The Simpsons Movie* teaser rubbed it in. 'In a time when computer animation brings us worlds of unsurpassed beauty ... . One film dares to be ugly!'

The prosecution claims that *The Simpsons* and *South Park* (and the subsequent *Family Guy*, 1999) aren't cartoons at all. Rather, they're illustrated radio, utilitarian pictures garnishing the prose of non-animators. Even the 'spectacles' in the films, such as *South Park*'s descent into Hell, aren't there to awe the audience, but to spoof cheesy live-action blockbusters. (The phrase 'illustrated radio' was coined by Chuck Jones, talking about the TV product swamping cartoons from the 1950s.)

It's an unquantifiable, unresolvable argument. Are cheap images a *material* part of a talk-led cartoon? For some, *The Simpsons*' banana-skin family and *South Park*'s carelessly bouncing cut-outs are as integral to their charm as the crafted retro stop-motion of *Fantastic Mr Fox**, another animated sitcom for adults. Moreover, even the crass cartoons have moments of high-speed lunacy beyond other media. Witness Bart Simpson's nude skateboarding in *The Simpsons Movie*, or Cartman's world-spanning performance of 'Kyle's Mom Is a Big Fat Bitch!', which is one long raspberry to Disney's 'It's a Small World'.

The defence might call Bob Godfrey, creator of Britain's *Roobarb* (1974) and the Oscar-winning *Great* (1975). 'A lazy animator will find good ways of not animating,' he said in 2006.

> I don't think animation is king, I think it's the second or third priority after whatever you're putting over. You put anything in the pot that contributes to the stew, cut-outs and photos, jumbled together ... . I call animators ballet dancers because they don't give a damn about the audience, all they care about are beautiful movements. Animation has to work the crowd, get to the audience.

DIRECTOR Trey Parker
PRODUCER Trey Parker, Matt Stone
STORY Trey Parker, Matt Stone, Pam Brady
ANIMATION Eric Stough, Martin Cendreda, Toni Nugnes, Fred Baxter, John Fountain

In feature form, *South Park* scores over *The Simpsons* in all the non-animated departments. Its jokes cohere far better, its songs are disarmingly excellent and its satire has grown more pungent since 9/11. The 'plot' involves America attacking Canada in reprisal for two foul-mouthed comedians (series regulars Terrance and Phillip) who've taught the South Park kids such useful phrases as 'donkey-raping shit-eater'. According with Aristotelian unity, Cartman saves the world by zapping Saddam Hussein with the filthy language he's learned.

From its dead-on spoof of the 'Belle' opening number in *Beauty and the Beast**, the score slams Disney formula, giving Satan a wistful 'I Want' number about ascending from Hell ('Up there, there is so much room/ Where babies burp and flowers bloom ...'). 'La Resistance' goes to Disney's Broadway sources to mock *Les Miserables*, but the film's catchiest song is the happily racist 'Blame Canada' ('They're not even a real country anyway ...'). After all that, the finale is surprisingly sweet, with nearly everyone getting a happy end – even if the uplifting moral *is* delivered by a giant, talking clitoris.

Spirited Away
Japan, 2001 – 124 minutes
Hayao Miyazaki
[Drawings with CGI]

DIRECTOR/STORY Hayao Miyazaki
PRODUCER Toshio Suzuki
SCORE Joe Hisaishi
ANIMATION Masashi Ando, Kitaro Kosaka, Megumi Kagawa, Takeshi Inamura, Atsuko Tanaka

As of writing, Hayao Miyazaki's *Spirited Away* is the top-grossing foreign-language film in the world, excluding Mel Gibson's *The Passion of the Christ* (2004), which was mostly in dead languages. *Spirited Away* was also the first non-Hollywood cartoon to win a Best Animated Feature Oscar, in 2003. True, there was no competing Pixar cartoon that year. For all John Lasseter's praise of his friend's film, could *Spirited Away* have beaten *Finding Nemo** or *The Incredibles**?

We'll never know. When *Spirited Away did* win the Oscar (on the heels of a Berlin Golden Bear, shared with Paul Greengrass's *Bloody Sunday*), Miyazaki fans celebrated the master's entrance onto the world stage. Yet it was, in some ways, an illusion. After the win, Disney (the film's US distributor) increased *Spirited Away*'s Stateside release, but it was wasted money. *Spirited Away* grossed a pitiful $10 million in America, having made more than twenty times that in Japan.

Nonetheless, mainstream critics had a new reference point in Japanese animation, supplanting *Akira**, *Ghost in the Shell* (1995) and *Pokemon* (1998). In Britain, *Spirited Away* opened a fortnight after Sylvain Chomet's *Belleville Rendez-Vous**. Together, the films helped spark the idea of a new wave of personal, surprising cartoons that were anti-Hollywood and anti-CGI (though both Miyazaki and Chomet use CGI in places).

In Japan, *Spirited Away* had come about during an uncertain time for its production studio, Ghibli. Miyazaki had been meaning to retire, and all the signs were his successor would be his friend and protégé Yoshifumi Kondo, the director of *Whisper of the Heart**. But Kondo died suddenly in 1998, and Miyazaki returned to work. For a time, he developed a period drama called *Rin the Chimney Painter*, but his producer, Toshio Suzuki, doubted if it would click with a twenty-first-century audience. Instead, he advised Miyazaki to make a film for the traditional cartoon audience: children.

Spirited Away tells the story of Chihiro, a little girl spirited to a magic world. Unlike the brave heroines of Miyazaki's previous films, Chihiro is passive, scared and listless. She's kicked into an adventure for her own good, stumbling into a haunted town, both quaint and otherworldly, where her materialistic parents turn into pigs. Chihiro is a sketchy protagonist by Miyazaki standards, but then it's enough for her to be amazed and vulnerable, conveying the peril and wonder of her journey.

And what a journey it is. It takes her though an old-fashioned palatial Japanese bathhouse that's domestic and epic, playful and menacing, catering for Japan's animist gods. The bathhouse draws on 'pseudo-Western' buildings from the pre-World War II decades when Japan modernised and Westernised; Miyazaki chose the style 'to make it ambiguous whether it was dream or reality'. The building holds a grumpy overworked spider-man with extendable arms, his squad of toiling soot-sprites, a witch like a Victorian ogre, a serpentine dragon, walking frogs and a shapeless, gurgling monster called No Face who takes a sinister interest in Chihiro.

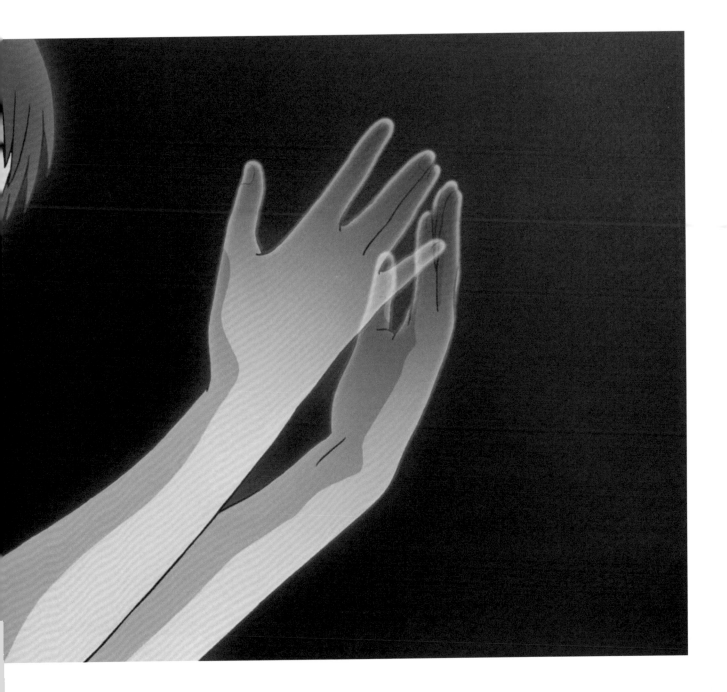

Miyazaki is notorious for starting his films before he's fixed his storylines. With *Spirited Away*, he changed his story during production when his first outline threatened to become a three-hour movie. We've barely found our feet before the story swings another way; Chihiro all but forgets her parents and starts a quest to save a mysterious magic boy who saved *her*. Towards the end, she gains the clear, resolute gaze of other Miyazaki protagonists, as she crosses the sea on a magic train.

Spirited Away is one of several films using animation to depict the power of memory. *Waltz with Bashir** and the films of Satoshi Kon (p. 212) highlight memory's subjectivity, as do shorts such as John Canemaker's autobiographical *The Moon and the Son* (2005). *Spirited Away*, though, focuses on a *collective* memory of an almost-forgotten Japan. The bathhouse was modelled on a Tokyo restaurant-hotel from the 1920s, but Miyazaki was more moved by 'old shops with decorative fronts', like those in the haunted town. The nostalgia overwhelms but sustains Chihiro, symbolised in the homely riceballs that she eats, sobbing, in a scene personally animated by Miyazaki.

Talking about one of his earlier films, *Porco Rosso** (which was set in Europe *circa* 1930), Miyazaki said there was 'something stirring' about the impossibility of returning to the past. He also acknowledged that foreigners who knew nothing of *Spirited Away*'s lost scenery would be on a level with Japanese children – his target audience – who were too young to recognise it. In his book, *Starting Point*, he links adult nostalgia to the humility of childhood. He speculated that, 'a sense of nostalgia is not simply something we acquire as adults, that it indeed may be a fundamental part of our existence from the very beginning. When I was a child and gradually expanding the range I dared travel from my home, I once found myself standing in an unknown part of town, overcome simultaneously by forlornness and homesickness.'

The point was developed in a very different Japanese animation a few years later. In the CGI adventure *Vexille* (2007), directed by Fumihiko Sori, an American woman soldier comes to a devastated future Japan. She finds a scrap of its heritage, a marketplace that might have come from *before* Japan's Westernisation. Surveying the bustling scene, the heroine is puzzled; she says it makes her 'nostalgic somehow'.

Summer Wars
Japan, 2009 – 114 minutes
Mamoru Hosoda
[Drawings with CGI]

DIRECTOR Mamoru Hosoda
STORY Satoko Okudera
SCORE Matsumoto Akihiko
DESIGN Yoshiyuki Sadamoto, Takashi Okazaki, Mina Okazaki, Tsuyoshi Hamada, Anri Kamijo
ANIMATION Hiroyuki Aoyama, Kunihiko Hamada, Kazutaka Ozaki, Shigeru Fujita, Tatsuzou Nishida

Japan's *Summer Wars* is a family comedy-drama that finds room for teen tensions and romance, the reconciliation of old and new Japan, the survival of love after death, a zippy virtual-reality universe, epic videogame battles and a goofily old-school 'teen whizzkid threatens civilisation' plot going back to the likes of the live-action *WarGames* (1983).

A hybrid with heart, *Summer Wars* is the successor (though not sequel) to *The Girl Who Leapt through Time**. It shares many of the same creative credits, including the director Mamoru Hosoda, and is just as accessible to outsiders. Though this is still a Japanese cartoon: wholesome by any live-action standard, but with a handful of gags and more sombre developments that you just wouldn't find in a Pixar, DreamWorks or Disney film *circa* 2009.

Summer Wars' protagonist is a boy, seventeen-year-old Kenji, whose androgynous appearance is *very* close to the heroine of *The Girl Who Leapt through Time*, both designed by Yoshiyuki Sadamoto. During summer vacation, the mathematically gifted lad is lured into the green countryside by the fair Natsuki, an older girl with an undisclosed task for him. They come to the Nagano castle-home of Natsuki's steely samurai-descended great-grandmother, where a family clan has gathered to celebrate her ninetieth birthday.

To Kenji's shock, Natsuki demands he pose as her boyfriend/fiancé. She's already constructed a fake backstory, which we later learn was swiped from someone else, foreshadowing the cyber-crimes to come. Kenji withers under the scrutiny of the horde of 'in-laws', but finds solace in a mysterious maths conundrum sent to his phone. Unfortunately, the sender isn't human; it's a Dennis the Menace A.I. plotting mayhem in the real and online worlds.

The film's title suggests a summer crowd-pleaser and so it is. There are echoes of *WALL·E**; instead of the giant luxury spaceship, we have OZ, a whimsical cyber-universe where Pokemon-style sprites race round an infinite shopping mall/theme park of mile-long shelves and soothing pastels. Also like *WALL·E*, *Summer Wars* revolves around its protagonists learning how to hold hands, as terrifying a prospect for a cartoon Japanese teen as it is for a Pixar robot.

Hosoda uses the hand motif in *Summer Wars*' saddest scene, when all laughs have been stilled. It's a moment that contemporary Pixar could never have done, and yet in a way it's more Pixar than Pixar, drawing attention to its own crowd manipulations and grace notes: a laterally tracking tableau of grief, a baby's cry that life must go on.

The wonderful world of OZ is nurtured by wise whales called John and Yoko, while the villain impersonates a sniggering Mickey Mouse. (The latter is a Japanese cartoon tradition that goes back to the evil Mickeys in a 1933 anti-Western cartoon, *Black Cat Banzai*). Reviewers thought OZ was based on Japan's

Superflat art school by Takashi Murakami, though Hosoda says he was going for cartoon simplicity and didn't have the style in mind. Then again, the whole 'virtual world' plot is effectively a remake of Hosoda's kids' featurette, *Digimon Adventure: Our War Game*, released in Japan in 2000, and spliced into the US *Digimon: The Movie*. If anyone complained, Hosoda could have pointed to Hayao Miyazaki's *My Neighbour Totoro**, which reworked the tots' film *Panda! Go Panda!* (1972) into art.

Indeed *Summer Wars* is a call for postmodern pluralism, which makes its fleeting jokey reference to Disney's *Fantasia** especially fitting (the villain poses as Mickey's Sorcerer's Apprentice). In a striking scene, the frictionless OZ world is fortified by the *Summer Wars* heroes, who build it up into a medieval Japanese castle. The script makes clear this is a mythologised past, but with a solidity that's borrowed from the clan home in the real world with its antique letters, photos, picture-scrolls and classically composed spaces. Other Japanese directors, such as Hideaki Anno (p. 135) and Satoshi Kon (p. 212), show reality dissolving into psychotic fantasy. *Summer Wars*, on the other hand, makes the virtual optimistically real.

Animators are often inspired by having kids. Hosoda was inspired by meeting his in-laws, having married after making *The Girl Who Leapt through Time*. *Summer Wars* presses the family-drama buttons, from the scenes of the rambunctious clan eating and joshing together, to the black-sheep pariah (modelled on a James Dean-esque film actor, Yusaku Matsuda) who comes home at last, to the computer-obsessed boy loner who launches a cyberspace kamikaze attack to save his mum and unborn sister. From Kenji's viewpoint, it's the story of how he must earn the right to belong, which he never thought he wanted. His eyes slither under great-granny's fierce gaze; at the end, they dance madly as he tackles the world's worst maths exam to *save* the world, while his now-real girlfriend becomes a magnificent virtual goddess with a million online supplicants. It's as ridiculous an outcome as any in a Japanese cartoon, but Hosoda makes it feel earned.

The Thief and the Cobbler
UK/US, 1995 – 72 minutes (US DVD version)
Richard Williams (US version 'completed' by Fred Calvert)
[Drawings]

You can buy Richard Williams's *The Thief and the Cobbler* on American DVD, but in a version so horribly defaced that you wonder if Hollywood *wanted* to destroy a legendary film. Produced over three decades at Williams's Soho Square studio in London, *Thief* employed generations of British artists and actors, plus esteemed Hollywood animators, to make (Williams said), 'the best animated film that's ever been made'. That ambition is visible even in the rough cuts and travesties left of *Thief* today.

Williams's early career entwined with George Dunning's, who released the maverick *Yellow Submarine** while Williams's epic was in early gestation. Dunning and Williams were fellow Toronto expats in London, and Williams helped set up Dunning's TVC company, before making his own half-hour film, *The Little Island* (1958), and founding Richard Williams Animation. By the late 1960s, Williams was making a feature about Nasrudin, a wise-fool sage from Middle East tradition. Around 1973, he fell out with his partners over copyright, and reconfigured his film *sans* Nasrudin. Several scenes and characters – notably an evil vizier voiced by Vincent Price – carried through to the new version.

The Thief and the Cobbler takes place in a sumptuous Arabian city, its ostentatiously intricate backgrounds following the Escheresque patternings of Persian art. The smelly Thief – replacing Nasrudin as the central figure – is obsessed with stealing three gold balls which shield the city from one-eyed barbarians. The Thief never speaks; the hero Cobbler – who must foil the invasion and save the balls – speaks once, in Sean Connery's voice. Other British actors on Williams's voice-track include Joan Sims (as a manically spry witch), Windsor Davies (leading a troop of crude brigands) and Anthony Quayle (as an addle-pated king).

Williams funded his film through work-for-hire: film titles, thousands of commercials and an Oscar-winning TV version of *A Christmas Carol* (1971). After unhappily supervising Fox's feature, *Raggedy Ann & Andy: A Musical Adventure* (1977), Williams got backing from a Saudi Arabian prince. The money paid for a spectacular sequence (*Thief*'s finale) in which the thief is hurtled, sprung and spun through the innards of a self-destructing war machine.

In 1982, Williams claimed only ten minutes of *Thief* were done, as his film came to resemble the endlessly rehearsed play in Charlie Kaufman's *Synecdoche, New York* (2008). 'You can change (animation) … . You can just keep fixing it.' Historian Harvey Deneroff claims that *Thief* was mostly a training exercise for Williams's animators, and that even much of the work by its Hollywood guest artists – Grim Natwick, Art Babbitt, Ken Harris and Emery Hawkins – was cut or redrawn.

Yet the footage was enough for Robert Zemeckis to hire Williams as the animation director on *Who Framed Roger Rabbit**, which reshaped the cartoon market and won *Thief* a deal in 1988. Williams had said he needed three undisturbed years to finish his film. Warners gave him until 1992, when it became clear that Disney's *Aladdin** would beat *Thief* into cinemas.

DIRECTOR Richard Williams
PRODUCER Imogen Sutton, Richard Williams
STORY Richard Williams, Margaret French
DESIGN Errol Le Cain
ANIMATION Neil Boyle, Tim Watts, Richard Williams, Art Babbitt, Paul Bolger, Ken Harris, Alex Williams

Williams's son Alex, an artist on *Thief*, claims there were ten to fifteen minutes of *Thief* left to animate when Warners withdrew its support. Fred Calvert, a Disney and *Sesame Street* (1969–) animator brought onto *Thief* by the insurers, asserted that Williams was 'woefully behind schedule and way over budget.' With Williams removed, Calvert subcontracted animation to other studios and forced the film into Disney formula, adding songs on a par with Disney DVD fare.

Calvert's version played in South Africa and Australia as *The Princess and the Cobbler* (1993). In America, it was picked up by Miramax which made heavy cuts, changed most of the voices (Price was kept) and added a cretinous voice for the Thief, rendering the film barely watchable. This version flopped in American cinemas as *Arabian Knight*, and now impersonates *The Thief and the Cobbler* on DVD. None of the *Thief*s now circulating – including an unofficial 'Workprint' and a fan-made 'Recobbled' cut – are the film Williams would have made.

The extant Williams footage, though, is extraordinary. Characters and perspectives zoom round the screen in a way that has nothing to do with the precision mechanics of CGI. The Thief and Cobbler race through abstract mosaics and rollercoaster down mathematical figures. Extreme close-ups segue into vast panoramas; incidental business is imbued with Wellesian hubris. The Thief crawls head-first down a tree, and the shot becomes an exercise in travelling perspectives and non-Euclidean geometry. Williams spent years perfecting one movement, where the twelve-fingered, cantilevered vizier shuffles and drops a deck of cards.

Yet the characters seem almost devoid of personality. Even Price's grinning villain (who speaks only in rhyme) has the substance of an exclamation mark. For all its exquisite design and movement, *Thief* feels close to Williams's early abstract fable, *The Little Island*, about blinkered idealists obsessed with Good, Truth or Beauty. One TV documentary on Williams shows an extract from the abandoned Nasrudin film; strangely, this unfinished fragment already feels richer in characters and caricatures. Williams insisted *Thief* was blockbuster material, which seems as unlikely as its hero's own exploits.

A Thousand and One Nights
Japan, 1969 – 128 minutes
Eiichi Yamamoto, Osamu Tezuka
[Drawings with live-action]
[This should not be confused with *1001 Arabian Nights*, a 1959 US cartoon feature made by the UPA studio, featuring Mr Magoo.]

The Japanese artist Osamu Tezuka (1928–1989) lived a myriad imagined lives and countless real ones. He created an estimated 170,000 comic pages. If Anglophone viewers know him, it's probably as the father of the character Astro Boy (called Mighty Atom in Japan), an android blend of Pinocchio and Superman. Astro Boy brought American and Japanese cuteness within kissing distance, his robot features a few circles away from Mickey Mouse.

Serious accounts of Tezuka warn against making careless comparisons between him and Disney. For one thing, Tezuka was a great cartoonist and a dreadful businessman. But much as Walt is forever misidentified as the inventor of US animation, so Tezuka is wrongly seen as the creator of Japanese comics, and of cartoons too. Like Walt, he emerged from a sea of pioneers, flooring them with a breakthrough hit. His *Steamboat Willie* (1928) was a story comic, *New Treasure Island* (1947), which sold 400,000 copies in a bomb-blasted country. *Astro Boy* followed four years later. By 1963, the boy-robot was starring in Japan's first major TV cartoon.

Like America's Winsor McCay, Tezuka was a comics pioneer (mimicking camera moves for motion and excitement) who also had a profound impact on animation. He produced dirt-cheap, crudely animated, much-loved TV cartoons on Hanna-Barbera lines. He also made stylistically ambitious experimental shorts for the festival circuit, such as *Jumping* (1984) and *Legend of the Forest* (1987). And then there were his feature-length sex films … .

'Tezuka didn't think of the audience for comics and animation as necessarily being limited to children,' says historian Frederik L. Schodt, who knew Tezuka. 'His goal was to expand the audience, and be able to depict anything he wanted.' Tezuka's wry adult short *Memory* (1964) turned a mushroom cloud into a naked woman in the year of *Dr. Strangelove*. Five years later, Tezuka's animation studio Mushi released the feature-length *A Thousand and One Nights*, promoted as 'Animerama', Tezuka's label for adult animated drama. Tezuka was director and designer together with Eiichi Yamamoto, one of *Astro Boy*'s TV directors.

A Thousand and One Nights is not, in fact, a sex cartoon, but just a cartoon interested in sex. Tezuka could claim fidelity to the source; indeed, the sexuality of *Arabian Nights* is only playfully half-hidden in films such as *The Adventures of Prince Achmed** and Disney's *Aladdin**. (What other Disney would have the villain call a seductive princess a pussy-cat?) In Tezuka's film, the sex helps drive stories that entwine and sprawl for more than two hours. Like Japan's later *Akira**, it's an exhausting epic, but more lucid for Westerners because it contains so many stories we know.

Aldin, a travelling water-seller, liberates, loves and loses a beautiful slave-girl in Baghdad, sets forth on sea adventures, wins a fortune and returns to Baghdad as a conquering tyrant. There's no genie, but rather

DIRECTOR Eiichi Yamamoto, Osamu Tezuka
PRODUCER Eiichi Yamamoto
STORY Osamu Tezuka, Kazuo Fukuzawa
SCORE Isao Tomita
DESIGN Osamu Tezuka, Eiichi Yamamoto
ANIMATION Kazuko Nakamara, Sadao Miyamoto

Ali Baba's cave, a flying horse and a man-eating giant perhaps inspired by Ray Harryhausen's monster in *The Seventh Voyage of Sinbad* (1958). Tezuka waves at other mythologies; his island of nude nymphs turning into snake-monsters suggest the Sirens mated with the Lamia. Finally, the tyrannical Aldin demands the building of a Babel tower to heaven. The whole is a celebration of stories piled on stories that still *entertains* as a story.

Compared to the adult *Fritz the Cat** released three years later, sex is treated reverently, with abstract animations of opening flowers and melting limbs. There's also humour – the hero climbs from an enfolding orifice, then collapses in exhaustion like a 'Looney Tune'. Much of the other animation is rudimentary, but always peppered with ideas. In the opening sequence, Aldin marches endlessly on the spot, his shadow rippling across white sand to a twangy Hendrix guitar. A lascivious shape-changing Jinn turns into a horse, then struggles to stand on four hooves. She also flaunts a disturbingly feminine bottom as a lioness, a shock from the studio which made the children's series *Kimba the White Lion* (1965) (see p. 119). In the finale, the Babel tower crumbles in impressively epic detail; a stone in the rubble bears the words, 'MADE IN JAPAN'.

Mushi produced two further 'Animerama' films before the studio collapsed in 1973. The trippy, goofy, likeable *Cleopatra* (1970) briefly opened in America to coincide with *Fritz the Cat*. It was retitled *Cleopatra: Queen of Sex*, but its supposed 'X' rating was a marketing ploy. Tezuka appears to have had no involvement in Yamamoto's 1973 *Belladonna of Sadness* (aka *The Tragedy of Belladonna*), a wholly serious medieval phantasmagoria about a raped woman rebelling against God and patriarchy, abetted by the satanic part of her psyche, which is drawn as a phallus and sensually voiced by the live-action Japanese film star Tatsuya Nakadi. Released the same year as *The Wicker Man*, which shared its folk-rock soundtrack and pagan liberation, *Belladonna* alternates between lambent static watercolours, scratchier scrolling tableaux and unbridled runaway animated orgies. In the most psychedelic, the impaled heroine gives way to hundreds of zanily anachronistic cartoon characters, in the spirit of *Yellow Submarine** and even of Disney's *The Three Caballeros**.

The Three Caballeros
US, 1944 – 72 minutes
Norman Ferguson
[Drawings and live-action]

The Three Caballeros is the strangest animated feature released by the Disney studio – if, that is, you count it as a cartoon at all. Large parts of this thrown-together film are in live-action, as Donald Duck and his feathered friends carouse through South America. One caustic reviewer called them 'ecstatic playboys, eternally rioting around torch singers and bathing beauties in a Technicolor Paradise'.

Caballeros was part of Disney's generally forgotten downtime between Bambi* and Cinderella*, when Walt supposedly said, 'We're through with caviar; from now on it's mashed potato and gravy.' His studio was starved of funds and foreign markets, battered by the successive flops of Pinocchio*, Fantasia* and Bambi. 1941 saw a bitter strike and horrendous downsizing. Of the studio's nearly 1,200 employees, more than half were gone by the year's end.

While the strike was in arbitration, Walt fled to South America for a goodwill tour, spending much time in Rio and Buenos Aires. Like Orson Welles, who went to Rio to make the ill-fated It's All True, Walt had state backing, from the Coordinator of Inter-American Affairs. (The body had been formed to fight fascism and promote 'Good Neighbour' policies towards the Latin states.) As well as the tour (a hit), Walt agreed to make several Latin-themed cartoons, some merged into longer packages.

The first of these was Saludos Amigos (1942), though it only ran forty-two minutes. It combined four fairly conventional cartoon shorts – Donald visits Peru and Brazil, Goofy becomes a gaucho – with home-movie footage of Walt's trip. The sequel, The Three Caballeros, starts in a similar vein. Donald receives several presents from his 'friends in South America', including a pair of short films, which he plays on a home projector. In one, a penguin journeys to South America for the sun; the other is a tale of a boy and his flying donkey.

Both are comforting Disney fare (the penguin story is narrated in feminine fashion by Sterling Holloway, already an upcoming Disney institution). However, they remind us of the gags Walt didn't normally allow into his features. For example, the donkey story has a Rashomon-style joke, where the adult narrator is supposedly recalling his childhood, but still talks with the boy hero and subverts his own story (when he can't remember some scenery, the boy finds himself sitting on a rock, a tree, then a rock again).

About twenty minutes in, Donald opens a present to find José Carioca, a dapper cigar-puffing Brazilian parrot (with an accent but no speech impediment), who'd débuted in Saludos Amigos. From this point, Caballeros heads off in random directions with no regard for pace, structure or tonal coherence. We lollop from cartoon knockabout (Donald fighting a Mexican piñata and losing, or being converted into psychedelic music soundwaves like the ones in Fantasia) to dissolving landscapes and townscapes, colour sketches and picture stories. The picture-book motif is extended when Donald and José catch a train through a chalky night flatland.

DIRECTOR Norman Ferguson
STORY Homer Brightman, Ernest Terrazas, Ted Sears, Bill Peet
ANIMATION Ward Kimball, Fred Moore, Eric Larson, John Lounsbery, Les Clark, Milt Kahl

The more boisterous scenes show the influence of playful Disney animator Ward Kimball, who drew Donald jitterbugging with Mexico's Carmen Molina. He also animated *Caballeros'* title song with its 'Looney Tunes' gags, when Donald and José are joined by Panchito, a noisy but forgettable Mexican rooster. On the other side, the blossom-coloured paintings and backdrops were created or inspired by art supervisor Mary Blair, whose style would prevail in 1950s Disney. The cartoon/live-action mixes were facilitated by Disney's old colleague, Ub Iwerks, who drew *Steamboat Willie* (1928).

Some combination shots seem obvious now, as when Donald and José are rear-projected with Brazil's Aurora Miranda on an unrolling cartoon street, but then the film wrongfoots us by putting the pair in the foreground instead. Two male dancers transmogrify into silhouetted fighting cocks in mortal combat, then morph back into humans with a smoothness worthy of MTV. Later, the singing face of Mexican starlet Dora Luz is doubled in a lusty Donald's beady pupils, one of the film's 'What were they *thinking*?' moments.

For *The Three Caballeros* is infamous for its ending, an overwrought lust-fantasy *à la* Tex Avery, whose saucy *Red Hot Riding Hood* was a hit in 1943. Donald chases girls on Acapulco Beach (actually the Disney studio's parking lot), and through discordantly ruptured dreamscapes, before things wind down with some hoofing cacti and relatively tame firecrackers. The critic Brian Sibley saw *Caballeros* as Disney's first feature that was 'uninhibitedly modern in its energetic and iconoclastic animation'. Today's average viewer, though, would probably turn off when the travelogue starts interrupting the cute cartoons.

Tokyo Godfathers
Japan, 2003 – 88 minutes
Satoshi Kon
[Drawings]

DIRECTOR Satoshi Kon
STORY Keiko Nobumoto, Satoshi Kon
SCORE Keiichi Suzuki
DESIGN Kenichi Konishi, Satoshi Kon
ANIMATION Kenichi Konishi, Shinji Otsuka, Hideki Hamasu

As this book was being proofed in August 2010, the news broke that the Japanese animation director Satoshi Kon had succumbed to pancreatic cancer at the age of 46. It was a devastating shock, as Kon was one of the most vital animation directors in the world, and had far more to give. From the 1990s, Satoshi Kon established himself as a Japanese auteur whose work is reliably excellent yet playfully unpredictable. Born on Hokkaido, Japan's northernmost island, in 1963, Kon grew up a fan of animated TV sci-fi sagas such as *Space Battleship Yamato* (1974, American title: *Star Blazers*) and *Mobile Suit Gundam* (1979). His early career was as a comic artist and animation designer, specialising in backgrounds and layouts. He worked with Katsuhiro Otomo, assisting on his mammoth comic-strip version of *Akira* though not the film version; however, his brother Tsuyoshi contributed to the soundtrack. Yet the big influences on Kon's own anime are live-action films, including those by *Monty Python* animator Terry Gilliam (*Time Bandits*, 1981, *Brazil*, 1985) and Walter Hill's 1972 version of Kurt Vonnegut's novel, *Slaughterhouse-Five*.

Like those pictures, Kon's anime jump between subjective time frames, unreliable perceptions and shaky realities. After writing 'Magnetic Rose', the hallucinatory space-opera segment of the film anthology *Memories**, Kon directed *Perfect Blue* (1997), a gory splintered psycho-thriller told from the viewpoint of an unhinged female pop singer. Watching the film, we're unsure if the killer pursuing the heroine is real, the singer's delusion or even the singer herself. *Millennium Actress* (2001) is a magic-realist biopic of a starlet who races through her own movies, from geisha dramas to monster flicks. The lighter-hearted *Paprika* (2006) has a 'dream detective' dancing through wonderlands. It feels like a riposte to Kon's waspish TV miniseries, *Paranoia Agent* (2004), in which people stampede *en masse* into fantasy and cause Armageddon.

Tokyo Godfathers, though, is an initially straightforward-looking story about three homeless people in Japan's capital. There's a self-abasing wino who asks the police for a bin to put himself in; a girl runaway whose sullenness makes her story arc all the more exquisite; and an exuberant middle-aged drag queen, who's perhaps inspired by the cross-dressing Japanese celebrity Akihiro Miwa (see p. 167). On Christmas Eve, the trio discovers an abandoned baby girl and sets out to find her mother.

Among other things, *Tokyo Godfathers* is a case of an animation director choosing a dark subject which wouldn't usually get into cinemas, and educating foreigners in the process. At the film's New York première, Kon was shocked when people expressed surprise that Tokyo *had* homeless people. It's especially ironic, as Kon's subject (if not style) recalls Ralph Bakshi's early films about the marginal groups in New York (see p. 75).

Kon, like Bakshi, had used abrasive animated sex and violence in his film *Perfect Blue*, but *Tokyo Godfathers* is an almost Capra-esque fantasy. Its ensemble comedy recalls British underdog TV sitcoms such as *Porridge* (1974) and *Only Fools and Horses* (1981). In one scene, the trio arrives at what they thought

was their destination, only to find a demolished house; the wino walks through the doorway anyway, muttering sourly, 'I'm home.' The mischievous plot relies on an outrageous set of screwball coincidences and near-misses, perhaps engineered by the angelic baby. This thread is signposted from the opening credits, where spilled paint and a skidding vehicle *just* miss the three protagonists as they walk through Tokyo with the child. But the darkness is never schmaltzed. The girl runaway has stabbed her father in a family row; a gang of hoodlums beat up homeless people for sport. Both scenes were taken from contemporary Tokyo headlines.

Bakshi played horrendous violence as slapstick, while Disney's *Bambi** counterpointed high tragedy with cute comedy. Kon uses both comedy and tragedy at once. In his finale, the baby is kidnapped by a screaming, suicidal woman, who's then chased by the homeless heroes in a manic Keystone Kops climax. It's a provocative clash of tones but hugely affecting, culminating in an electrifying dénouement on a rooftop ledge. Kon called it 'two-faced humour,

where you cannot tell if you should be laughing or feeling sorry for the characters'.

The highly realistic Tokyo scenery, supervised by Kon's art director Nobutaka Ike, is poeticised by snow and lighting. A beautifully sombre interlude sees the characters walk down a railway track, the flat white snow set against the dulled dark city. The three godfathers go through creative cartoon distortions that owe nothing to the cheesy 'superdeformities' in much TV anime. The transvestite Hana's rubbery face bulges and grins alarmingly in the early scenes, yet by the end we know him as human, even dignified. His striking animation – particularly a bravura stand-up rant in a hospital corridor – was handled by Shinji Otsuka, who'd previously turned a boy into a blob-monster in *Akira**'s climax.

The film's title refers to *Three Godfathers*, a much-filmed and imitated Western novel about three robbers who find a baby in the desert. The most famous version was John Ford's *3 Godfathers* (1948); another variant is the CGI cartoon *Ice Age**.

Toy Story
US, 1995 – 77 minutes
John Lasseter
[CGI]

Blue sky and clouds resolve into wallpaper, before which are 3D cardboard boxes. The 'camera' hunkers down, encouraging us to see the crayoned doors and windows as a kid would, as imaginatively living architecture for a Wild West adventure. One box bears a paper 'Wanted' poster: it's Mr Potato Head! In a blink, the toy is thrust before its drawn signifier, waggling a plastic gun.

Toy Story ushered in a new cartoon mainstream and a generation of post-Disney studios. The film employed about seven times fewer artists than *The Lion King**, leading Hollywood to question the viability of moving drawings. With hindsight, *Toy Story*'s innocent opening images look portentous, collapsing 2D drawings into 3D objects and changing toon history forever.

At the time, though, it was a parodically low-key way to start an animated film. Contemporary Disneys opened with spectacle; a rush towards Ayers Rock in *The Rescuers Down Under* (1996), a multiplane-style glide to the castle in *Beauty and the Beast**. Both films relied on the CAPS system, co-created by Disney and Pixar, which split layers of art into dimensional travelling images.

Toy Story has in-jokes about blockbusters, but the film has more parallels with Nick Park's plasticine *The Wrong Trousers* (1993), so much so that you could almost switch Park and Pixar's characters into each other's mini epics. The film starts from the notion of a secret life of toys, as explored in Pixar's short *Tin Toy* (1988), and traditionally animated in the likes of Disney's 1933 *The Night before Christmas* and Richard Williams's 1977 feature, *Raggedy Ann & Andy: A Musical Adventure*. The magic of the scenario is kept, suitably updated, in the famous early scene where inch-high toy soldiers flipflop their way downstairs to recce the humans.

Toy Story, though, ups the psycho-warfare. Pixar's toys aren't cute projections of their child owners, but grown-ups whose appearances deceive. A naive-looking Bo Peep is a sultry seductress; a T-Rex has 'New Man' neuroses. In the office-style hierarchy, cowboy Woody (Tom Hanks) is on top of the playpen, but is threatened by the new spaceman toy, Buzz Lightyear (Tim Allen). The irony is that, as critic William Leith pointed out, Buzz is the only toy with a child's script. He believes he actually *is* a spaceman.

Probably *Toy Story*'s best-known shot has Buzz the alpha-male standing on the bed with hands on hips, baring his plastic white teeth. A later reveal has Woody standing on a new bedspread, regarding a giant picture of a soaring Buzz (and we already know Woody has 'laser envy'). But Buzz's castration is cruel, when he sees a TV ad showing Buzzes lined on shelves like soup cans. 'Not a Flying Toy!' reads the caption, but Buzz tries, breaks his arm off and ends up in drag with girl dollies. (In one draft, a macho Barbie would have saved the day.)

On the standard production account, Disney chairman Jeffery Katzenberg first suggested the idea of the toys having adult personalities, then pushed Pixar to make the film more and more 'edgy'. After a

DIRECTOR John Lasseter
PRODUCER Ralph Guggenheim, Bonnie Arnold
STORY Joss Whedon, Andrew Stanton, Joel Cohen, Alec Sokolow
SCORE Randy Newman
DESIGN Bob Pauley, Bud Luckey, Andrew Stanton, William Cone
ANIMATION Rich Quade, Ash Brannon, Pete Docter, Michael Bernstein, Kim Blanchette

legendarily disastrous version in which Woody was characterised as a smart-alec boor, Pixar's staff rallied and saved their film from the suits. Yet in the final version, a mutant toy resembles John Carpenter's Thing, a cute toy alien is casually tossed to a ravening dog, and there's a great deal of sometimes wearing bickering.

Toy Story seems placed, sometimes uneasily, between the Pixar brand to come, its future competitor DreamWorks, and the gnarly miniature visions of The Nightmare before Christmas*. A properly Gothic Toy Story would have made the doll-splicing kid, Sid, the hero, but the animators acknowledge the uncanniness of toys beloved by Mamoru Oshii and Jan Svankmajer. Woody and Buzz look as alive as 1990s Pixar can make them, but the film doesn't deny the slight nausea we feel each time they blink and unfreeze from doll-hood. Woody exploits this to traumatise Sid ('So play nice!'), breaking the law that toys throw themselves to the ground as found objects when humans pass. Yet it's the stodgy, stolid Buzz who's the better actor, surviving a weak drunk scene to perplexedly realise his worth in dawn's early light.

Toy Story 2 (1999) smooths the original's rough edges but adds wit, pathos and fiendish plot permutations that complete the first film. Woody finds a meta-fictional 'past' in a TV puppet Western, which gives him a new family but seduces him away from toyhood. A non-Pixar Toy Story 3 was cancelled when Disney and Pixar merged; Pixar's version appeared in 2010 and is, as of writing, the highest-grossing animated feature ever made. Another film, Disney's CGI Bolt (2008) reworks Buzz's arc from the first Toy Story, playing up its debt to The Truman Show (1998). In Bolt, the title dog learns he's a TV star, a devastating comedown for a canine who thought he was a superhero.

Up
US, 2009 – 96 minutes
Pete Docter
[CGI, released in 3D]

Before the computers are switched on, says *Up*'s director Peter Docter, the creative process of developing a film feels something like water.

> It's as though we're in the pool, splashing around, looking for things, and then at some point we jump out and analyse. I've never worked on a film where I've intentionally said, 'I want to make a film about *this*.' It's more that you step back and say, 'Oh, I see what I'm saying.'

Docter made *Up* from an especially strange set of objects. One of them is the main character Carl, a curmudgeonly brick-shaped widower with a letterbox mouth, who's sighed and growled and grumped by *The Mary Tyler Moore Show*'s Ed Asner. Then there's Carl's clapboard house, lifted into the clouds by gaily coloured balloons. It's a dinky, decorous building, pervaded by Carl's late wife Ellie, who's embodied in an empty armchair and a miniature picture-portrait. The flying house is redolent of Henry Selick's stop-motion film, *James and the Giant Peach* (1996), where the fruit was lifted by seagulls, but Carl's house is freighted with dollar-book Hollywood symbolism.

Docter leads us into the film by the hand, showing us Carl and Ellie's first meeting as children. Ellie is a gap-toothed tomboy voiced by Docter's daughter, and she's as fearsome a discovery for Carl as any fantasy monster. Carl and Ellie grow up, get married and grow old in a montage that evolves from winsome comedy into underplayed weepie. At the end, the old Ellie exits, leaving Carl alone. The sequence builds on the beginnings of two previous Pixars, *The Incredibles** (where the young heroes also marry and age) and *Finding Nemo** (where a brutish tragedy is conveyed through a black-out ellipsis).

Carl's world implodes without Ellie, and he makes his miracle escape. The multicoloured cloud of balloons burst from a sack, tearing Carl and his house from the earth into the blue morning sky ('So long, boys!'). He's blown toward South America, where Carl plans to fulfil his and Ellie's childhood dreams. En route, there's a knock on the door and the discovery of a rosy-cheeked boy scout, Russell, cowering on the porch. Carl and Russell reach the *tepuis*, sheer-walled tropical table mountains, and crash into funny animal territory. Russell teams up with a talking dog ('It's a *talking dog*!') and a giant emu-like bird, all of whom pester Carl.

Unlike *Spirited Away** or *WALL·E**, whose adventuring heroes were ciphers, *Up* is firmly anchored to Carl's stiff figure as he turns liberation into a burden. His house may float but he's mostly earth-bound, tugging his dream on a tow-rope like one of Werner Herzog's monomaniacs. Next to him, *Up*'s other elements look flimsy, and Carl's narrative destiny seems oppressively familiar as he bonds grumpily

DIRECTOR Pete Docter
PRODUCER Jonas Rivera
STORY Pete Docter, Bob Peterson, Tom McCarthy
SCORE Michael Giacchino
DESIGN Ricky Nierva
ANIMATION Scott Clark, Shawn Krause, Dave Mullins, Michael Venturini, Simon Allen, Dovi Anderson

with Russell, lets him down at a vital moment, then has a second chance.

For Carl's redemption, Docter develops a twist from *Monsters, Inc**, his previous Pixar film. In it, a cuddly monster scared kids for a living but stopped after seeing himself through a child's eyes. In *Up*, the late Ellie provides the vital perspective, as her scrapbook assures Carl they had a wonderful life and his breast-beating quest is redundant. It's touching because we want to see Carl happy, but it would have had more force if his tribulations weren't diluted by so many silly adventures.

In the last airborne battle, the derring-do and flying dogs fall awkwardly between Miyazaki's *Laputa** (a cartoony but serious action-adventure) and Wallace and Gromit (who have straight adventures in a silly world). *Up*'s last image is more suggestive, framed as something the characters will never know. Carl's house has finally landed exactly where he wanted, by a gauzy waterfall on an unreachable mountain. It suggests closure, yet at the same time it takes us back to Carl and Ellie's airy childhood dream, subverting the folksy, *Wizard of Oz* message of fulfilment in your own backyard. Is Docter quite sure what he's saying?

Wallace & Gromit in The Curse of the Were-Rabbit
UK/US, 2005 – 84 minutes
Nick Park, Steve Box
[Stop-motion with CGI]

One of the first bits of stop-motion in *Wallace & Gromit in the Curse of the Were-Rabbit* involves a stone garden gnome. As a fluffy intruder breaches a proud English night garden, snuffling pumpkins and cauliflowers, the statue grindingly turns its head (invoking Ray Harryhausen's monstrous Talos) and triggers an alarm. In a kitchen, a stove comes on, a kettle sings, spokes and winches turn … and a wooden finger prods someone's bed.

This is Wallace and Gromit's world, where spades are spades, people are plasticine and technology pokes you with its thumb. The homely surfaces and textures are defined by touch, for what else is plasticine for? Later, the guileless inventor Wallace is brow-beaten by the thug-snob Elmer Fudd villain, voiced by Ralph Fiennes. The characters' noses don't just meet; the cad's pendulous hooter bends as it presses into Wallace's friendly sphere.

Yet the film's key clay anatomy is not a nose but the brow-cum-eyebrows of Wallace's dog Gromit. The ledge over Gromit's eyes puckers, arches and glares, conveying annoyance, resignation and undying love. More minimal than Disney's mute stars (Dopey, Tinker Bell), Gromit is closer to Manfred, the woolly mammoth in *Ice Age**, but far more expressive. In *Were-Rabbit*, Gromit and Wallace's lead animator was Merlin Crossingham, but everyone knows their real dad is Nick Park.

The feature was the second collaboration between *Shrek**'s studio DreamWorks and Britain's Aardman Animations. Aardman had grown from the short films of schoolboy animators Dave Sproxton and Peter Lord, who founded the company in 1976. Aardman's early work, from the tabletop clay hero Morph to the quicksilver imagery in Peter Gabriel's phallocentric 'Sledgehammer' video, sank into Britain's *Zeitgeist* long before the studio's name was known outside festivals.

Park popularised the brand. A student at Beaconsfield's National Film and Television School, Park inched through Wallace and Gromit's début, *A Grand Day Out* (1989), until Lord and Sproxton took him under their wing. Few feature-animation directors are famous; Park became a star through his Oscar-winning shorts. *Creature Comforts* (1979) infused zoo animals with real people's voices. *The Wrong Trousers* (1993) and *A Close Shave* (1995) brought back Wallace and Gromit in more structured stories, drama moderating the whimsy, most memorably with *The Wrong Trousers*' menacing film noir penguin (animated by Steve Box).

Aardman's first feature with DreamWorks, *Chicken Run* (2000) by Park and Lord, was a witty but rarely inspired 'Great Escape with chickens'. It was unfortunately similar to Pixar's *A Bug's Life* (1998) (both the bugs and chickens resort to bodged-up flying machines). In *Were-Rabbit*, the heroes endeavour to bag a monstrous bunny. Like the live-action *Shaun of the Dead* (2004), it's a horror-film parody that respects its sources: *The Wolf Man* (1941), *The Invisible Man* (1933) and 1958's *The Fly*, all transposed to the England of Orwell's 'The Lion and the Unicorn', where proles have knobby faces and bad teeth.

DIRECTOR Nick Park, Steve Box
PRODUCER Claire Jennings, Carla Shelley, Peter Lord, David Sproxton, Nick Park
STORY Nick Park, Steve Box, Mark Burton, Bob Baker
SCORE Julian Nott
DESIGN Phil Lewis, Jan Sanger
ANIMATION Merlin Crossingham, Loyd Price, Ian Whitlock, Jay Grace, Seamus Malone

The story has fewer politics than a seaside postcard, though Wallace has a black neighbour and a weight problem (from his love of cheese). Park and Box focus on hitting their comic marks. There are joyous cartoon gags – a surprised rabbit is vacuumed up its hole and thinks it's off to bunny heaven – and criminally dreadful puns, such as a bullet made of '24-carat' gold.

New to the film are a chorus of rabbits (recalling the stunt sheep in *A Close Shave*) and rent-a-mob villagers. Helena Bonham Carter voices a dizzy mature aristocrat whose liaison with Wallace is conducted in innocent *double entendres* in an Eden-like greenhouse. The were-rabbit's transformation in a misty wood faithfully replicates horror-movie scares as ludicrous laughs. The creature's final, traditionally tragic, change may cause children a few tears before the inevitable happy ending.

Perhaps thanks to its parochial Britishness, the film won the Best Animated Feature Oscar but performed only modestly in America. A costlier CGI film, the disposable *Flushed Away* (2006), had similar returns, and DreamWorks and Aardman split in January 2007. Wallace and Gromit returned in a fourth (half-hour) adventure, *A Matter of Loaf and Death*, which captured more than half Britain's TV audience on Christmas Day 2008.

WALL·E
US, 2008 – 94 minutes
Andrew Stanton
[CGI with brief live-action]

WALL·E, Pixar's ninth feature film, is the story of a dowdy square robot alone on an abandoned, garbage-strewn Earth, and how he finds love and humanity. *Finding Nemo** director Andrew Stanton called on *Star Wars'* sound designer, Ben Burtt, to create an audiovisual world much like the one at the start of Lucas's film, where childish, childlike anthropomorphics whine and whir and squeal. The epic tale reimagines *2001: A Space Odyssey* (1968) with the whimsy of Wallace and Gromit.

At first *WALL·E* seems humourlessly photo-real, its quiet Earth too like the live-action empty worlds in films such as *I Am Legend*, released a few months earlier. Then *WALL·E* seems destined to shunt itself into one-note repetitions of a theme, such as the robot's cute antics in his planet-sized playground, or his pratfalling efforts to woo EVE, the white egg-shaped probe (inspired by the sleek lines of iPods) who descends from the sky. Both bots are babes in the wood; EVE blows up a shipyard in a tizzy, before WALL·E calms her by letting her play with his bubblewrap and Rubik cube.

WALL·E's joy, though, is how its situation develops in an organic, lyrical, musical way, its rhythms recalling *Bambi**'s shifting seasons. Many reviewers felt the film declined after its Earth opening, which is actually less than radical. It merely follows the precedents set by Kubrick and Lucas, and sneaks in more speech than all of *Belleville Rendez-Vous**. Later, though, WALL·E and EVE go into space to find humans in a 700-year holding-pattern vacation. The robots' automated choreography now has a goal; they must subvert a theme-park world that runs on rails. Thomas Newman's score leads the changes in tempo as WALL·E's ancient *Hello, Dolly!* video spreads the lost memes for love and adventure through the human and metal cast.

WALL·E's and EVE's acting is visibly constructed from simple, puppet-like gestures, recalling Wes Anderson's description of stop-motion (p. 67), 'That magical effect where you can see how it is accomplished.' Even on those terms, their expressions are severely limited. WALL·E's twitchy binocular head might be compared to the ears of Aardman's dog Gromit, but it lacks an eloquent brow. As in Pixar's inferior *Cars* (2006), *WALL·E*'s most lyrical scenes convey the joys of being a supple piece of moving metal, with a waltzing space-flight ('Define dancing') that matches anything by Hayao Miyazaki. There's also a surprisingly dark interlude in which WALL·E cares obsessively for EVE when she's shut down and effectively 'dead', with perversely funny overtones of Norman Bates.

Male and female, WALL·E and EVE are streamlined gender symbols without mouths or biology. WALL·E evokes a hyper-puppyish Chaplin's Tramp, while EVE is a mish-mash: fearsome or motherly (in space, she bears WALL·E in her 'arms'), giggling cutely or turning trigger-happy to zap the landscape with a laser. She's less a character than a post-*Alien* (1979) feminine construct; fittingly, *Alien* star Sigourney Weaver figures in the film as the ship's computer.

DIRECTOR Andrew Stanton
PRODUCER Jim Morris
STORY Andrew Stanton, Jim Reardon, Pete Docter
DESIGN Ralph Eggleston
ANIMATION Alan Barillaro, Steven Clay Hunter, Angus MacLane, Carlos Baena, Rodrigo Blaas

The gender essentialism turns overt when EVE nurtures a plant inside her egg-body; but there are shades of new man-ism in the ship's captain who protects the plant too, his devolved round body seeming feminine as well as infantile. It's impossible to imagine *WALL·E* with a female lead, but that's because of its roots in silent romantic comedy, not in stereotypically macho space opera.

The reviewers highlighted *WALL·E*'s political baggage, as it first reveals an Earth under mountains of consumer garbage, then humanity's vacuous, push-button existence in space. But the film's too gentle for satire: even DreamWorks' *Antz** had bigger dystopian teeth. With its affectionate child-robots, whose kisses are fairy-blue sparks and whose touches have intimacy without flesh, *WALL·E* feels like the offspring of *Star Wars* and Miyazaki's *Laputa**, another high-flying epic proclaiming humans should return to Earth.

The finale falters; WALL·E is slow-tortured like a luckless Pinocchio, while the emotional and mechanical rhythms are undercut by bathetic *Titanic* jokes. But then EVE rushes WALL·E back to Earth, frantic to save him. The sound drops out, leaving us with two barely animate implements in the dust, WALL·E's mind seemingly gone, and the moment left to float. It's Pixar's most haunting scene, and a Walt-worthy piece of manipulation. Stanton confessed he never thought of *not* bringing WALL·E back, but he just *loved* making the viewer think otherwise.

Waltz with Bashir
Israel, 2008 – 90 minutes
Ari Folman
[Flash animation with drawings and CGI]

Waltz with Bashir depicts Israeli soldiers' memories of the 1982 conflict in Beirut, and of the events leading up to the murder of thousands of Palestinian refugees by the Phalangist Christian militia, Israel's allies. The choice of subject is all the more provocative in an Israeli film, though we're spared the horror of the war crime until the last minutes, when cartoon reconstructions give way to real footage of heaped corpses and shrieking relatives. *Waltz with Bashir* treats these images as a hidden wound that it circles, probes and finally tears open, as the live-action overwhelms everything that came before.

The film is constructed from the accounts of former Israeli soldiers. Ari Folman, director and on-screen investigator, presents his own flashback, a haunting tableau of soldiers emerging naked from the sea under the yellow light of illumination flares. Of the voices we hear, most are of the real witnesses to the events, with actors reading the other testimonies.

Early on, one of Folman's interviewees tells him, 'It's fine if you draw but don't film.' On one level, *Waltz with Bashir*'s animation seems to play a similar role to artists' sketches in court cases, a way to present what might be politically unacceptable in live-action. However, Folman himself stressed interior experience over exterior history. 'Animation is the only way to tell this story, with memories, lost memories, dreams and the subconscious.'

The character animation in *Bashir* is crude; the figures sometimes resemble jerky Gerry Anderson puppets. However, the limitations are less obvious to Anglophone viewers, just because there's so much talking, forcing us to focus on the subtitles more than the speakers' limited expressions. As with much Japanese animation, the emotional weight is mostly carried in the voices, the compositions and the plain or sickly pastels.

Much of the often expressionist action is stylised, distanced. However, real emotion breaks through, as in what could have otherwise been a mawkish moment; a soldier, facing death on a beach, suddenly remembers washing dishes as a child beside his mother. In other scenes, *Bashir* can seem overwhelmingly male, complete with a porn-video scene that earned the film its British '18' certificate. It feels far from the female sensibility of *Persepolis**, another film that deployed cartoon autobiography to comment on the Middle East. (*Persepolis* and *Bashir* premièred at successive Cannes Festivals in 2007 and 2008.)

Yet femininity pervades Folman's film too. There are recurring images of a sea which supports and carries weary men. In one of the fantasy sequences, a soldier imagines himself cradled by a giant nude sea-nymph. Masculinity, meanwhile, is symbolised in the film's opening-titles fantasy, where savage dogs run through a city to a pulsing drumbeat. This, however, recalls nothing so much as heavy-metal album covers, and the comic-strip aggression feels misplaced in a film ending in such shattering reality.

Except that Folman highlights how violence seems unreal even to people in combat zones. There are pop-video montages and disjointed interludes; a bloody skirmish is dissected in slow-motion to the music of

DIRECTOR/STORY Ari Folman
PRODUCER Ari Folman, Serge Lalou, Yael Nahlieli, Gerhard Meixner, Roman Paul
SCORE Max Richter
ANIMATION Yoni Goodman, Tal Gadon, Gali Edelbaum, Neta Holzer, Asenath Wold, Sefi Gayego

Bach. As the Israelis struggle into Beirut, citizens watch them from balconies and windows, as if viewing a film. We hear of a soldier who dissociates from the carnage to such a degree that he admires the 'great (action) scenes' he's in. He's shocked back to reality by an arbitrary sight, the death agonies of race horses in a blasted Hippodrome. But even his revelation is shown through a consciously 'artful' shot, his face mirrored in a horse's fly-encrusted eye.

Bashir's artificial relationship to its subject is conspicuously unresolved, as elusive as the memories Folman chases in himself and others. In a film that uses animation to convey the subjective, to depict the myriad of personal memories rather than the official, locked history, does the last cut to live-action betrays *Bashir*'s whole project?

The film's shock ending has even been accused of being a crass catharsis, making dead Palestinians ciphers for the virtuous Israelis' breast-beating. In interviews, Folman himself said the Israeli soldiers – as opposed to their leaders – had nothing to do with the massacre, though viewers, seeing the events as Folman depicts them, may reach different conclusions.

In the end, Folman foregoes meta-textual critiques in favour of brute human nature; no animated image equals the raw, transgressive sight of real flesh-and-blood people in hell. At the end of *Bashir*'s screening at the Annecy animation festival, there was an extended silence as the screams faded and the credits rolled, before the 1,000-strong audience rose in a stunned standing ovation.

Watership Down
UK, 1978 – 88 minutes
Martin Rosen
[Drawings]

From Pepperland to Hampshire; from Edwardian day-glo to symphonic green pastures. *Watership Down* was the next major British cartoon feature after *Yellow Submarine**, but director Martin Rosen had no time for stylistic adventures, though his material was symbolic. Based on Richard Adams's bestselling novel, *Watership Down* concerns a band of rabbits whose leaders have the souls of legends (Moses, Ulysses). Fleeing their doomed warren, the rabbits are threatened by men, beasts and a totalitarian rabbit Reich, led by the monstrous General Woundwort.

Watership Down doubly transforms the English countryside through the eyes of artists and rabbits. This isn't *Bambi**'s sublime wilderness, or the mid-Atlantic Hundred Acre Wood in Disney's contemporary *Winnie the Pooh* cartoons. *Watership Down*'s watercolour backgrounds show barbed-wire fences, farms, pylons, roads and railways. The rabbits move through this occupied territory, clinging to wood and water (they learn to use boats), and seeking the Downs' rolling sanctuary. Anticipating *My Neighbour Totoro**, *Watership Down*'s drawings recover rural landscapes from tame quaintness, as the intrepid protagonists peek up from the ground, then burrow, hide or run through the vastness.

The film was made in a rundown London leatherworks that, as every report noted, was off Warren Street. The first director was John Hubley, the modernist pioneer of Mr Magoo and *Rooty Toot Toot* (1951). After a year, he was thrown out, the cartoon equivalent of Akira Kurosawa being turfed off Hollywood's *Tora! Tora! Tora!* (1970). The American producer, Martin Rosen, took over; new to animation, he was utilitarian about its worth. At first, he'd considered making *Watership Down* with live rabbits, or actors in rabbit suits (an idea picked up by the comedy TV show, *The Goodies*, 1970, when it spoofed the film). Having decided on a cartoon, Rosen proclaimed *Watership Down* different from previous animated films, which were unsubtle and unchallenging. 'Demands,' he said, 'are made on (*Watership Down*'s) audience which they have not been used to in animation before.'

His film is indeed demanding. It challenges us to tell many similar-looking rabbits apart in cross-cutting action scenes; to watch furry animals tear each other up in a notoriously gory climax; and to put up with an ending so elliptical that only one rabbit gets a proper goodbye (and we'd last seen *him* pinned down by a cat). The rabbits move awkwardly, jerk their heads annoyingly and have only occasional presence. Fiver, a Cassandra figure, stands out because his whole weakly sloping design connotes terror, which turns to prophetic enlightenment when he follows a black shadow-rabbit into the night. His anathema is Cowslip, a flopsily effeminate, poetry-spouting wretch voiced by Denholm Elliott. It's an uncomfortable stereotype by modern lights, but one of the film's more interesting quirks. Keehar, a prima donna seagull, is the best character just because his theatrics suit his form.

The bitty merits sit uneasily with the 'quality' British voices – including John Hurt, Michael Hordern and

DIRECTOR/PRODUCER/STORY
Martin Rosen
SCORE Angela Morley
ANIMATION Philip Duncan, Tony Guy, Arthur Humberstone, George Jackson, Edric Raddage, Bill Littlejohn

Ralph Richardson – and the classically styled score, which jars in turn with Mike Batt's infamous 'Bright Eyes' ballad, sung by Art Garfunkel (who disliked it). What *is* compelling, though, is how the rabbits' world is progressively defamiliarised by the constant threats, the below-ground excursions into rough earth tubes and the bloody battles that leave tranquil scenery unruffled. Even the dialogue is peppered with untranslated rabbit expressions ('Embleer Frith!' is a blasphemous oath).

Some commentators claim that the film's few abstract sequences – including a mythical 'creation of the world' prologue with childlike designs and playful animation – are too good for Rosen and must be leftovers from Hubley's treatment. However, several contemporary reviewers disliked the 'arty' prologue almost as much as 'Bright Eyes'. In any case, the film's darker expressions – a field that fills with blood, a screaming chorus of bodiless, mad-eyed rabbit heads – would set the tone for Rosen's next (and last) animated film, *The Plague Dogs*, released in 1982. Animated in San Francisco, it was a better film technically and dramatically; it was bleak and cruel, with ugly shocks; and it was a cartoon about dogs. It bombed.

When the Wind Blows
UK, 1986 – 80 minutes
Jimmy Murakami
[Drawings, miniatures and live-action]

DIRECTOR Jimmy Murakami
PRODUCER John Coates
STORY Raymond Briggs
SCORE Roger Waters
DESIGN Richard Fawdry, Errol Bryant
ANIMATION Tony Guy, Bill Speers, David Unwin, Dianne Jackson, Richard Fawdry, Jimmy Murakami

A British cartoon Armageddon, *When the Wind Blows* followed the lines of two live-action TV films, *The Day After* (1983) and *Threads* (1984), made in America and Britain respectively. All three show the build-up to a nuclear war, the holocaust itself and its ghastly aftermath. However, *When the Wind Blows* confines itself to just two characters – the married OAPs Jim and Hilda Bloggs, voiced by John Mills and Peggy Ashcroft – and one setting, a remote cottage on the South Downs.

Here, Hilda irons clothes, hangs washing and tries not to be ruffled by Jim's excited preparations for war, even when he starts unscrewing doors and painting the windows white. As the script interminably reminds us, Jim is slavishly following the Civil Defence leaflets of the time, especially the notorious *Protect and Survive*. The film misses a trick, though, in not showing the animated Public Information films of that name, whose unnerving minimalist graphics made America's *Duck and Cover* (1951) seem Disneyesque.

The apocalypse is abstract: we see the flash, then pan over the verdant Sussex landscape to a horizon of roiling blackness, with flickering sketches of crashing trains and disintegrating houses (no humans are shown). The approach is closer to *Akira** than to an earlier Japanese animated film, *Barefoot Gen* (1983), which showed the Hiroshima bombing in horrifically graphic detail, with melting eyeballs and children reduced to ash. It was based on the memories of a Hiroshima survivor, Keiji Nakazawa.

After the bomb, the Bloggs' house is a squalid tip in a sullen grey wasteland. Jim and Hilda cling to their Blitz spirit, presume they've survived the worst, and think their bleeding gums and blotched skin are passing ailments ('Have you got lipstick on, dear?'). Even when they're flopping and vomiting in the last scenes, they think help's coming, though Hilda's last line is a gentle 'No more, love, no more.'

When the Wind Blows was the mutant sequel to the lyrical featurette, *The Snowman* (1982). Both films were animated by TVC London, and based on Raymond Briggs's picture-books. In the case of *Wind*, too many of its images look like pale copies of the source strip, but its patchwork of techniques is appealing. There are pencil-drawn interludes and time-lapsed skies. The drawn Bloggses share the screen with cut-out props in a scale model house, shot by a camera converted to single frames. The hybrid look recalls vintage Fleischer cartoons which sometimes used physical miniatures ('setbacks') for backdrops.

British viewers who saw *Wind* in the cinema were leafleted by CND members, but also by the pro-nuclear Families for Defence, which proclaimed, 'Jim and Hilda are safe with NATO.' Briggs said his book was apolitical, but the film finger-points in its pre-credits footage, showing a nuclear convoy rumbling through England. The Japanese American director was Jimmy Murakami, who'd lost a relative to the Nagasaki A-bomb and a grandfather to a conventional bomber that dropped its spare load after a raid.

Briggs said Jim and Hilda were based on his late parents, 'fairly simple, uneducated people'. The film, though, seems to trash their whole generation, presenting the couple as sexagenarian infants and snidely displaying World War II images to the tune of 'Rockaby Baby'. (Jim and Hilda were supposedly kids in the war, hence their 'simple' nostalgia; however, a 1986 audience would identify the pensioners with the generation who served.) After the bomb, Hilda complains she's missed *Woman's Hour*, and she and Jim *sunbathe* in their blasted garden. *The Spectator*'s Peter Ackroyd called them 'an unbearably stupid couple'.

However, the last scenes choke off these objections, as Jim and Hilda plunge into their terrible decline. Previously, their drawing was only non-Disney adequate, carried by a wordy script and dignified voice-actors. As the couple decay from fall-out, though, they take on putrescent life. The flawed drawing congeals with their on-screen sickness, more bearable than live-action, but with a haunted, primitive sadness. Next to Japan's *Grave of the Fireflies**, another animation about slow-dying characters, *Wind*'s drawing is more repellent, but the couple is all the tenderer.

Whisper of the Heart
Japan, 1995 – 110 minutes
Yoshifumi Kondo
[Drawings]

Whisper of the Heart was released by Japan's Studio Ghibli in 1995, a few years before the world-famous *Princess Mononoke** and *Spirited Away**. But the nine-year-old studio was already a recognised brand. 'Like Disney's prince and princess romances, Ghibli films have formulaic elements that identify them as surely as a brand logo,' wrote Mark Schilling in the *Japan Times*. 'There is usually a spunky young heroine … a feline familiar … vaguely European settings … and, most distinctively of all, flying scenes animated with a breathtaking dynamism and infectious joy.'

A delightful film, *Whisper* reflected a practical problem for any studio with a personal stamp. Could it outlive the people who founded it? 'I'd like to retire before someone suggests it to me,' Miyazaki told *Animerica* magazine in 1993. *Whisper* was Ghibli's first cinema film by a 'new' director, Yoshifumi Kondo. No newcomer, Kondo had worked with Miyazaki since the 1970s as an animator and designer. Some of his most striking work was on Miyazaki's 1978 TV cartoon, *Future Boy Conan*. Kondo drew the boy going mad with grief after his paternal guardian dies. The lad becomes feral, smashing huge boulders on the ground. It's comparable to the scenes of child trauma in *My Neighbour Totoro**, but in a far rawer cartoon form.

Whisper's production was a literal handover. Kondo directed from Miyazaki's storyboards, based on a girls' comic by Aoi Hiiragi. Unlike Miyazaki's films, *Whisper* has a contemporary Tokyo setting and few 'magic' elements. Like Miyazaki's films, there's an outgoing girl protagonist, a junior high-schooler called Shizuku. We see her learn to express herself through her budding art – she wants to be a writer – much like the trainee witch in Miyazaki's *Kiki's Delivery Service**. But *Whisper's* theme takes longer to emerge from a purposefully generic teen drama.

At the start, Shizuku is trying to solve a mystery; why all the library books she's borrowing have the same male name on the reader's slips. 'I wonder if he's nice?', she asks herself. Her surroundings are Miyazakified; her apartment home is cramped, but the sunny town *mise en scène* is radiantly detailed. (For a scuzzy rejoinder, watch the film *Tokyo Godfathers**.) Schilling describes Shizuki walking down a shaded street, 'the light and shadow playing on her slender form, celebrating her youth with all its promise, hope and uncertainty'.

True to Ghibli tradition, the girl sees her surroundings as an adventure and she the adventurer. She follows a mysterious stray cat over walls and up alleys to a wondrous antique shop, magic in her mind and perhaps reality too. Like *Tokyo Godfathers*, *Whisper* delights in piling on fateful coincidences. The brief fantasy dream scenes meld with the story; they also bring in Ghibi's signature flying, but it's our immersion in the real-ideal world that lifts the film. The most natural elevation involves not flying but singing, as Shizuku is forced into an impromptu song recital, struggling to rein in her gauche spontaneity

DIRECTOR Yoshifumi Kondo
PRODUCER Hayao Miyazaki, Toshio Suzuki
STORY Hayao Miyazaki
SCORE Yuji Nomi
DESIGN Yoshifumi Kondo, Kitaro Kosaka
ANIMATION Kitaro Kosaka, Atsuko Tanaka, Hiroyuki Inoe, Shinji Otsuka, Masashi Ando

– though she can't help but glance sideways at the annoying boy she likes.

For *Whisper* is a commonplace teen romance, 'a love story of the type one might find in an ordinary girl's comic', as Miyazaki put it. The answer to the library-slip mystery is magnificently corny, the last romantic declarations even more so. When I saw *Whisper* in a cinema, the end provoked gales of laughter from a largely female Japanese audience, though it's a film you laugh with, not at. Notably, the end was made sappier by Miyazaki himself.

'Why am I proposing we film *Whisper of the Heart*?', he wrote.

It is because, no matter how hard middle-aged men try to point out the naïveté and fragility of such dreaming, we can never deny the longing for an encounter with the opposite sex, so wholesomely and honestly depicted in the original story.

It echoes Walt Disney's remarks half a century before, about cartoons appealing to 'that fine, clean, unspoiled spot deep down in every one of us'.

A domestic hit, *Whisper* was also embraced by foreign viewers, despite their bemusement at its extensive use of John Denver's 'Country Roads' (a Japanese karaoke standard). But Kondo never directed again. In 1998, after supervising animation on *Princess Mononoke*, he died of an aneurysm aged forty-seven. In the following years, Ghibli released more films by junior directors. As of writing, the most recent is 2010's *The Borrower Arrietty*, directed by Hiromasa Yonebayashi.

Who Framed Roger Rabbit

US, 1988 – 104 minutes
Robert Zemeckis
[Live-action with drawings]

DIRECTOR Robert Zemeckis
PRODUCER Robert Watts, Frank Marshall
STORY Jeffrey Price, Peter S. Seaman
SCORE Alan Silvestri
ANIMATION Richard Williams, Andreas Deja, Russell Hall, Phil Nibbelink, Simon Wells, Wes Takahashi, Sean Turner

In the 1980s, American animation was revitalised by two films which many purists don't see as animation, but rather effects films for the kids of Spielberg and Lucas. One was *Tron* (1982), whose rudimentary videogame tanks and motorbikes had the run of three-dimensional virtual space. The other was *Who Framed Roger Rabbit*, a mash-up of live-action and animation from a mindset that would have baffled Walt Disney. Directed by Robert Zemeckis, *Roger* was fannish, knowing and in love with plot and technical hybrids.

Though it fitted the high-concept 80s, *Roger* could have been from an earnestly inquiring *Mad! Magazine* gag-strip. How would a film noir like *Chinatown* (1974) look with cartoon characters? In *Roger's* world, Hollywood's pen-and-ink stars – most prominently those from Disney and Warner Bros. – mingle with humans in 1947 Hollywood, recreated at Britain's Elstree Studios. The human protagonist, a sloshed private dick called Eddie Valiant (Bob Hoskins), takes photos of a sex-on-legs Toon torch-singer, Jessica, *in flagrante* with her human sugar-daddy. This may be the first dirty photos scam in mainstream animation since the silent insect film, *The Cameraman's Revenge* (1912) (see p. 174).

Jessica's husband, the bob-tailed critter Roger Rabbit, is framed for lover-boy's murder, and Eddie finds himself a patsy in a twisty mystery that few viewers will bother following, though the solution's soon revealed if you listen to the dialogue. In opening out his world, Zemeckis doesn't tell us if World War II happened (were Hollywood's Toons a deterrent?) or address the socio-metaphysical tangles of presenting cartoon caricatures as an oppressed race. Rather, he prefers to show us Eddie's glory-days cuttings, back when the gumshoe and his late brother cleared Goofy of spy charges and saved Donald's kidnapped nephews, Huey, Dewy and Louie. The film is punctiliously geeky about following through on classic toon tropes. When tweety birds appear round a character who's been clonked on the head, the animators trouble to show us (if we notice) how Roger collects them up, while Eddie just bats them away.

The human-Toon world is as impressive now as it was twenty years ago, though with some shark-looks-fake moments, as when Eddie is thrown into the garbage by a bouncer gorilla. Following *Tron's* lead, the Toons are liberated by the busy live-action camerawork, moving round convincingly in real space, with all the shifts that entails in size, lighting and perspective. The spatial freedom extends into the animation. In the manic opening vignette, Roger's cartoon kitchen expands to giant dimensions that amaze the eye. Toontown, the Toons' own world, seems a bit staid by comparison; the out-of-control budget was squeezed, and cartoon fans will recognise the layers of recycled animation. The entrance, though, is perfect; a curtain in a tunnel, drawing jauntily apart with Warners' cartoon music sting.

Cartoonwise, *Roger* is inspired by Warners and MGM far more than by Disney (1947 was in the middle of Walt's 'mashed potato and gravy' downtime) but its spirit is closest to Spielberg, *Roger's* executive producer. The frantic action, in-jokes and period details take precedence over artistically structured gags. The

best jokes are simple homages, such as Eddie getting Roger to take an explosive drink by adapting the 'Rabbit Season! Duck Season!' gambit of Bugs Bunny ('You do!' 'I don't!' 'You don't!' 'I do!'), itself taken from vaudeville. Soppy and winsome, Roger can't convince as a classic cartoon star, but works as a foil to the stumpy, far funnier Hoskins. In any case, the Toons are all upstaged by Christopher Lloyd's villain, who has scene-chewing speeches and a delicious twist transformation more David Lynch than Disney.

Today, however, we remember mostly the Toon femme fatale Jessica, with her buoyant curves, throbbing pout, breathy voice (spoken by Kathleen Turner, sung by Amy Irving) and perfectly formed one-liner: 'I'm not bad, I'm just drawn that way.' Later there was a scandal about her *real* dirty pictures when fans found a knickerless Jessica in subliminal frames, but Mrs Rabbit had already returned arrested adult humour to Hollywood animation. Disney might have picked up this thread. Instead the Mouse kept *Roger* at arm's length, releasing it under its Touchstone label, leaving kidult animation to *The Simpsons* (1989–), and capitalising instead on the fad for cartoon babes. Next year, its *The Little Mermaid* sported what critic Pauline Kael called 'a teenage tootsie in a flirty seashell bra'.

Yellow Submarine

UK, 1968 – 87 minutes, extended to 89 minutes in the 1999 reissue
George Dunning
[Miscellaneous techniques]

It was a glorious false dawn. We thought it was the beginning of a marvellous new period in feature animation, doing things in the mainstream that were previously confined to arthouses. We would change the way animation was perceived, establish London as a world centre, and start a whole new art style. It was very exciting. As for Disney, we understood it was a historical period which was over, which had become one giant cliché.

The 'false dawn' was the 1968 British film, *Yellow Submarine*. The description was John Challis's, who worked on *Submarine* as a junior animator fresh out of art school. I interviewed him in 1999, which was the year a six-foot Blue Meanie (voiced by the original actor Paul Angelis, who doubled in *Submarine* as Ringo) joined Liverpool's Lord Mayor to celebrate '*Yellow Submarine* Day'. If *Submarine* didn't change animation, it endures as a pop-art icon, confounding critics who scorned its flower-power. As of writing, a CGI remake is being developed by Robert Zemeckis. Challis might be wryly amused by the production studio: Disney.

In the original, the Beatles – Paul, John, George and Ringo – voyage in the Yellow Submarine to save the Edwardian world of Pepperland, which has been conquered by the big-eared Blue Meanies. Along the way they pass through whimsical fantasy realms, eminently suitable for a family audience, from a sea of cackling monsters dreamed by Edward Lear, to a sea of holes drawn from fashionable Op Art. The best setting, though, is the Beatles' TARDIS-like multidimensional madhouse, where zany objects rush in and out of slamming doors, referencing Tex Avery and Claes Oldenburg. The Czech-born designer Heinz Edelmann spoke of 'overloading' the audience with impressions. The animation itself is ramshackle, although that proves highly effective in portraying the bushy, gibbering Blue Meanies in the Pepperland scenes. The flat Carnaby Street colours are bright-going-on-psychedelic, but with room for charcoal-toned photos in the haunting 'Eleanor Rigby' sequence, where many of the staff and crew cameo.

The film was made in London's Soho Square by the studio TV Cartoons (TVC), which had already made a Beatles cartoon series for the US market. There are many clashing stories of *Submarine*'s unruly making, of who came up with what and why, told with unreliable hindsight. The maze of stories is explored exhaustively in *Inside the Yellow Submarine* by Dr Robert R. Hieronimus. Yet *Submarine* stands for itself like few other films. The Canadian director George Dunning knew it when he received the Beatles concept sketches from Edelmann, now widely seen as *Submarine*'s true author. The Beatles are emphatically 2D, day-glo-coloured figures, like a child's imitation of the *Sgt. Pepper* cover. 'It was really marvellous, because it [the design] had that solved, attended-to quality,' Dunning said. 'You could see it wasn't Mickey Mouse. It wasn't this, it wasn't that – it was just there.'

Submarine's scripting was chaotic, but the story settles around the two most endearing characters. One is the soft-hearted drummer Ringo ('But I don't have an imagination!'), the Beatles' established fall-guy, who'd

DIRECTOR George Dunning
PRODUCER Al Brodax
STORY Lee Minoff, Al Brodax, Jack Mendelsohn, Erich Segal, Roger McGough
SCORE George Martin
DESIGN Heinz Edelmann, Jon Cramer, Dick Sawyer
ANIMATION Jack Stokes, Bob Balser, Alan Ball, Reg Lodge, Tom Halley, Dave Livesey

nearly been sacrificed in Richard Lester's *Help!* The other star is a newcomer, the cotton-tailed Boob or 'Nowhere Man'. A delightful twirling clown-faced fluffball, he comes over as an intellectual Winnie the Pooh ('So little time, so much to know!'), and was voiced by comedian Dick Emery. Another actor, Geoffrey Hughes, went from Paul McCartney in *Submarine* to the sixteen-stone scouser Eddie Yeats in *Coronation Street* (1960–). He was luckier than Peter Batten (George), arrested toward the end of recording for deserting the British Army. The marketers strove to give the impression that the real Beatles voiced *Submarine*, fooling the American film paper, *Variety*.

Dunning, a former colleague of the experimental animator Norman McLaren, implicitly snubbed *Submarine*'s artistry. 'The artistic validity of long animated films is often a question of their relative vulgarity,' he said. Yet while critics mocked the idea of a radical Beatles film, *Submarine* pre-empted them. Its revolution is almost absurdly nostalgic, from the Beatles' music-hall quips to the reimagining of 'Lucy in the Sky with Diamonds' as a Busby Berkeley routine loosely painting live-action dancers in peacock colours. When the Beatles do reach Pepperland, it's to find they've been there all along, as Sgt. Pepper's Lonely Hearts Club Band.

Of *Submarine*'s twelve Beatles songs, four were new for the film (not including the title track from the *Revolver* album). One of them, 'Hey Bulldog', was cut after the première, but restored for the 1999 reissue. The excellent incidental music was by George Martin.

Select Bibliography

General animation

Animation World Network, website founded by Ron Diamond and Dan Sarto <www.awn.com>.

Anipages Daily, a blog run by Benjamin Ettinger <www.pelleas.net/aniTOP/>.

Beck, Jerry (ed.),˙*Animation Art* (London: Flame Tree Publishing, 2004).

Beck, Jerry (ed.), *The Animated Movie Guide* (Chicago, IL: Chicago Review Press, 2005).

Bendazzi, Giannalberto, *Cartoons: One Hundred Years of Cinema Animation* (Bloomington: Indiana University Press, 1995) (English edition translated by Anna Taraboletti).

Cartoon Brew, a blog run by Jerry Beck and Amid Amidi <www.cartoon.com>.

Clarke, James, *Animated Films* (London: Virgin Books, 2007).

Edera, Bruno, *Full-Length Animated Feature Films* (London: Focal Press, 1977).

Grant, John, *Masters of Animation* (London: Batsford, 2001).

Harryhausen, Ray and Tony Dalton, *A Century of Model Animation* (London: Aurum Press, 2008).

US animation

Barrier, Michael, *Hollywood Cartoons: American Animation in Its Golden Age* (New York: Oxford University Press, 1999).

Barrier, Michael, *The Animated Man: A Life of Walt Disney* (Berkeley: University of California Press, 2007).

Gabler, Neal, *Walt Disney: The Biography* (London: Aurum Press, 2007).

Gibson, Jon M. and Chris McDonnell, *Unfiltered: The Complete Ralph Bakshi* (New York: Universe Press, 2008).

Paik, Karen, *To Infinity and Beyond! The Story of Pixar Animation Studios* (San Francisco, CA: Chronicle Books, 2007).

Stewart, James B., *DisneyWar: The Battle for the Magic Kingdom* (London: Simon and Schuster, 2005).

Thomas, Frank and Ollie Johnston, *The Illusion of Life: Disney Animation* (New York: Hyperion, 1995).

Asian animation

Clements, Jonathan and Helen McCarthy, *The Anime Encyclopedia* (revised and expanded edition) (Berkeley, CA: Stone Bridge Press, 2006).

Lent, John A. (ed.), *Animation in Asia and the Pacific* (Eastleigh: John Libbey, 2001).

McCarthy, Helen, *Hayao Miyazaki: Master of Japanese Animation* (Berkeley, CA: Stone Bridge Press, 1999).

Miyazaki, Hayao, *Starting Point 1979–1996* (San Francisco, CA: VIZ Media, 2009) (English edition translated by Beth Cary and Frederik L. Schodt).

Nausicaa.net, a website focusing on Studio Ghibli's animation. The current version, *Ghibliwiki*, is at <www.nausicaa.net/wiki/Main_Page> although I prefer the older page at <www.nausicaa.net/miyazaki>.

British animation

Kitson, Clare, *British Animation: The Channel 4 Factor* (Bloomington: Indiana University Press, 2009).

Lord, Peter and Brian Sibley, *Cracking Animation: The Aardman Book of 3D Animation* (new edition) (London: Thames & Hudson, 2004).

Index

List of Illustrations

While considerable effort has been made to correctly identify the copyright holders, this has not been possible in all cases. We apologise for any apparent negligence and any omissions or corrections brought to our attention will be remedied in any future editions.

The Adventures of Prince Achmed, Comenius-Film/BFI; *Akira*, Akira Committee; *Aladdin*, © Walt Disney Company; *Alice*, © Condor-Features; *Alice in Wonderland*, Lou Bunin Productions Inc.; *Allegro non troppo*, Bruno Bozzetto Films; *American Pop*, Columbia Pictures Corporation; *Animal Farm*, Halas & Batchelor/Louis de Rochemont; *Avatar*, © Twentieth Century-Fox Film Corporation/© Dune Entertainment III LLC; *Bambi*, © Walt Disney Productions; *Batman Beyond*, © Warner Bros.; *Beauty and the Beast*, Walt Disney Productions; *Belleville Rendez-Vous*, © Armateurs/© Champion Inc./© Vivi Film/© France 3 Cinéma/© RGP France; *Cinderella*, Walt Disney Productions; *Coraline*, © Laika, Inc.; *Dumbo*, © Walt Disney Productions; *The Fabulous World of Jules Verne*, Czech State Film/Kráty Film; *Fantasia*, Walt Disney Productions; *Fantastic Mr Fox*, © Twentieth Century-Fox Film Corporation/© Indian Paintbrush/© Monarchy Enterprises S.a.r.l.; *Fantastic Planet*, Films Armorial/Service de Recherche ORTF/Ceskoslovensky Filmexport; *Ferngully: The Last Rainforest*, Fai Films/Youngheart Productions; *Finding Nemo*, © Disney Enterprises, Inc./© Pixar Animation Studios; *Fritz the Cat*, Fritz Productions/Aurica Finance; *Ghost in the Shell 2: Innocence*, © Shirow Masamune/© Kodansha – ITNDDTD; *Grave of the Fireflies*, Shinchosha; *Happy Feet*, Warner Bros. Entertainment Inc./© Village Roadshow Pictures; *Hoppity Goes to Town*, Paramount Pictures/Fleischer Studio; *How to Train Your Dragon*, © DreamWorks Animation LLC; *The Hunchback of Notre Dame*, Walt Disney Pictures; *Idiots and Angels*, © Plymptoons; *The Illusionist*, Djano Films/Ciné B; *The Incredibles*, © Disney Enterprises, Inc./© Pixar Animation Studios; *The Iron Giant*, Warner Bros.; *Ivan and His Magic Pony*, Soyuzmultfilm Studio; *The Jungle Book*, Walt Disney Productions; *King Kong*, © RKO Radio Pictures; *Kung Fu Panda*, © DreamWorks Animation LLC; *Laputa: Castle in the Sky*, Tokuma Shoten/Studio Ghibli; *Lilo and Stitch*, © Disney Enterprises, Inc.; *The Lion King*, Walt Disney Pictures; *A Midsummer Night's Dream*, Prague Puppet and Cartoon Film Studio; *Monsters Inc.*, © Disney Enterprises, Inc/© Pixar Animation Studios; *My Life as McDull*, Lunchtime Productions; *My Neighbour Totoro*, Tokuma Group; *Nezha Conquers the Dragon King*, Shanghai Animation Film Studio; *Night on the Galactic Railroad*, Asahi Shimbunsha/TV Asahi/Nippon Herald Films; *One Hundred and One Dalmations*, Walt Disney Productions; *Persepolis*, © 2.4.7. Films/France 3 Cinéma; *Pinchcliffe Grand Prix*, Caprino Filmcenter A/S; *Pinocchio*, Walt Disney Productions; *The Polar Express*, © Warner Bros. Entertainment Inc.; *Ponyo*, © Nibariki – GNDHDDT; *Princess Mononoke*, © Nibariki TDDG; *Le Roman de Renard*, Ladislas Starewitch; *A Scanner Darkly*, © Warner Bros. Entertainment Inc.; *The Secret Adventures of Tom Thumb*, bolexbrothers/BBC Bristol/Sept/Manga Entertainment; *Shrek*, © DreamWorks LLC; *Sita Sings the Blues*, Nina Paley; *The Sky Crawlers*, Production I–G/Nippon Television Network Corporation/Bandai Visual/Warner Bros./D-Rights Inc./VAP/Yomiuri TV/Hakuhodo DY Media Partners/D.N. Dream Partners/Yomiuri Shimbun/Chuokoron-Shinsha/Hochi Shinbun; *Snow White and the Seven Dwarfs*, Walt Disney Productions; *Spirited Away*, © Nibariki TGNDDTM; *The Three Caballeros*, Walt Disney Productions; *Tokyo Godfathers*, Tokyo Godfathers Committee/Columbia TriStar/TriStar Pictures; *Toy Story*, © Walt Disney Pictures; *Up*, © Disney Enterprises, Inc./© Pixar; *Wallace & Gromit in The Curse of the Were-Rabbit*, © Aardman Animations Limited; *WALL·E*, © Disney Enterprises, Inc./© Pixar; *Waltz with Bashir*, © Bridgit Folman/© Films d'Ici/© Razor Film/© Arte France Cinéma/© Noga Channel 8; *Watership Down*, © Watership Productions Ltd; *Who Framed Roger Rabbit*, Touchstone Pictures/Amblin Entertainment/Silver Screen Partners III; *Yellow Submarine*, King Features Entertainment/Subafilms/Apple Films/TV Cartoons.